Through the Eyes of Innocents

Through the Eyes of Innocents

CHILDREN WITNESS WORLD WAR II

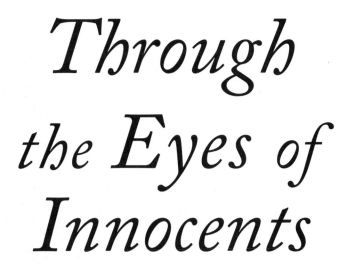

Emmy E. Werner

Westview
PRESS

A Member of the Perseus Books Group

Copyright © 2000 by Westview Press, A Member of the Perseus Books Group

Published in 2000 in the United States of America by Westview Press, 5500 Central Avenue, Boulder, Colorado 80301-2877, and in the United Kingdom by Westview Press, 12 Hid's Copse Road, Cumnor Hill, Oxford OX2 9JJ

Find us on the World Wide Web at www.westviewpress.com

Designed by Heather Hutchison

Library of Congress Cataloging-in-Publication Data
Werner, Emmy E.
    Through the eyes of innocents : children witness World War II /
Emmy E. Werner.
        p.   cm.
    Includes bibliographical references and index.
    ISBN 0-8133-3535-3 (hc)
    1. World War, 1939–1945—Children.   2. Children—History—20th
century.   I. Title.
    D810.C4W45   1999   99-42028
                                                                  CIP

The paper used in this publication meets the requirements of the American National Standard for Permanence of Paper for Printed Library Materials Z39.48-1984.

10   9   8   7   6   5   4   3   2   1

For my husband, Stanley Jacobsen,
and in memory of Richard Jacobsen,
and my mother who sent me back to school
when the world I knew lay in rubble

Contents

Illustrations

Cartoons

Acknowledgments and Credits

MANY THANKS TO MY HUSBAND for typing the manuscript of this book and to Rob Williams, Michelle Trader, David Toole, and the staff at Westview Press for shepherding it through the production process. Twelve individuals who were children or teenagers in World War II were kind enough to participate in interviews in which they reflected upon the impact of the events depicted in this book on their later lives. My heartfelt thanks go to Keith Barton, Isao Fujimoto, Sara Glickstein, Stanley Jacobsen, Larry Lauerhass Jr., Harriet Neufeld Williams, Annegret Ogden, Peter Palmié, Nancy Rogers, Sir Michael Rutter, Dinah Towns, and Kiyoko Yamasaki for the time they gave me and the thoughtfulness with which they responded to my questions. Many thanks to Kathleen Philipps Tebb for transcribing the interviews efficiently and with good cheer.

Grateful acknowledgment is made to the following individuals and institutions for their permission to reprint excerpts from previously published material and to quote from unpublished diaries, letters, interviews, and oral histories in their archives:

The Allied Museum, Berlin, for permission to print translated paragraphs from a child's letter to Gail Halvorsen, the "Chocolate Pilot."

The American Friends Service Committee Archives for permission to print "thank you" letters and drawings from German and Japanese children in the AFSC archives in Philadelphia, Pennsylvania.

C. LeRoy and Joanne R. Anderson of Missoula, Montana, for permission to reprint excerpts from *No Longer Silent: World-Wide Memories of the Children of World War II* (copyright 1995).

To CARE in Atlanta, Georgia, for permission to reprint photographs and to quote excerpts from interviews conducted with CARE Package recipients on the occasion of CARE's 50th anniversary (CARE and CARE Package are registered marks of the Cooperative for Assistance and Relief Everywhere, Inc.).

The Eisenhower Center for American Studies, Metropolitan College, University of New Orleans, for permission to quote from the Anthony D. Duke and the Joseph McCann oral histories in the Eisenhower Center

Archives, and the Herbert Meier oral history in the Stephen and Hugh Ambrose German Veterans Collection.

John S. D. Eisenhower of Trappe, Maryland, and Edward Koehnen of Dayton, Ohio, for permission to print twenty-two letters exchanged between Major General Eisenhower and Mary Louise Koehnen, in the archives of the Dwight D. Eisenhower Library in Abilene, Kansas.

The University of Hawaii at Manoa (James F. Cartwright, University Archivist) for access to diaries from the Sacred Hearts Academy and the Boy Scouts, and to essays, written by students from Punahou School and the University of Hawaii, in the Hawaii War Records Depository (Files 24.01, 24.02, and 50).

The Douglas MacArthur Memorial Archives and Library (Colonel William Davis, Director, Jim Zobel, Archivist) in Norfolk, Virginia, for permission to print the letters of Patricia A. Coyle, Joan Dooley, Lorraine Fader, and Clive Oldroyd, written to General Douglas MacArthur.

The Minnesota Historical Society Press in Saint Paul, Minnesota, for permission to reprint excerpts from *Dear Poppa: The World War II Berman Family Letters* (copyright 1997).

UNICEF, New York, for permission to reprint both excerpts from *I Dream of Peace: Images of War by Children of Former Yugoslavia* (copyright 1994) and a copy of UNICEF's first greeting card.

Many thanks to Dr. Bruce Jentleson, Director of the University of California–Davis Washington Center, for providing a research travel grant that enabled me to collect pictorial material from the U.S. Army Signal Corps and the Wartime Relocation Agency at the National Archives in College Park, Maryland.

Special thanks also to Katharine Williams and her mother, who located photographs of the evacuation of British children and of German boy soldiers at the Imperial War Museum in London, and to Bonnie Hardwick, who introduced me to the photographs of Europe's children by Thérèse Bonney in the special collections of the Bancroft Library at the University of California at Berkeley.

Emmy E. Werner

Prologue

$\mathcal{A}$FTER MY MOTHER DIED, we readied our home on the river Rhine for a new occupant. We packed and stored things she had treasured—among them an old photo album with fading pictures. One caught my eye: Three children, dressed in their Sunday best, are lined up on the steps that lead from our house to the rose garden. They are ten-year-old cousins who have met with their parents for a summer reunion on a hot day in August. The year is 1939. I am the oldest, born in late May, two weeks older than my German cousin Helga. The youngest of the three is cousin Eddy, son of a French army officer who lives in Strasbourg. He had come to visit his aunts and uncles and to be treated to his favorite dessert: sweet raspberries from our garden, served with rich toppings of whipped cream. We clown for the camera, our dresses and shirts stained red from the berries. We look as if we have no care in the world!

Two weeks later, on September 1, 1939, World War II broke out in Europe. Young Eddy, Helga, and I were now declared "enemies." Our fathers, uncles, brothers, and cousins would soon fight each other in a war that would eventually engulf the whole world. Six years later, when the fighting finally stopped, some 55 million individuals had been consumed in the global conflagration. Military casualties alone, including both Allied and Axis soldiers, had reached the staggering figure of 15 million killed and more than 25 million wounded.

By the spring of 1945, all of the adult males in our three families had died on the battlefields of Europe or languished in crowded prisoner of war camps in France and Siberia. Women and children who had been our neighbors or schoolmates were dead as well—killed by indiscriminate saturation bombing, machine gun fire from low-flying enemy planes, artillery shells, and shrapnel from anti-aircraft guns.

World War II would become the first modern war in which more civilians than soldiers were killed or maimed. By August 1945, when the Japanese surrendered, some 40 million civilians had died on both sides of the conflict. Many of the civilian casualties were ordinary children—like us—children who had once smiled contentedly in the summer sun. My cousins and I looked different now than at age ten—unkempt, dirty, hungry—used to foraging in the ruins of bombed-out houses and in abandoned beet, potato, and turnip fields. But we had survived a global conflict in which more children had been killed and maimed than in all previous wars in the world.

French children play with German weapons.

The odds had been against us, for among the nations involved in this bloody epic, Germany and the USSR suffered the most casualties, with a total of some 29 million soldiers and civilians killed.[1] More than half of all deaths in World War II came from these two countries: Germany, with 9 million dead, lost 12 percent of its prewar population; the USSR, with 20 million dead, lost 10 percent. In Japan, 2 million soldiers and civilians died—some 2 percent of the population. Though equally painful for each individual family who lost a loved one, there were fewer casualties among the Western Allies: Some half million American families would receive a letter informing them that one of their men had died in military service in the Pacific or in Europe. British deaths, including colonials, amounted to some 757,000; a fourth of these were civilian deaths due to aerial bombing. The French listed 210,671 killed.

Helga, Eddy, and I were lucky. We were alive. Our fathers were gone, but we could count on our mothers to give us emotional support and whatever meager sustenance they could find for us. But there were 20 million children in devastated Europe who became orphans of the war. Their fathers had died on the battlefield; their mothers had been killed in air raids or while fleeing from their homes in the face of the approaching enemy. These youngsters had to fend for themselves—often lingering for years in displaced persons camps that sprung up all over the continent after the war had "officially" ended.

All of this happened long ago, and the faces of Europe and Asia, where the faraway battles were fought, have changed beyond recognition. Soon the children of World War II will be the only survivors of a decade in human history when the civilized world was close to the abyss and then, miraculously, discovered a reservoir of extraordinary goodwill in the Quakers, CARE, and the United Nations Children's Emergency Fund—the quiet helpers who showed us in the dark days after that war what it meant to be one's brother's keeper.

I would like to tell the story of the children of World War II through their own words, based on letters, diaries, and journals they kept during the darkest decade of the twentieth century, from the outbreak of the war in Europe in 1939 to 1949, when the rehabilitation efforts of the international community began to offer the survivors some sustaining hope. My primary sources are some two hundred eyewitness accounts of children and teenagers from a dozen countries, representing both Allied and Axis nations: Germany, Austria, Japan, the United States, England, France, Holland, Belgium, Denmark, Norway, the former Soviet Union, and Poland. The war experiences they describe took place on three continents: Europe, the United States, and Asia. As corroborating evidence, I also include interviews with a dozen adults from opposing sides of the war who reflect on their wartime childhood and its impact on their later lives.

A caveat is in order here: The children who speak in this book are not Jewish—hence they were spared, with few exceptions, the horrors of political persecution and concentration camps. The trauma and the magnificent spirit of survival of their Jewish contemporaries have been chronicled in many books about and eyewitness accounts of the Holocaust.[2] This book tells the story of ordinary gentile youngsters who lived in extraordinary times and who saw the effects of the deadliest war in human history close up—with children's eyes.

The twelve chapters in this book deal with experiences shared by the children of World War II, regardless of whether they were on the side of the

Allied or the Axis powers, the occupiers or the occupied, the victors or the vanquished. The focus will be on their shared reactions to the war, the hardships they endured, how they coped with them, and how the war experience shaped their lives. These stories about the last surviving eyewitnesses to the bloodiest conflict of the twentieth century show us humanity's capacity to endure against all odds.

The first chapter deals with the events unfolding in Europe between September 1939 and December 1940, as seen through the eyes of children whose daily routines changed, suddenly and dramatically. German and British children write about their first experiences with blackouts, air raid drills, gas masks, and bombs, and about the departure of their fathers and brothers to the front. Polish, Dutch, Belgian, and French children tell about the invasion of their homelands by German troops.

Chapter 2 covers the year 1941, when the children of Western Europe get to know their occupiers and when Germany invades the Soviet Union. British children meet their first prisoners of war; Dutch and Danish children learn that the enemy has a human face; teenagers in Holland and Norway join the resistance; and Russian children witness the siege of Leningrad and the fighting around Moscow.

Chapter 3 deals with the impact of the mass-scale evacuations of millions of children in Great Britain and Germany in the wake of increasing air attacks on heavily populated cities. British children are shipped into the countryside and overseas, to Canada, the United States, New Zealand, Australia, and South Africa. German children are evacuated to the rural south and to neighboring countries that have been occupied. The voices are those of the evacuees, of the children and caregivers in the host families, and of some of the teachers who accompanied the evacuated children.

Chapter 4 focuses on the entry of the United States and Japan into the war: the attack on Pearl Harbor, as seen by Hawaiian children, and its repercussions on life on the U.S. mainland. American children from the West Coast to the Midwest and the Atlantic seaboard are now an active part of the home front. Barrage balloons, scrap collections, and victory gardens become part of their daily routine—so does letter writing to relatives who serve overseas and to the generals who command them.

Chapter 5 deals with the lives of Japanese American children in internment camps. In Arizona, California, Wyoming, and Utah, native-born children of Japanese descent, citizens of the United States, keep diaries and journals of their lives behind barbed wire. Each school day, they recite the pledge of allegiance in class. Occasionally they are visited by a relative who serves in the U.S. Army.

Chapter 6 chronicles a unique wartime correspondence between a seventh-grade school girl from Ohio and General Dwight D. Eisenhower.

Over the course of eighteen months, between April 1942 and August 1943, the young girl writes Ike about the daily events on her home front; he shares his impressions of people and places, as he visits the Allied troops in Europe and North Africa.

Chapter 7 contains eyewitness accounts of youngsters in battle. Among them are underage GIs who participated in the Normandy invasion and German boy soldiers who "manned" the anti-aircraft artillery batteries that surrounded their hometowns or who fought in the last-ditch defense of their fatherland, from the Battle of the Bulge in December 1944 to the Battle of Berlin in April 1945. The last photo ever taken of Hitler—which is now in the Imperial War Museum in London—shows him decorating one of these boys, age twelve, with an Iron Cross.

Not all the eyewitnesses of the battles fought in World War II were boys: One of the most moving accounts of the war comes from a Japanese girl—Tomiko Higa—who surrendered to the Americans in the Battle of Okinawa. She was only seven years old when she approached an American unit in June 1945, waving a bamboo stick with a piece of cloth tied to it, the palm of one hand stretched out as if she was offering a greeting of peace.

Chapter 8 relates the experiences of children who survived the firestorms of Hamburg, Berlin, and Dresden and who witnessed the bombings of Tokyo, Hiroshima, and Nagasaki. The German cities were destroyed by "conventional" bombs—incendiaries, explosives, and phosphorous; Hiroshima and Nagasaki were leveled by atom bombs. The eyewitness accounts of the children who survived these bombings are eloquent testimonies to the horror of war as it descends on helpless civilians and to the heroism of ordinary people who managed to live through it.

Chapter 9 tells the stories of children who learn through a letter or the tearful announcement by an adult that a family member has been killed—either on the battlefield or on the home front—or that a relative or close friend is missing in action. As fighting in Europe intensified and as the saturation bombing of enemy cities became a daily routine, many European children had to confront such a loss. So did a Hawaiian girl whose father was killed by the freak explosion of an undetonated bomb in Honolulu; a ten-year-old Lakota Sioux whose brother was killed in Europe during the American invasion; and a Japanese girl whose mother died in Hiroshima.

Chapters 10 and 11 focus on children's survival during the postwar years, when the situation for many people was even more desperate than during the actual war. Bitter winters and poor harvests led many children in Europe to near starvation. The devastated cities of central Europe were filled with orphans who fended for themselves in the ruins of bombed-out houses, and with millions of refugees who had fled from the East or who had been forcefully expatriated.

Even those who remained in their homes faced a grim struggle to survive. Once well-to-do families ate weeds and beets for sustenance and chopped fine furniture for firewood to warm at least one room where everyone huddled together. A flourishing black market undermined any attempt at rationing by the government. The essays included in Chapter 10, written by school children in 1946–1948 on the theme "How I live today," give a vivid account of what it was like to be a young person during that period. Children and teenagers who were displaced persons "on the run" tell in their diaries what it was like to survive without a family or country.

But in the midst of despair and devastation came glimmers of hope. The first CARE Packages began to arrive in France in May 1946. UNICEF, founded in November 1946, shipped supplies of milk and medicine to Europe and Asia, and the Quakers began their "Friends Relief Service," which provided a daily midday meal of 350 calories for millions of hungry school children until 1949. Chapter 11, based on interviews and letters from the archives of UNICEF, CARE, and the American Friends Service Committee, tells of the heartfelt gratitude of children from war-torn Europe and Japan for the unexpected kindness of the strangers from across the sea.

The last chapter sums up the themes that are woven through the narratives of the children of World War II and examines the impact that war has had on their adult lives. The message they share today across the boundaries of time and place with other child survivors of modern wars is an extraordinary affirmation of life, shaped by their hardiness and resourcefulness, by their strong bonds to their families and communities, and—above all—by the life-sustaining power of hope.

I

War Breaks Out

THE CHILDREN OF EUROPE were asleep when World War II broke out. At 5:45 A.M. on September 1, 1939, German troops poured across the Polish frontier and converged on Warsaw.

At dawn my mother woke me up and said: "Kind, es ist Krieg" (We are at war, my child). We sat near the radio all day, listening for news, and watched an endless parade of trains and trucks, filled with soldiers, pass by our house, heading east. When the trains stopped, we brought fruit and flowers from our garden to the men in uniform. That was Friday. On Sunday, September 3, Great Britain and France declared war on Germany. My brother was drafted the next day.

Other children, in other towns, remember the trains filled with soldiers, and the news that blared from the black box radio, and the men leaving, one by one. One of the most moving collections of essays about that time was written by a group of school children from Nuremberg at the end of 1945 and published in 1980 under the title *Als Ich Neun Jahre Alt War, Kam Der Krieg* (The war came when I was nine years old). The essays were intended to help the children come to grips with their past in a lofty exercise called *Vergangenheitsbewältigung* (overcoming the past).[1]

A thirteen-year-old boy wrote in his essay: "When we mobilized we were sent home from school which I enjoyed very much. At home I was bewildered by the worried faces of my parents. In the days and weeks to come I watched with great interest the soldiers who passed by. I thought: 'It's too bad I can't be with them.' The radio announced their victories. In school we followed their progress on the map."

Another youngster remembered:

> It was a Sunday morning when I got up and went to the kitchen to drink coffee. The radio was on and suddenly the music stopped. A gruff voice announced that France had declared war at 6 A.M. and that the German people were prepared to fight. People were surprised and bewildered. In school the next day, the principal wrote our names down on a list for our ration cards. I didn't understand what that meant, but my mother explained: "These ration cards will give us a certain amount of food for each month . . . ." People wondered, "What will happen next? Will the war end well?"

A seven-year-old learned that week that her father was being drafted. When she saw him in uniform on a visit to his barracks, he told her and her mother that he would be sent with a troop transport to Poland. "We said good-bye to him at the bus stop. That was the saddest hour in my life," she wrote. "I didn't know if I would ever see him again." She didn't. Her father would be killed in action—one of more than 8 million military casualties that the German army sustained before the war would end in utter defeat.

Only once on September 1, 1939, did Hitler speak the truth when he addressed the Reichstag: "I am asking of no German man more than I myself was ready throughout four years to do [in World War I]. I am from now on just the first soldier of the German Reich. I have once more put on [the uniform] that was near and dear to me. I will not take it off again until victory is secured, or I will not survive the outcome."[2] He didn't. But the children did not know yet what was to come.

TEN-YEAR-OLD JANINE PHILLIPS had spent her summer holiday in the Polish countryside and was ready to return to Warsaw for the beginning of her school term when she heard the news that her country had been invaded. In *My Secret Diary*, she wrote on September 1, 1939:[3]

> Hitler has invaded Poland. We heard the bad news on the wireless . . . that the German forces have crossed the Polish border and our soldiers are defending our country. Everybody was stunned. . . . Grandpa turned the switch off and looked at our anguished faces. He knelt in front of the picture of Jesus Christ and started to pray aloud. . . .
>
> Soon after tea, Uncle, Aunt and Papa arrived from Warsaw with some more bad news. Papa said that we were not going back to Warsaw because it was safer to stay here in the village. . . . I wondered what will happen to our school, but Mama said that when a country is fighting for its survival, there is no time for schooling. . . . Please, Dear God, let our brave soldiers beat the nasty Germans.

On September 2, newspaper headlines warned the German people who huddled around the radio on the other side of the border: "Deutsche hören keine Auslandssender" (The German people do not listen to foreign broadcasts): "(1) Listening to foreign news will be punished by incarceration in a maximum security prison. (2) The spreading of foreign news will . . . be punished by death."[4]

Still, some of us managed to listen to the BBC behind closed doors, with the radio covered under heavy blankets. Dinah Towns heard the broadcast announcing Britain's entry into the war in her home, some thirty miles north of

London. She remembered: "My dad was listening to the wireless radio, and he said, 'There will be a war.' And then my dad got his papers to be called up in the army. I remember him opening the mail and sitting and staring at these papers and my mom stared at these papers, and he said, 'Well, I have to go.' He was 39 at the time, and he went into the Royal Signal Corps."[5]

Janine heard the news in her Polish country refuge. On September 3, she wrote:

> Magnificent news. England is going to thrash the Gerries in no time at all. . . . England has declared war against Germany. This welcome news came from the loudspeaker like a blessing from Heaven. I am so glad that we have some good friends abroad. . . . Everybody is greatly relieved. I shall have to learn some English because I know only one word, "Good-bye," and that's hardly enough to carry on a conversation with English soldiers. . . . I should like to thank them for helping us beat Hitler but if I haven't learnt sufficient English to say so, I'll just have to hug them and they'll know what I mean.

Two weeks later, on September 17, the Soviet army marched into eastern Poland. On September 28, Warsaw surrendered unconditionally. German newspapers reported the signing of a German-Soviet border and friendship pact and encouraged the ringing of church bells in celebration of the joint victory. They rang for seven days—each day for one hour at noon—in every German town. Janine wrote in her diary: "We are overwhelmed with sorrow. Polish resistance has collapsed."

A FRENCH BOY by the name of Jean-Louis Besson was learning about the reality of war as well. "Everyone in the house is upset," he wrote. "My father and uncle Eugene agree that we can't let Hitler keep invading other countries—our allies—and do nothing about it. Fortunately there is the Maginot line. The Germans won't be able to invade France like the last time!"[6]

But nothing of consequence happened in France in the fall of 1939. "Hitler is afraid of the French army," said Jean-Louis's uncle. By the end of September, the boy's father was drafted into the French artillery and began producing shells. But his letters home were depressing. His company was not making many shells because their work was so badly organized. They had the powder, but the rest of the parts were missing.

In England, meanwhile, children learned about blackouts, gas masks, and how to build an air raid shelter and put out incendiary bombs, should the Germans attack. But the fall and winter of 1939 turned out to be a "phony

*A French boy writing
to his father, who is
away in the army.*

war" for Great Britain. At the beginning of the blackouts there were more
casualties from road accidents than from enemy actions. White lines were
painted along curbs, and men were encouraged to leave their white shirt-
tails hanging out at night. An ingenious farmer painted white stripes on his
cows in case they strayed onto the roads.

Gas masks were distributed to everybody—grown-ups and children alike.
The masks were considered a lark by most mischievous little boys. They
learned to spit on the inside of the mica window to prevent it from misting
up. Gas masks, they soon discovered, were great for making rude noises, and
they fogged up anyway. Dinah Towns learned to practice her 3Rs with her
mask on. "We would sit there, saying our time tables," she remembered,
"looking like we came from the Planet of the Apes."

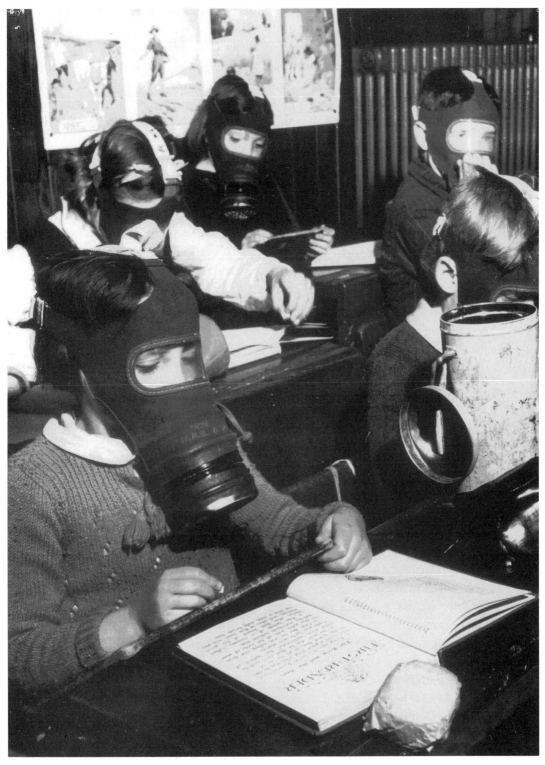

British children at a gas-mask drill.

The British government had a special Mickey Mouse gas mask designed for under-fives. It was brightly colored in red and blue. Young children laughed at the funny faces and enjoyed putting them on. A BBC radio broadcast encouraged their mothers to do the same: "Are your little ones used to seeing you in *your* mask? Make a game of it, calling it 'Mummy's funny face.' Then if the time comes when you really have to wear it, you won't be a terrifying apparition to the child." To everyone's relief, the gas masks never had to be used.

What came in handy was the training of volunteer air raid wardens who taught civilians how to cope with air raids. Every home received a leaflet explaining how to prepare for such emergencies as fire bombs falling through the roof. People were told to keep buckets of sand handy to extinguish fire, and to keep a bath or tank full of water—just as the Germans were taught to do in the years to come.

In the fall of 1939 the British government began to deliver air raid shelters to areas most likely to be attacked by German planes. The Anderson or garden shelter was the most common type of shelter, but it was never very popular. If the siren sounded at night, people disliked snatching up their sleeping children and dashing outside into this cold and damp refuge.

More popular were the Morrison or table shelters, which could be set up in the living room. At night two adults and two children could sleep comfortably in it, although one "war boy" remembered that seven visiting relatives could crowd in as well. Another child liked it because you could play Ping-Pong on its top. The Morrison was not as strong as the Anderson shelter, but raids seemed less scary to the children in the familiar surrounding of one's living room.[7]

But at the beginning of World War II, the British were still safe. The sea and air battles that were to take place in the fall and winter of 1939 centered on a group of islands north of Scotland—the Orkneys—that stretch out across the North Atlantic. There German planes swept across the skies, and German submarines moved silently through the sea, close enough so that the islanders could spot their periscopes when they rose above the water.

Sixteen-year-old Bessie Shea, who lived on a farm on one of the islands, kept a diary of the events she witnessed between September 1939 and May 1940. Bessie's story begins with the sighting of a German submarine on September 5, 1939.[8] That same day, three enemy spies were caught on her island. The next day, as she was taking the cattle out of the barn, she heard the sound of German aircraft and the explosion of anti-aircraft shells over Kirkwall, the island's capital.

On September 8, she relates the capture of two German ships. The crews of both vessels were taken prisoner, but three seamen managed to escape on a motorboat. Two of her neighbors gave chase and discovered the Germans the next morning in the harbor of a neighboring island. "They caught them," she wrote, "found them unresisting and friendly; gave them cigarettes and were about to make them a pot of tea, when a tug appeared and unceremoniously ordered the Germans aboard at gunpoint."

In October, the Orkney Islands were visited by King George and Winston Churchill. Because of concern for the safety of the naval base at Scapa Flow, orders had gone out to post additional aircraft guns on Bessie's island. The concerns proved justified. On October 14, Bessie's diary entry reads: "Two air raids over Kirkwall while I was in town. The *Royal Oak* was blown up in Scapa Flow and about 800 lives lost—many young boys in training."

By mid-November, air raids throughout the Orkneys were a common occurrence, and naval battles had begun in the North Atlantic. Bessie noted in her diary that three German seaman had been captured after they had been adrift at sea without food for several days. By now Bessie had learned to recognize the sounds of German planes as they flew over her island. They made a clacking noise that was very different from the sound made by British aircraft.

As the days progressed, the routines of Bessie's life changed little, though she missed the dances and Bible classes that had been canceled for fear of an impending invasion. Still the cattle had to be milked, and the chores on the farm had to be completed. In the stores food and clothing were still plentiful.

But on November 22, 1939, Bessie came literally eye-to-eye with an enemy plane. She had grabbed her binoculars when she heard its clacking sound and ran outside. "When it came nearer," she wrote, "I saw a cross on the wings— a black cross in blue circle—with a white or yellow circle outside that. It clacked away . . . then came back again and circled right over us."

Ten days later, on December 3, Bessie's diary entry read: "The Germans are not all bad. A U-boat sank a British ship and the crew took to the boats. The submarine came up and stood by. Some of the British were soaked and shivering, and the Germans served up hot food and drinks to them, and waited till a British vessel arrived to pick up the survivors. Then the U-boat commander shouted, 'Tell Churchill we have some humanity!'"

IN POLAND, MEANWHILE, ten-year-old Janine had a hard time seeing any humanity in the occupiers. She blamed them for the demise of her little dog, Gabriel, who nipped at the leg of a German soldier. "Gabriel doesn't like strangers," she explained in her diary. The soldier pulled out his revolver and shot the dog on the spot. Janine and her brother wrapped their pet in a clean cloth and buried him. On his headstone, the children inscribed the words "Here lies little angel Gabriel who bit the big devil!"

Janine had some scruples about hating the Germans. In her diary entry of October 25, she wrote: "I asked Father Jacob today if it were a sin to be nasty to the Gerries. Father Jacob scratched his head and said that under normal circumstances it would be a sin. But taking into consideration the fact that . . . the Germans are occupying our country, God probably would be prepared to give us some sort of dispensation."

A week before Christmas, as heavy snow fell on the Polish countryside, Janine and her brother had a chance to get even with Hitler—or at least the snowman they had made in Hitler's image. He had a mustache from an old broom, a swastika on his left arm, his right arm raised in salute, and Grandma's old chamber pot on his head. She wrote on December 19: "We armed ourselves with sticks and bottles and had a go at Hitler with unbelievable pleasure. . . . Finally he collapsed and was reduced to a mere heap of snow. Wojtek stuck a little white and red flag on top of the rubble signifying our victory. We stood to attention and sang the Polish national anthem."

Across the border, German newspapers urged their readers on Christmas Eve to be prepared for greater things to come. The motto for 1940 was "Wir wollen kämpfen und arbeiten!" (We will fight and work!). Winter had settled on Europe. Bessie Shea on the Orkney Islands reported in her diary that there was a lot of snow on the ground and that the weather was clear and sunny. "On heavenly days like this one can't realize that there is a war!" she wrote. And in mid-February, Janine noted that the frost had eased in the Polish countryside and that "people are feeling more cheerful on the whole."

By then little Janine had met a friendly German—"well, as friendly as one could expect from one's enemies." A German lieutenant had come to her house and asked her mother to prepare a reunion dinner for himself and his wife; he had offered to pay all expenses and had invited her whole family to the party. "Lieutenant Kirshstein, although a German, was also a decent fellow," wrote the little girl in her diary. "It was hard to dislike him."

In Great Britain, government rationing of butter, meat, bacon, and sugar had gone into effect on January 1, 1940. On the last day of that month, Bessie Shea noted in her diary that three ships were sunk near Scapa Flow—two destroyers and a coast guard patrol boat. Bodies washed ashore the next day and the next week. A member of the coast guard, going past the place where the bodies had lain one dark night, nearly jumped sky-high when something gripped his trouser leg. It turned out to be a small white dog!

On February 9, Bessie found a 100-pound keg of Danish butter on the beach. She also spotted an empty cask. That day two German U-boats had been sunk in nearby waters. Two weeks later, she learned of the loss of a British destroyer that was part of a convoy. The German High Command reported on February 26 that some 496 enemy vessels with more than a million tons of goods had been sunk by the German navy since the war began.

The air war was beginning to heat up as well. On the evening of March 16, while Bessie was shopping in the village, she heard the sounds of approaching German aircraft. Running out of the store, she saw giant sparklers going up and great flashes from the fleet in Scapa Flow. "It looked like fireworks and was really lovely," she wrote in her diary. She counted a dozen enemy planes and suddenly saw a tremendous flash. "Did I run?" she asked rhetorically. "The shells were right above me and the flashes at my very nose so I went hell for leather." The Germans hit a battleship that night. All-out war had come to the Orkneys!

Barely a week later, on March 22, Bessie reported: "The last convoy that went out past here was attacked off the east coast by . . . Germans. Three ships were damaged, one had to be abandoned." Still, the people on the islands managed to get on with their lives: Bessie participated in a local concert and was proud of her good recitation. And she was looking forward to a dance, sponsored by the Territorials, soldiers of the volunteer reserve forces, who had recently arrived on her island and installed additional anti-aircraft guns and searchlights. "The Lancaster men are nice," she wrote, "though we have difficulty understanding their speech, and they have the same difficulty with us, unless we speak English."

The German air raids over the Orkneys continued without letup. When the planes approached, there were now flashes of big guns and a big display of light from thirty-seven new searchlight batteries. "I marched around for some time," Bessie wrote in her diary, "whistling 'Run, rabbit, run' not very tunefully, I'm afraid, for I was a bit excited. Every raid we get, I long to be at the guns! These raids seem to rouse the Viking in me!"

On April 9, she learned from an American radio broadcast that Germany had invaded Denmark and that German soldiers were parading in Danish towns. Norway was at war with Germany as well. Some 100 German ships, mainly armed trawlers, minesweepers, and a few battleships, were heading for the Norwegian coast.

That same day German newspapers printed a terse message from the German High Command: "Deutsche Wehrmachtsteile sind heute morgen . . . in Dänemark und Norwegen einmarschiert, um den bewaffneten Schutz dieser Staaten zu übernehmen" (German troops marched this morning into Denmark and Norway to take over the armed protection of these countries).

On May 10 Bessie Shea wrote in her diary: "Norway is almost gone—and Germany has invaded Holland and Belgium . . . dropping hundreds of men by parachutes. . . . There have been great ructions in Parliament. . . . Churchill has almost supreme power now." In Berlin that day, Hitler challenged the soldiers on the Western front: "Der heute beginnende Kampf entscheidet das Schicksal der deutschen Nation für die nächsten tausend Jahre. Tut jetzt Eure Pflicht!" (The struggle that begins today will decide the fate of the German nation for the next thousand years. Do your duty now!)

LUCIEN HUT WAS NINE years old when war came to Holland on May 10, 1940. He remembered how it began: "At six in the morning, my middle brother woke us up because of the sound of airplanes. . . . My mother and father rose up . . . turned on the radio and the first thing we heard was that the Germans had invaded Holland and we were at war. As we looked out, we could see that the planes were dropping hundred of parachutists."[9]

Four days later, on May 14, Rotterdam was given an ultimatum to surrender or to be bombed. The bombing that began at 1:45 P.M. that day lasted for only a few hours. When it was over, the heart of the city was in shambles. At the beginning of the attack, Lucien's parents took in an elderly lady who forcefully directed the whole family to sit on their beds and to place cooking pans on top of their heads for protection. "I remember the whole family sitting there," wrote Lucien later. "We just got hysterical, laughing. It was such an odd sight to see somebody with such a thing as a turkey pan on their heads."

What Lucien saw after the bombardment was heartbreaking. Many streets were in flames; many stores were burning. But in one of the churches that was bombed out, the organ was miraculously still working, and there was a German officer playing Bach's preludes and fugues. Lucien remembered: "It touched me very deeply. I mean it was a real wreck of a church but he played the organ. Now you can't tell me that man was altogether bad."

JULES WAS ONLY FOUR years old when columns of German troops marched through the streets of his home town in Hasselt, Belgium. His childish reaction was one of fascination rather than fear. Years later, in an interview with Kati David in *A Child's War* he could still see the men in uniform in his mind's eye:

> Papa has counted them. There are twenty-seven of them. . . . The one that walks alone on the side is the boss. . . . Papa says that he is a lieutenant. . . . All of them walk straight. But he walks even straighter. They fling their legs up. All at the same time. . . . It's so nice to look at. . . .
>
> Papa also used to be soldier. . . . He still has his cap. . . . When I heard the soldiers, I quickly went to fetch his cap. I put it on and . . . stood outside on the front step. And when they passed by I held up my hand against it. And the lieutenant saw it. He looked at me and I

saw his head moving! I shouted, "Maman, Maman! He saluted me! The lieutenant saluted me!" But Maman was not happy at all. She doesn't like the soldiers.[10]

On May 20, 1940, about the time the young boy Jules saluted the German soldiers, Bessie Shea wrote in her diary: "The war gets more serious. Holland gave in last week, the Germans are half way through Belgium." Her diary ended on May 25 with a last desperate entry: "The Germans are right through the French lines now. . . . The news is getting worse and worse. What if Hitler wins? *He can't*. In all human reason he can't."

The next day, the British Expeditionary Force, which had been sent to help the Allied forces on the continent, began the massive evacuation of some 338,226 men from Dunkirk across the Channel. On June 4, the day their withdrawal from the continent was completed, a defiant Winston Churchill addressed the House of Commons: "We shall go on to the end. . . . We shall fight on the seas and the oceans. . . . We shall fight on the landing grounds, we shall fight in the fields and in the streets, we shall fight in the hills: We shall never surrender."

That same week Jean-Louis Besson was watching the collapse of France in Vitre, a small town in Brittany. In *October 1945: Childhood Memories of the War*, he wrote: "Every day cars pass through town on their way from Paris or from the east of France. The cars have mattresses, tables, and chairs tied to their roofs and entire families crowded inside. The Germans have entered France. The Maginot line didn't stop them; they went around it by way of the Belgian border. . . . The refugees think they may not advance all the way to Brittany."

The English soldiers left town in the wake of the refugees. They headed toward the coast, where ships took them home to regroup. "There are too many Germans for them to fight," concluded the boy. To everyone's surprise, the Germans arrived soon afterwards. Jean-Louis saw tears stream down his uncle's face as the invading troops passed in front of his store on their motorbikes and trucks, in perfect formation.

The next day, their landlord, a doctor, had two visitors: German officers asked permission to stay in his house—only in the guest room, so as not to bother anyone. "They speak French very well," noted the boy. "The doctor says they are very proper, for enemies. . . . Everyone agrees that the German soldiers are very disciplined."

Two weeks later Jean-Louis' father returned, without socks and with holes in his shoes. For the once proud artillery officer the war was over. "We are so happy to have Papa back with us," wrote his son. On June 22, France

French refugee girl with a doll.

signed an armistice treaty with Germany. The citizens of Strasbourg, home of my cousin Eddy, changed their address to Strassburg as they had done once before, when Bismarck defeated France in the nineteenth century. They would revert back to the French spelling in May 1945 when the war ended in Allied victory.

Even after the French had asked for an armistice, Churchill reiterated Britain's resolve to continue the war. In a fiery speech in the Parliament he exhorted his countrymen: "Let us therefore brace ourselves to our duties, and so bear ourselves that, if the British Empire and its Commonwealth last for a thousand years, men will say: "This was their finest hour." On July 10, within weeks of his defiant stand, the first heavy bombing of British and Welsh docks took place, marking the beginning of the Battle of Britain. By late August, the first German bombs fell on central London. The British air force retaliated by bombing Berlin.

REGINA SCHWENKE was five years old when a squadron of British bombers first attacked the capital city of Germany. In a book of childhood memoirs, entitled *Und Es Wird Immer Wieder Tag* (Daybreak always comes again), she describes her first night in the communal air raid cellar in her apartment building.[11] It contained some broken-down furniture—old benches, tables, beds, and mattresses—and it was musty and cold. The children each had a bag with games, picture books, colored pencils, and papers to keep themselves occupied. Someone brought a flask of tea and coffee. People felt safe and secure until the first bombs shook the house and some of the women and children began to cry.

During a break in the bombing her mother was called outside by the air raid warden, who asked her to identify the mangled body of a man who had tried to dispose of an incendiary bomb that had landed on the roof of their apartment building. The bomb had exploded in his hand. He could not be saved. The children, meanwhile, went asleep in the cellar. When they awoke the next morning, they went on an expedition with their aunt to search for shrapnel from the anti-aircraft guns and fragments from the bombs—a hobby that all of us "war children" would indulge in for years to come.

Like stamp collectors we would hunt after each air attack for the biggest and most exotic looking metal pieces, carefully examining their shape, weight, and jagged edges. As our collections grew, we would trade with other children, if we had duplicates or yearned for an unusual specimen. With increasing savvy—and repeated exposure to air raids—we would be able to tell at a glance whether these scraps were of German, French, British, or American origin. British children—I found out later—were just as resourceful in this hobby. They had plenty of opportunity to indulge in it.

ON SEPTEMBER 1, 1940, the "Blitz" began in earnest. That day, Jill, a little English girl in a convent boarding school in Hamshire, wrote a letter to her parents: "Dear Mummy and Daddy: We had an exciting time on Thursday. You see we had an air raid warning in the night. It was funny, mistresses in dressing gowns, Nuns half dressed. . . . We were down in the shelter about an hour. We played games and went nearly to sleep. We said the Rosary, too. The next day we were very tired so we had to rest. Most of the school went to sleep."[12]

In the late afternoon of September 7, a Saturday, the first great air attack on London began. It was kept up by successive waves of German bombers until dawn on Sunday morning. The next evening, the attack was renewed and continued throughout the night. Vast damage was inflicted on the city. The assault went on all the following week, night after night. On Sunday, September 15, the Luftwaffe decided to carry out a daylight assault, but most German planes were routed, and fifty-six were shot down before they could deliver their bomb load. It was a turning point in the air war.

Three days later, the German High Command in Berlin reported that British planes had attacked civilian targets in northern and western Germany. German newspapers assured their readers: "Die Vergeltungsflüge gegen London werden mit steigender Heftigkeit fortgesetzt" (The retaliation flights against London continue and are being steadily escalated).

London was to take a terrible pounding for fifty-seven consecutive nights, until November 3, 1940, from a daily average of 200 German bombers. Many other British cities, Coventry above all, suffered great damage. But British morale did not collapse. The same would be true for the Germans when they were subjected to British and American saturation bombing in the years to come.

Alice Brady, an American social worker, recorded in her diary, *Children Under Fire*, a conversation she overheard between her nephew and niece on a night in early November when the bombardment of London was especially heavy. A bomb dropped quite near and shook the house. Said eleven-year-old Terence to his younger sister, "That one sounded as though it fell in the garden, go and see if it's done any harm." His sister replied disdainfully, "If you are interested, go out yourself. I'm not going to be Hitler's housemaid."[13]

That same week air raid rescue workers were about to abandon a devastated house in their London neighborhood, thinking no one could possibly be alive, when they heard a small quavering voice singing "God Save the King." They started digging and rescued a little five-year-old. On the way to the hospital one of the members of the rescue squad asked him, "What made you sing God Save the King?" The little boy explained: "My daddy was a miner and he told me when the miners are buried they tap and sing. I was squeezed so tight I couldn't tap, and I have only been to school a little while and 'God Save the King' was the only song I knew."[14]

During the Blitz in London, there was only one absolutely safe place to be: deep below the streets, in the tunnels of the underground railway system. Families brought their camp beds and blankets to the platforms and stayed there all night until the first trains began to rumble in the morning. It was uncomfortable but safe, and children entertained themselves by singing songs and listening to stories.

Sometimes there was not enough time to make it to the underground shelters. Sixteen-year-old Josephine Kenney was the seventh of eleven children from an Irish/English Catholic family who lived in Cricklewood, a subdivision of London, during the Blitz. She wrote:

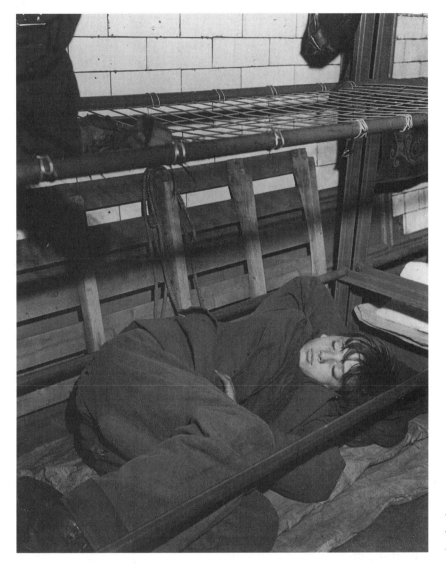

London boy in a subway during the Blitz.

At night I lie in bed listening to the air raid sirens. It has gotten to the point where rather than getting up and going to the shelter, we all just pull the covers up over our heads, put cotton in our ears, and pray the next bomb does not have our names on it. This may sound fatalistic, but it is my life. We must carry gas masks and helmets with us at all times to protect us from debris and poisoning from unexpected attacks. I often ask what kind of life this is for a teenager to lead, but all I can think of is if I do survive how it will effect me in the long run?[15]

Children in the countryside around London remembered the bombing as well. Dinah Towns, who lived some thirty miles north of the capital, would watch when the city was being bombed and count the searchlights and the barrage balloons that were supposed to keep the planes from coming in over London. She remembered the planes going to Coventry on a Saturday afternoon: "They would go in formation, right over where we lived," she said, "and they would be going quite low because they were loaded with bombs. But on the way back, we could tell that some had been shot down, because they were out of formation."

Some of the bombs intended for London or Coventry would go off in Dinah's neighborhood:

> The sirens would go off and you would run to the garden shelter. It was covered with dirt, a bench on each side, and always had water in it. When you would walk in you would slosh, slosh, slosh. Grandma and Grandpa lived across the street and sometimes when the siren would go off, and if we didn't wake up, they would come and bang on the door: "Get into the shelter!" So we would jump up in the middle of the night and run in there. We would listen for the all clear—that was an even pitch, whereas the warning was up and down—and then we would dash out and collect the shrapnels.

The bombing stopped abruptly in mid-November. Losses of German planes over England had been so severe that the Luftwaffe never recovered from the blows received over Britain that late summer and fall. When Christmas came that year, the German High Command announced: "Die deutsche Luftwaffe hat am 25 Dezember keine Angriffshandlungen unternommen Auch der Feind griff deutches Reichsgebiet nicht an" (The German air force has not launched any attacks on December 25th. The enemy has also refrained from attacking targets within Germany).

In London, Alice Brady and her nephew sang carols on Christmas Eve. She wrote in her diary:

> We had a quiet night, the first for a long time. We cycled over to Chapel Royal H.C. on Christmas morning and the boy choir, the only one in or near London not evacuated, sang beautifully "Unto us a Son is Born". . . . Then on to the hospital to take our gifts to the family. . . . Doctors and nurses have been wonderful, carrying on with their general patients as well as receiving and treating casualties, night after night. But Christmas night this time was really a "Silent and Holy Night," no enemy action. Many extra services were held in church shelters. . . . Everyone seemed to have had a good time and deeply appreciated the temporary cessation of hostilities.

In occupied Paris, Jean-Louis Besson sang in the children's choir during Christmas Mass, wearing a white surplice and red soutane for the festive occasion. His family had returned from their refuge in Brittany and settled in their apartment near the Church of Saint Jean-Baptiste-de Belleville after the signing of the armistice.

In Berlin, Regina Schwenke celebrated a quiet Christmas with her family, her grandparents, and a few neighbors. Her father, who had been transferred by the German army from Poland to France, had sent some "rare" gifts: cookies, chocolates, bonbons, cigarettes (for trading), coffee, and cocoa. She also received a special costume for Malwine, her beloved doll.

On New Year's Eve, German newspapers printed the special orders of the Führer to his troops: "Das Jahr 1941 wird die Vollendung des grössten Sieges unserer Geschichte bringen" (The year 1941 will bring the completion of the greatest victory in our history). Fate would have it otherwise!

2

Meeting the Enemy

Y SPRING 1941, Western Europe had been under German occupation for nearly a year. The Luftwaffe still flew sorties over Great Britain, and the RAF reciprocated by bombing cities in the north and west of Germany that were commercial and industrial centers. On April 21, 1941, three-year-old Michael Foreman had his first encounter with an incendiary during an air raid on the naval base of Lowestoft—Britain's nearest town to Germany. In *War Boy*, he remembers:

> I woke up when the bomb came through the roof. It came through at an angle, overflew my bed by inches, bounced up over my mother's bed, hit the mirror, dropped into the grate and exploded up the chimney. . . . It was a firebomb. My brother Ivan appeared in pajamas and his Home Guard tin hat. Being in the Home Guard, he had ensured that all the rooms in our house were stuffed with sandbags. Ivan threw sand over the bomb, but the dry sand kept sliding off. He threw the hearth rug over the bomb and jumped up and down on it, until brother Pud arrived with a bucket of wet sand from the yard. This did the trick.[1]

When the RAF bombed Berlin, Hamburg, or Frankfurt, German children would go through the same gyrations. I was twelve then and volunteered for the *Luftschutzwache* (air raid watch) in our school. We became experts at spotting incendiaries that had penetrated the roof of our schoolhouse or the classroom ceilings. Armed with buckets, we would race to throw sand over the eight-sided metal sticks before they exploded. In large metropolitan areas, like Berlin, children were paid a small stipend for their duties—fifty pfennig during the day, one mark for the night to check the perimeters of schools and to report or contain any damage.

The losses of the German Luftwaffe in the Battle of Britain had been so severe that they could never be made up in the years to come. They also had an unexpected consequence. The airmen who were shot down and survived were the first German soldiers English children encountered. They discovered to their astonishment that the enemy had a human face. Robin, who was seven years old at the time, remembered in *A Child's War*: "My encounter with the prisoners of war was an interesting experience. To discover that people I feared and hated—that I had been taught to fear and hate—were just like us, and not at all the gruesome, terrifying enemies one heard talk about. I suppose this was one of my first lessons in understanding other people, in not accepting first impressions as complete and final and irrevocable."[2]

Keith Barton, one of my colleagues at the University of California, was only three years old when three German POWs were billeted with him and his mother in their "one down and one up" house at the outskirts of London: "My first memories are of these three people who suddenly turned up at our house. They were very friendly, but they talked different. They made toys for me, including a wooden car, and they said 'Guten Morgen' when they left for their jobs in the barracks in the morning and 'Gute Nacht' when they came back."[3]

Dinah Towns, age five, who grew up in the countryside halfway between London and Oxford, lived right next to a prisoner of war camp: "My gran had a shop there, and they would work on the farms and they would go to her shop to buy their cigarettes. One of them became very friendly with my parents—a German boy, named Tony. He married an Irish girl after the war and his father-in-law, who just died, left him the farm."[4]

Children in occupied Europe had a chance to meet the enemy face-to-face as well, but their meetings were tinged with a strong feeling of ambivalence: Many regarded the German soldiers as alien and potentially hostile—and learned to ignore them or to keep a distance. Christian Søe was in the first grade when German troops were stationed in his hometown in eastern Jutland. "My childish reaction was one of general astonishment rather than fear over the many uniformed men with military trucks, motor cycles, and horses," he recalled later.[5] For a long time the children had no direct contact with the invaders. Always say "nicht verstehen"—I don't understand—he was told by his elders.

In school, Christian and his fellow classmates were taught patriotic songs from Denmark's proud past. They became a very important part of his young life. His teacher in the small country school he attended would get the children all fired up about the deeds of brave Noels Ebbesen, who killed a German tyrant in the nearby town of Randers. "That was six hundred years earlier," the boy remembered, "but it might as well have been last month when our teacher talked about him. He drew no obvious parallels with the present, but I don't think anyone who listened could have missed them."

Danish children became familiar with anti-Nazi songs. One of Christian's favorite was a parody of "Lily Marlene":

First we take Goebbels, by one of his legs,
Next we take on Göring, and beat him with a stone,
Then we'll hang Hitler from the noose,
Right next to Herr von Ribbentrop,
The big Nazi swine, the big Nazi swine.

But half a dozen older and partly invalid German soldiers lost their alien and fearsome quality for the boy. They were stationed in the little mission hall of Christian's town and were headed by an officer who gained respect among the local Danes for his courteous demeanor. Soon after their arrival, Christian's mother, a parson's widow, was asked to serve as an occasional translator for them, and thereafter two or three German soldiers would sometimes come to the boy's home to talk to "Mutter Søe," to join in the family's board games, and to listen to the evening news on the BBC because they trusted London more than Berlin as a source of information.

"We children soon learned to follow the basic line of their German," remembered the boy.

They would talk about their families and show small photos from back home. Werner from Hanover and one or two of the others became familiar enough for us to think of them as adult friends. . . . We all knew that people on some neighboring farms helped a German deserter who had fled into the countryside by putting out food for him in their barns. . . . In the end we heard that he was caught and taken to Aarhus for execution by a firing squad.

Six-year-old Jytte Christensen, who lived in Nyborg, a few miles east of Odense, the birthplace of Hans Christian Andersen, has similar memories of the occupation of Denmark: "We saw the German soldiers walking through the town, always singing, but they did not make any trouble. The private soldiers did not hurt anybody. They probably would have preferred to stay home rather than going to war."[6]

But her most awful memory of the war was seeing a young man hit by a hand grenade that a German soldier, in panic, threw after him when he was loitering near a railroad bridge. "He lay dead beneath our window, covered with blood. My mother went down with a blanket to cover him."

In occupied Holland, school children were required to learn the German language, and their textbooks changed from ordinary reading texts to being more politically oriented. Dutch children learned now more about Germany, its power, and especially that the Germans were out to save the world—to the great dismay of teachers and parents. Lucien Hut, who went to elementary school in Rotterdam, remembered that most of his teachers were under strict guidance by the German administrators who observed their teaching in the classroom. If they went out of line, it cost them their jobs or they were sent to work camps to reform.

By 1941, Dutch children experienced constant interruptions during their school days. There were daily alerts for air attacks: British planes, going to Germany, flew over Rotterdam with regularity and sometimes bombed and strafed in Allied territory to disrupt or destroy military efforts.

But Lucien also experienced examples of kindness and humanity on the part of both the occupiers and the occupied. Lucien's mother was bitterly anti-Nazi and enjoyed causing them discomfort, but she could also appreciate that many German soldiers were victims of circumstances beyond their control. Once, on a tram, a lone German soldier asked her where he could find a public toilet. "Ja," he said in German, "I really need to go to the bathroom." Lucien's mother pointed him in the direction of a well-known whorehouse. The soldier was very polite, said "Danke Schön," and headed for the brothel!

But the boy also learned that his mother had a mellow heart when it came to soldiers who were lost and homesick. A neighbor, who was a supplier for German boats, introduced her to two young sailors, Willie and Hans, who brought food to Lucien's family, visited them on occasion for a home-cooked meal, and befriended the boy. Said he: "In retrospect, I find this an extremely good side of my mother. She could realize that there were Germans who were barbarians, but not everyone could be called a barbarian, not every German. She was quite a lady."[7]

*F*OURTEEN-YEAR-OLD JAN, who lived in Amsterdam, was not as forgiving. He and four of his best school friends—Piet, Charlotte, Hendrik, and Jos—decided to form a secret society—the SS5—to do all they could to make life unpleasant for the Nazis. One of their first acts of resistance occurred after a German officer entered their classroom one day and, in a fit of fury, ripped out the picture of Queen Wilhelmina that was displayed in a prominent place on the wall.

The next day, two large words appeared right across the empty frame that had held the queen's picture: TEMPORARILY ABSENT—the handiwork of Charlotte, the only girl in SS5. Charlotte also discovered the hotel in which the officer was staying. She kept track of his car, and at night she decorated the back with a large **W** in orange paint and emptied the rest of the bucket on the back seat.

Two weeks later, SS5 scored another victory of sorts. They had distributed white carnations, spiked with pieces of broken razor blades, to friends and neighbors who wore them in their buttonholes to celebrate the birthday of Prince Bernhardt, the queen's consort. Jan's diary, published in *Children of the Resistance*, records what happened on that occasion: "Crowds are everywhere wearing white carnations. We exchange merry greetings as though it's our own birthday. The Nazis are furious. To our delight they have issued an order: Tear every carnation from button hole or dress. We did not resist as fingers bled and the streets were spattered with the blood of the cursing and cursed Nazis. A notable victory for SS5."[8]

Later in the year, members of SS5 escalated their acts of sabotage. Reported Jan in his diary:

> Our artists Jos and Charlotte are enjoying themselves these dark nights. They are specializing in painting false road signs. Other young people do the same, and many Nazis are fished out of the canals. We hope the eels have a good time. Hendrick's favorite hobby is cutting telephone wires. He has become quite an expert and was especially pleased when one night he disrupted half the telephone system in Amsterdam. Little Jos is sticking to arson. Piet and I have passed our tests with Farmer Smit (a member of the resistance movement) to drive a truck.

The truck, driven by the boys, delivered beets but also parcels that their schoolmaster had given them and that were tied to special points on the railroad lines. At night, when the boys were on their return journey, they heard a terrific explosion. The next morning they learned that a German ammunition train on its way to Belgium was derailed and destroyed.

Jan's diary ends on a note of caution: "So far fortune has favored us, but we must exercise greater care. Hendrik has had a narrow squeak. He offered to repair a handpress on which patriotic news sheets were being printed. But for the quick presence of mind of Jos, who was on guard, six people would have been caught. . . . Hostages are being seized on the slightest provocation. We have to be extra careful."

Days later, Piet and Jan were arrested by the Gestapo, tortured, and hauled before a military court. Even the Nazis balked at executing anybody under the age of sixteen. They were sentenced to four years of imprisonment. SS5 had now become SS3, but Charlotte, Hendrick, and Jos carried on with their works of sabotage until Allied troops swept into Amsterdam three and a half years later and all political prisoners were freed.

Thirteen-year-old Willemien van de Zand never forgot her first encounter with a trainload of Dutch Jews. She was waiting for a train that would take her from her relatives' village in the countryside to the town of Nijmegen, where she lived. She had arrived at the train station far too early and sat down in the empty train that was waiting. Suddenly she noticed German soldiers chasing everyone away from the platform. Another train pulled in on the other track, opposite hers. It was a freight train. Suddenly she saw hands sticking out of the little windows on the top of the wagon. A railwayman tried to give the person behind the window something to drink, but a German soldier drove him away with the butt of his gun.

The girl made herself as small as possible because she realized she was not supposed to see what was going on. Then a group of about twenty-five Jews arrived, carrying little suitcases. She saw a few boys who were about her own age, twelve or thirteen. They were taken to the end of the train on the opposite track. Suddenly the train moved off. "I was rigid with fear," she recalled. "I knew what was happening. . . . At night back home I was unable to talk about it. In bed I cried my eyes out and was finally able to tell my sister. I felt somewhat better after this, but I often think back at that moment and see it very clearly before me, just like a film, but in slow motion."[9]

Lucien Hut had a similar encounter near a Jewish pastry shop in Rotterdam on a Sunday morning when he was twelve years old. He watched a German soldier batter in the closed door of the store with the butt of his rifle. Then, in a matter of minutes, the soldier appeared with the youngest child in the family, picked him up by the arm and foot, and threw him into a waiting truck. The second two children followed. "I heard the parents scream," the boy remembered, "and saw them hug their hands on their heads. The Germans shoved them into the truck, too, and that's the last we ever saw of them."

OLA AUSTBO was eleven years old when he learned about the persecution of the Jews in his native Norway. The example of his uncle, who was a leader in the resistance movement, and of his teachers who refused to promote Nazi ideology in their classroom made a lasting impression on him. In order to monitor ship traffic along the west coast of Norway, a large German flotilla was stationed near his hometown on the island of Bom Mel Oy. Day in, day out, Ola, together with other loyal townspeople, kept a close surveillance of the German ships and relayed their movements to the underground movement.

At night, he would listen, secretly, to forbidden news broadcasts from England, which contained coded messages for the resistance. One of their most important underground activities was transporting political refugees from Norway to Scotland, Shetland, and England, including Jews. Ola remembered the fishing boats that would glide silently into the fjords on calm, moonlit nights. They delivered ammunition and other war supplies

*Refugee children
hiding in a barn.*

destined for different parts of the country and then picked up their precious human cargo.

Often the boy was awakened at the crack of dawn by German soldiers
who came to search his house for unauthorized persons. Luckily, none of
them caught the many "guests" who had vanished in the night. If he asked
his parents who these people were, the answer was, "They are just people
travelling through."[10] Thanks to the efforts of the local underground, over
three thousand persons were transported from his island across the North
Sea and reached a safe haven. Ola's uncle was not so lucky. He was arrested

and taken to jail, where he was interrogated and tortured. Later, more people from his village were arrested and sent to concentration camps. Many of them did not return.

In midsummer, on June 22, 1941, one year after France had capitulated, Germany's armies poured across the Niemen River and penetrated swiftly into Russia. My brother and two of my uncles were among the infantrymen. We would never see them again. Like Napoleon and his troops who had crossed that same river on the same date in 1812 on the way to Moscow, the Germans would eventually meet the same fate as the French—defeat and retreat in the snow.

Ten-year-old Lucia K., who lived on the outskirts of Berlin, heard the news of the invasion on the radio. Her father, who knew his history, said simply: "Das ist das Ende" (This is the end). But no one else would believe such a dire forecast, for throughout the summer and fall, the advance of the German troops into Russia was inexorable. Within a few days, whole armies were encircled and hundreds of Soviet planes were destroyed on the airfields. Tens of thousands of prisoners of war began to pour in.

By August, the city of Leningrad (Saint Petersburg) was cut off from the rest of the mainland. Its population would be trapped in a siege that lasted 900 days. On October 2, German troops began their offensive to capture Moscow. Two and a half weeks later, on October 19, a state of siege was announced in the Soviet capital. By November 28, German tanks were only twelve and a half miles away from Moscow.

In my home state of Hessen, children in middle school were told to delete the good things that had been written about Russia in their *Realienbuch*—books that had been printed two years earlier when the Soviet Union and Germany had signed a nonaggression pact. Because of an acute paper shortage no new books had been printed, so the youngsters did the editing themselves. It was a remarkable history lesson!

Yuri Kirshin was nine years old when Germany invaded the Soviet Union. In *No Longer Silent* he looks back at the events that took place in 1941 in his hometown of Unecha in the Bryansk region. The German attack did not come entirely as a surprise to his community. The school children had already been prepared for war. They learned to shoot, received basic instructions on how to take care of wounded soldiers, and learned about air defense and gas masks. At the tender age of nine, Yuri passed the necessary exams and, after that, proudly carried an "Air Defense and Chemical Defense Badge."

Yuri was in a Youth Pioneer Camp some fifteen kilometers away from his hometown when the Germans invaded Russia. His father, a retired officer, immediately volunteered for combat duty. Before going to the front, he came to say good-bye to his son. The farewell meeting was hard for every-one: "I was crying," Yuri recalled, "and it was the first time I had ever seen tears in my fathers eyes."[11]

Yuri's mother stayed with her three sons—ages nine, six, and two months—in Unecha. In August 1941, his town was occupied by German troops. A short time later, all the Jews were prohibited from leaving town and had to wear six-pointed stars made out of white cloth. No one was al-lowed to speak with them. Later, all Jews were arrested and interned in a nearby poultry farm that had been converted to a prison.

During the German occupation (which lasted a year, until the town was lib-erated by the Soviet army), food and clothing for the civilian population were scarce. If someone was fortunate enough to have a good article of clothing, it was traded to the peasants for potatoes and flour. Whenever he could, Yuri would fish to supplement the meager diet. Still, he was hungry all the time.

Yuri's hometown was an important railway junction that connected Moscow with Golan. During the first months of the war, German planes were bombing the town. After the Germans invaded Unecha, Soviet pilots bombed it in turn. The boy saw many civilians killed as a result of the con-stant air raids. He also witnessed an incident in which a German set fire to a truck loaded with Russian soldiers—within 100 meters from where Yuri stood! Three of the men were burned to death. The boy helped bury their bodies in a common grave—a sight he would never forget. But he was still enough of a child to be enamored of war games. "Every day," he remembers, "we passionately argued who would play the part of the Soviet troops and who—the Germans." There were no volunteers for the role of the invaders.

N. P. DOVBENKO was only a few months older than Yuri when he learned about the German invasion. He lived in the village of Golu-bichi in the Chernigov region and was in the third grade when war burst into his life. Within a few days all the men in his village had left for the front. Old people, the women, and teenagers had to take it upon themselves to harvest the collective fields. But they were unable to thrash the sheaves before the Germans came at the end of August.

The boy's father, a member of the Communist Party, had been a political instructor for the Soviet army. He was called immediately to the front. Fear-ful of reprisals by the approaching Germans, his mother burned his spare badges of rank and uniform, all issues of the *Bolshevik Magazine,* and the volumes of Lenin and Stalin in the kitchen stove. She then took her three young children, ranging in age from one to nine and a half, to Grandmother Ulita's house and rounded up the cow, piglet, and poultry. At Granny's house they could count on the safety of a shelter in the kitchen garden. On August 30, the Germans began to shell the village with mortar fire.

The shelling lasted all day long. When it grew dark, the Soviet heavy artillery opened fire on the enemy. The boy and his family fled into the shelter and huddled under a feather bed and pillows. The boy finally fell asleep in spite of the deafening bursts of heavy shells. He woke up to silence and then the whispers of his mother and grandmother. They said, "The Germans are in the village." He remembered:

> When the sun rose we left the shelter. Beside it, under the apple tree
> . . . the Germans had laid the wires [of a field telephone communication
> system] at night, noiselessly, so that not one of my relatives had heard
> them. Some time later we saw a German for the first time. He was
> walking along the street toward the highway. Coming up to Uncle
> Seraphim's house, he asked for some milk, and, after drinking some, he
> thanked him and went on walking.[12]

On the first day of occupation, a rumor spread that a battle was expected in the village. The boy's mother asked her neighbors to drive her and her children to another settlement where her sister lived. Some two kilometers before they reached her home, the youngsters saw dead German soldiers lying in a row on the roadside. Victims of a Soviet air attack, they had been found in a rye field by the German burial team. The boy remembered:

> Hardly had we passed this unusual graveyard when . . . Germans
> gathered around our carriage. They detected two loaves of home-made
> bread, a large piece of fat and a jar of honey. . . . They took it all . . .
> but, thank God, they did not take away the carriage. . . . When we ar-
> rived at Aunt Masha's place we stayed for the night . . . in a shelter
> Uncle Sasha arranged in the kitchen garden. Once again we heard an
> artillery cannonade through the night.

After two days at Aunt Masha's house, on September 3, the little family trudged back home. They started early and walked in the fields, avoiding other villages along the way. A kilometer away from the house he had lived in before the war, the boy witnessed a battle between Soviet fighter planes and a German anti-aircraft artillery battery. Lying in a potato field, the children and their mother prayed that they would be safe from the splinters of shells exploding in the air. "Luckily, the Germans could not shoot down a single plane," he remembered. "When it was over, we got to our feet and started for home."

At the end of September 1941, the boy heard from an eyewitness that his father had been killed in action. His mother took the children and all her belongings to Granny's home, so she would be safe and have some company.

In the middle of November, the boy resumed his schooling in the junior grades of his school. For two years, while under German occupation, he would meet the enemy face-to-face. German troops, carrying military equipment, came occasionally to his village to stay for the night or to havea short rest. Sometimes, they would give him lollipops or biscuits, perhaps mindful of their own children, whom they might never see again.

L YUDMILA ANOPOVA, daughter of the Russian novelist Akindin Kadykov, was ten years old when she experienced the siege of Leningrad. "At first they tried to save the children," she remembers. "They knitted me a little shoulder bag. I had to leave alone, without my parents, with a troop of other children, carrying the same little shoulder bags. We assembled at a factory . . . and then all returned home."[13]

The evacuation had been canceled. The city was surrounded. The siege had begun. Every few hours of the night, the little girl was awakened by bomb raids or artillery barrages. Trying to get dressed, she would lace her boots in a hurry, grab her bundle, and stumble in the dark night, over a road pockmarked with shell holes, to the neighbor's air raid shelter. In the shelter, she would waste no time taking her place on a bench in the center, alert to the rumbling sounds in the distance where the bombs were dropping. But she was worried about something else: "It's not [the bombs] I'm afraid of. I am hiding my right foot from the other people. I've just noticed that I am wearing my grandmother's boot, laced up by one eyelet. . . . I am so clumsy. It's five sizes too big. How could I have not seen that—even half asleep? What a muddlehead I am! I can't stand it—all those people throwing such indifferent glances in my direction."

Famine descended on Leningrad in early winter when all provisions in the town were burned. Once again there was an evacuation—this time Russian troops from the front line were retreating to the center of the city under heavy fire. The Germans cut off the water supply. The worst winter in Lyudmila's memory began.

Her family and neighbors lowered sledges, saucepans, and milk churns from the fourth floor of the house where they lived. They made their way slowly to the Neva River, across snow drifts, and scooped freezing water from the iceholes. On both sides lay the abandoned corpses of the dead. Some were clothed, some covered in shrouds. It wasn't long before the little girl ceased to be afraid of death.

Her parents boarded the windows of their home with plywood. It was dark everywhere. The only warmth was in the kitchen by the iron stove, where everyone huddled around the table. A tiny wick, a twisted piece of cloth dipped in oil, gave a semblance of light. The family no longer took notice of the shells exploding around them, no longer went down to the air raid shelters. Lyudmila remembered:

> I read to myself all day. And such wonderful books! About the young princess who became Catherine II. I draw pictures of little houses, trees, woods. But I'm hungry every moment of the day. Provisions are sold on ration books. We stand in a long queue at the shop. . . . For our six ration books we get a little millet, some dry onion, now and again a piece of frozen meat. We stand there for hours. We are frozen but we wait and suffer in silence.

One day, the bakery chief in the breadshop where her father worked treated the little girl to the crumbs that fell off in the enormous ovens. She ate a whole loaf of them. By evening, she thought she was dying. By morning it had all passed—the pain, the feeling of satiety. But the smell of the bread crusts remained with her forever, long after she finally escaped the besieged city.

Sixteen-year-old Ina Konstantinova was living a comfortable life with her parents and a younger sister near the town of Kashin, northeast of Moscow, when she first learned that Russia was under attack. On June 22, 1941, she wrote:

> Only yesterday everything was so peaceful, so quiet, and today . . . my God! At noon we heard Molotov's speech broadcasted over the radio. Germany is bombing our nation. The country is endangered. I can't describe my state of mind as I was listening to this speech! I became so agitated that my heart seemed to jump out. The country is mobilizing; could I continue as before? No! I ought to make myself useful to my Homeland, to the best of my ability, in its hour of need. We must win![14]

The next day she noted: "This is the second day of the war. Only the second day, but these two days were more eventful than the past two years. Our region was placed under martial law. . . . Papa has already been mobilized. . . . And what about me? If only there was a way of making myself useful at the front! Immediately, without hesitation, I would volunteer for service in the combat zone."

Instead, Ina joined a voluntary aid detachment. Ten days later she was summoned for duty to the district committee of the Red Cross. Together with other volunteers she was issued bandages, respirators, and medical bags. Early in the morning, on July 3, she was sent to the train station to help unload the wounded. That night she wrote in her diary: "I'll never forget the blue eyes of a soldier . . . flashing from an unbearable pain. How he suffered! I'll never forget this dark-haired youth with both legs torn off. . . . But what I remember best was the mood of the soldiers. They all believed in victory, all were cheerful. . . . No, I could never fully describe what I lived through this night. I was completely tired out. But it didn't matter!"

Two weeks later, on July 16, she noted in her diary that the Germans were bombing Leningrad and advancing toward Moscow. Military detachments were marching along the streets of her town. "Even the atmosphere has changed somehow," she writes. "What does the future hold in store for us? I am anxious to finish training and to go to the front. I dream of . . . defending our Homeland and making us happy again!"

On August 5, she reported: "Every night Moscow is subjected to air raids. The enemy troops are coming closer and closer. How awful! But, never mind, they will soon be stopped." Ina had to wait four long months before the Red Army counteroffensive began on December 5, 1941. On December 17, she wrote: "We heard good news over the radio today. The Germans are receiving a sound beating and are on the run. Well, that's splendid! Soon we'll likely hear a communiqué from the Informburo to the effect that our troops have entered Berlin. What a holiday it would be! I can't wait!"

Ina would not live to hear that news. At age seventeen, she volunteered to become a saboteur and spy in the partisan underground movement, behind the enemy lines. One day, the dugout in which Ina and her platoon of partisan scouts were hiding was discovered and surrounded by a detachment of German soldiers. When she realized that she and her comrades were trapped, Ina ordered them to leave while she stayed behind to cover their retreat with submachine gun fire. She was found the next day lying dead under a nearby pine tree.

On December 11, 1941, German newspapers informed their readers: "Deutschland ist von heute ab im Kriegszustand mit den Vereinigten Staaten" (Today, Germany is at war with the United States). A week later, on December 18, 1941, a cryptic announcement came from the Führer's headquarters: "Im Zuges des Übergangs aus den Angriffsoperationen zum Stellungskrieg der Wintermonate werden z.Z. an verschiedenen Abschnitten der Ostfront die erforderlichen Frontverkürzungen vorgenommen" (As part of the transition from an attack to a defensive operation during the winter months, several segments of the Eastern front will be shortened).

It was an extraordinarily cold December. My classmates and I spent the evenings knitting socks, caps, and woolen mittens as part of our contribution to the war effort. Children everywhere were wrapping Christmas presents for fathers, brothers, cousins, and uncles who were in faraway places. The radio played "Leise rieselt der Schnee" (Snow falls silently)—my favorite Advent song.

On the last day of the year that was to have brought the completion of the greatest victory in German history, the newspapers announced: "Schwere Abwehrkämpfe an der Ostfront! Haussammlung von Woll-und Wintersachen! Skier abgeben! Alles für unsere Soldaten!" (Heavy defensive fighting on the Eastern front! House-to-house collection of woolen winter clothing! Donate your skis! Everything for our soldiers!)

From the Russian front, the father of seven-year-old Elsbeth Emmerich had sent his family a homemade Christmas card. "Weit ist der Weg zurück ins Heimatland" read the caption next to the drawing of a Santa Claus with a little Christmas tree.[15] It was the favorite song of homesick German soldiers, sung to the tune of "It's a long way to Tipperary—It's a long way back home." By the time his Christmas greetings reached his wife and children, he had been killed in action near Leningrad.

In Paris that December, Jean-Louis Besson spent a lot of time freezing in the cold, standing in line for food. Like the other children in occupied Europe, and in Great Britain and Germany as well, he had a ration card. Because he and his sister were under the age of sixteen, they had the right to more bread, milk, and meat than the adults in the family.

The lines in the stores were especially long when products were sold that did not require any tickets, like leeks, potatoes, or rutabagas. People became very ingenious. They found that one could make all sorts of dishes with potatoes, even cake for Christmas, if one had a little flour. Jean-Louis's mother grilled barley instead of coffee and called it an *ersatz*, the German word that means substitute. And so they celebrated the holidays as best they could!

To keep warm, Jean-Louis and his family used balls of compressed dust of low-grade coal, which they burned in the big furnace in the kitchen, where he, his sister, and his parents huddled together. At night, his mother warmed the beds with a brick heated in the oven and wrapped in a rag. Once in bed, the children couldn't move if they wanted to stay warm.

On a visit to his aunt and uncle's house in Versailles, Jean-Louis's cousins proudly showed him a Ping-Pong table in the attic that they had transformed into a global battlefield. Armies, tanks, and planes were represented by little pieces of painted wood decorated with rosettes (for the Allies) or swastikas (for the Germans). The naval battles were the most impressive part, and the armored ships, with their chimneys and cannon turrets, looked absolutely real to the boy.[16]

As 1941 drew to an end, people in France and elsewhere in occupied Western Europe listened to the forbidden BBC broadcast from London. The radio commentator assured them that 1942 would be the beginning of the defeat of the German occupiers. Events to come would prove him right!

3

Leaving Home

$\mathcal{D}$EAR MOTHER, I AM NOT AT ALL JOLLY.... Please come as soon as you can. I am fretting and I have cried three times. . . . I am going to come home if I can. Lots of Love. . . . Aldyth."[1] The sentiment expressed by a little English girl on a hastily written postcard to her parents was shared by millions of other children who were evacuated from their homes in World War II—both in Great Britain and in Germany.

Among the first child evacuees from "Greater Germany" (Gross-Deutschland) to Great Britain were some 10,000 unaccompanied Jewish children who were sent to England between December 2, 1938, and September 1, 1939. In an act of mercy, not equaled anywhere else in the world at that time, the British government offered entry visas to children, ranging in age from three months to seventeen years, who were either full, half, or even a quarter Jewish.

"Operation Kindertransports" was a voluntary effort, spearheaded by Jews and Christians, especially the Quakers, who placed the nearly destitute youngsters in hastily established hostels, schools, and private homes across Britain. The effort saved the lives of thousands of youngsters from political persecution. Fifty years later, in 1990, some two hundred and fifty child survivors told their stories in a moving collection of memoirs, *I Came Alone*, which pays tribute to their parents who let them go to safety, never to see them again, and to the generosity of their British hosts who welcomed them into a new home.[2]

The "Kindertransports" ended abruptly on September 1, 1939—when Germany invaded Poland. Fearing that the war might start with immediate bombings by the Germans, Britain started transporting its own people; as part of an official government scheme, nearly 1.5 million British citizens were moved by September 3 (a few hours after war had been officially declared) from endangered cities—such as London, Liverpool, Newcastle, and Manchester—into reception areas in the countryside. Most of these evacuees were children. Beginning three months prior to the start of the war and continuing into the first weeks of the war itself, another 2 million people evacuated themselves by private arrangements with friends and family.

British child evacuees.

The Evacuation of British Children: 1939–1945

About half of the children in England and a third of the children in Scotland moved to safer areas—most of them for only a short time. Because the expected air attacks did not start, over half of the evacuees went back home again before the year was over. Accommodations for evacuees were usually settled in one of two ways: Either reception officers assigned billets at random, or foster parents were allowed free choice from groups of children that were gathered either in a hall or in the streets. Many of the children and their foster families have eloquent memories of these "auction sales" of children. Dinah Towns's family, living about thirty miles from London, were at the receiving end of the evacuation scheme. She remembers:

> The buses would come down from London and they would go to the village square and you had to go see what they had and claim the children. There were three children that nobody seemed to want, so they decided my mom should have them. In the evening the school master

British child evacuees.

came around with these three little girls and asked if we could take them because we had the room. It must have been devastating to these children to be passed around like that. They had their best clothes on, which wasn't very much because they were poor, and a bag with their rations—margarine and a tin of corned beef. They all had lice, so I remember my mom burning all their clothes and these little children crying. Then my mom got them leftover clothes from me and my sister. There was no counseling for them. When I look back I feel sorry for these children.[3]

Evacuation drew attention to the problems of urban poverty. Some very poor evacuees from city tenements had never had water from a tap or used an indoor toilet or slept in a bed. Some had never worn underwear or a set of pajamas and arrived sewn into their one set of ragged clothes. However, despite all the problems, there were many cases of child evacuees and their foster families becoming closely attached to each other, as they did eventually in Dinah's family. There one of the girls stayed for the entire duration of the war.

For many child evacuees from the cities, rural life became an adventure. The BBC News on October 29, 1939, reported the impressions of a London boy who saw his first cow:

> The cow is a mammal. It has six sides, right, left and upper and below. At the back is a tail, on which hangs a brush. With this it sends the flies away so they do not fall into the milk. The head is for the purpose of growing horns and so that the mouth can be somewhere. The horns are to butt with, and the mouth is to moo with. Under the cow hangs the milk. It is arranged for milking. When people milk, the milk comes and there is never an end to the supply. How the cow does it I have not realized, but it makes more and more. The cow has a fine sense of smell: one can smell it far away. This is the reason for the fresh air in the country. . . . The cow does not eat much but what it eats, it eats twice so that it gets enough. When it is hungry it moos and when it says nothing it is because all its inside is filled up with grass.[4]

Once bombing actually started and intensified in the summer of 1940, the decision was made to evacuate again. In September 1940, the second official evacuation went into effect. About 1.25 million individuals, mostly school children, were moved—many of them for the second time. This second time, too, many evacuees drifted back to the cities, in spite of the dangers.

Susan Isaacs, in her *Cambridge Evacuation Survey,* took note of the opinions of 300 London school children who had been sent to Cambridge during the second evacuation of 1940. She enlisted the help of teachers, who asked the children to write two essays, one on "What I like in Cambridge," and the other on "What I miss in Cambridge."[5]

The replies from the eight- to fourteen-year-olds were quite candid. One fourteen-year-old girl started her critical essay with the stark declaration: "Cambridge people, in most cases, are snobs."

Some of the North London children were placed in rather grand manor houses that employed maids, which led to mixed reactions. One twelve-year-old wrote: "I have all our meals with the maids and not with the lady of the house. The maids are very nice." Another girl, age fourteen, was not impressed: "I am sometimes unhappy at my billet, as the maids quarrel a lot and make it awkward for us."

The posh food at the manor houses also got mixed reviews. One fourteen-year-old girl wrote: "We have very nice food, such as venison, pheasant, hare and other luxuries which we cannot afford at home"; but a classmate of hers commented: "I miss my proper English food because my people are continental and their taste is much different than ours."

What the children missed about home and family was teasing and rough play and a freer, rowdier life. Homesickness was an acute problem with many evacuees. It was buffered in Cambridge by the presence of school teachers who had traveled with the unaccompanied children and who provided a sense of cohesiveness and continuity in their lives.

In the summer of 1940 children were sent overseas as well: As the air raids increased, there were offers to take British children to the United States, Canada, Australia, New Zealand, and South Africa. The Children's Overseas Reception Board (CORB) was set up. The cost of travel was met by the government, with contributions from the parents depending on what they could afford. Some 2,500 children were sent overseas by CORB; another 14,000 were sent privately overseas, more than one-third to the United States. American seamen offered to "seavacuate" British children without taking wages—but only if poor as well as rich children were carried.[6]

Not all the children whose parents wanted them to go overseas to safety were pleased with the idea. Eleven-year-old David Wedgewood Benn, son of a prominent labor M.P., wrote a letter to his parents, published in *The Times* in July 1940:[7]

> *I beg you not to let me go to Canada (I suppose you know that we are probably going?) A) Because I don't want to leave Britain in time of war. B) Because I should be very homesick. I am feeling likewise now. C) Because it would be kinder to let me be killed with you . . . than to allow me to drift to strangers and finish my happy childhood in a contrary fashion. D) I would not see you for an indefinite time, perhaps never again. Letters would simply redouble my homesickness.*
>
> *P.S. I would rather be bombed to fragments than leave England.*

Others relished the adventure of "seavacuation" despite lifeboat drills and bouts of seasickness. Among them was thirteen-year-old Morag Donald of Bishop, Scotland, who won first prize in the poetry contest that took place in the summer of 1940 on the HMS *Batory*.

Dubbed "The Singing Ship," the *Batory* sailed from Liverpool to Australia and New Zealand. On its marathon voyage of sixty days, the ship called at Capetown, Bombay, Colombo, Singapore, Fremantle, Melbourne, and Sidney. Morag wrote about her experience at sea:[8]

When the waves roll high and the sea breeze blows,
Then you never want to sail any more,
You just lie in bed with a basin by your head
Or stumble feebly down the corridor.
When lying on deck covered up with rugs
And you see others leaning o'er the rail,
Oh you feel so queer
You think your end is near,
And you wish you'd never left
Sweet home to sail.
You can't eat a bit, you can't sleep at night,
Your tummy seems to turn all 'round and 'round;
If you're feeling very bad, your head will ache like mad,
And you'll start to faint and swoon upon the ground.
Very soon it's gone—you're better again—
You feel as happy as the birds in spring
You sing all day as you run and play,
And your troubles to the wind you'll fling!

M ARGARET BEAL was fifteen years old when she traveled from her home in Scarborough, Yorkshire, to Canada. She kept a diary of her journey:[9]

Friday, August 9th, 1940
We finally got the word to set off. . . . We were singing songs, and . . . we got into buses and were taken to Glasgow station and were put on the boat train. Everybody looked at us as we went along the street, and we waved to everybody.

The boat train took us to Greenock. . . . We then went aboard the tender. It was blowy weather, but we stood on deck and watched the land get further and further away. Finally we pulled alongside the liner, which is called *Antonia.* . . . It is not a very big ship, but a very nice one. . . . They feed us marvelously, and our waiter is very nice. . . . The bunk is very comfy and I had a good night's rest. We have lifeboat drill and must not move without our gas masks.

Five days later, Margaret had a spell of seasickness: "Got up and felt rotten. Didn't want to move, but they made me go up on deck. Felt a bit better there and had a sleep, had half an apple and luckily didn't bring it up straight away."

On Monday, August 19—in the afternoon—the children sighted land. "At last we drew into Halifax," wrote Margaret, "and imagine our joy when a newsreel cameraman came aboard and took our pictures." They disembarked and went to the customhouse. It was past midnight when Margaret and her companions boarded the train to Winnipeg.

Her diary entry on August 20 reads:

> Everybody waves at us as we go past, and when we stop in the stations, people come and talk with us and give us sweets galore. . . . All the people over here talk so nicely. . . . We are always seeing soldiers, and sometimes their trains draw alongside ours, whereupon we talk to them. Lots of them give us sweets and things, and when we move away they all wave and stick their thumbs up, and we do the same.

Two days later, on August 22, the train reached Winnipeg. Margaret noted in her diary: "There were people on the platform to see us . . . and there were newspaper men who took our pictures. . . . It seems that the people were told that we were passing through all the stations, and that's why they were all there to see us."

The next day, the children enjoyed a bus tour of the town. Wrote Margaret:

> It was fun driving through the city and seeing all the shops. . . . Coming back we were given the newspapers with our photos in it, they are very good. It was funny, on the platform I said to someone that Peter Parson was a brat. Evidently the person to whom I said this was a reporter, because in the *Winnipeg Free Press* it said, "Little Margaret Beal, who had taken Peter Parsons, aged 6 (he is 11) under her wing during the journey said she would rather stand five million bombs than Peter for one hour, but there was a smile on her face when she said it."

Margaret Beal and Peter Parson were lucky. Three weeks later, in the third week of September 1940, seventy-seven children drowned in a cruel, icy sea when the *City of Benares* was torpedoed by a German U-boat off the coast of Ireland. Thirteen children survived, among them Jacky Keely, age nine, who was traveling with his sister Joyce, age six. In an interview with Ruth Inglis for her book *The Children's War: Evacuation 1939–1945,* Jack remembered:

> We took the train to Liverpool with two coachloads of children . . . and set sail on the *City of Benares* at 6 P.M. on Friday, the 13th. We knew we were headed for Canada, but we had no idea of the distance involved. The first days on the *Benares* struck us as being a huge lark. We had full waiter service and all the ice cream we wanted. . . . We had two

destroyers with us for . . . about three days. On the fourth day [September 17] a German submarine got under and up the middle of the ship. We were all in bed and there was a tremendous explosion. I was plummeted into the water [the *Benares* sank in thirty minutes] and was bobbing about in the water. I saw a raft with two men on it. . . . I pulled myself onto the raft and the two men sat on me as I lay under them. It was the only way they could keep me on. I wasn't scared, but my teeth were chattering like a German machine gun. The three of us seemed to be on that raft for an eternity. We lived on some biscuits we found in a . . . cupboard. There was also some tinned milk and some water. I felt fogged the whole time. It was rather like having the flu. We were down to the last can of milk when we saw a warship. It was the HMS *Hurricane*, a wonderful sight after forty-eight hours at sea. It took us back to Glasgow, and we were there for four or five days. It was all a nightmare, but I don't know, it didn't quite sink in, any of it.[10]

Jack's six-year-old sister, Joyce, drowned, probably just as he was being pulled aboard the raft. The CORB program was brought to a close after that disaster. It ceased to operate after October 1940.

The evacuation experiences of the British children who went overseas were generally happier than those of youngsters who had been sent to the English countryside and who were often jeered at in towns and called "vaccies," "vacs," and "skinnies" by their new classmates. The American-based evacuees were often fostered by relatively affluent or at least comfortable middle-class families who became an extension of their own. That experience is perhaps best expressed by twelve-year-old Caroline and ten-year-old Eddie Bell from Oxford, who spent their first Christmas away from home in New Milford, Connecticut. In *Thank You Twice or How We Like America* (1941), they wrote:

It was a lovely, frosty night with no moon but lots of stars. . . . As we got near the village we began to pass little lighted Christmas trees in front of the pretty white houses. We had never seen any before as there are none outdoors in England. . . . We wandered around the village green looking at the lighted trees and the candles in the windows. Then we decided to walk all the way home, singing carols as we went. . . . We bellowed out: "Good King Wenceslaus" and other familiar English songs. When we ran out of carols, we started on hymns. . . . It was a peaceful sort of a walk. . . . Of course we thought of England, and the blackness over it, and the people we loved there. But we all hid from each other what we were thinking, and at least the Germans had promised not to bomb that night. . . . When we go back we think the thing we will love most and remember best about America is this Christmas, and especially the little lighted Christmas trees. They make you feel that Americans don't want to keep their Christmas happiness just to themselves, but wish everyone to have a part of it. That gives you a warm and happy feeling.[11]

The last large wave of evacuation in Great Britain came in June 1944, after the first flying bombs and V-2 rockets fell on southeast England and London—an area that became known as "buzzbomb alley." Again, many evacuated children continued to drift home—often within weeks after their arrival in a "safe area." Ten-year-old Alan Skitton remembered that their destination was kept secret until the children arrived. "Being chosen was like being bidded for in a slave market," he recalled. "It was distressing because my friend and I were left towards the end. Two boys together were not the favorite catch."[12]

He and many other children returned for reasons similar to the ones he expressed in his letter to his parents:

> *Dear Mum and Dad,*
>   *I like the place and the people but I would like to come home. I went to the school today but I didn't like it so much as our school. . . . I amuse myself by going to the fields or looking at books. I am wearing my long socks, but I don't want to anymore. Was it hot yesterday. . . . We have no garden to play in. . . . I wish I could go home.*

A few days later came a message to his mother from the woman who was taking care of the boy: "I am sorry Alan is not settling down. . . . He still cries rather a lot. . . . I have done everything possible to make him happy and comfortable . . . but of course [he] misses [his] garden."

By March 1945, as the war entered its final phase on the European continent, there were only 400,000 evacuees left in the English countryside, and these were mainly from London. Six months later, after the end of World War II, there were some 38,000 children left who had no homes or parents to go back to or who had been abandoned by their families. Local authorities took care of the "unclaimed" children.[13]

Most British observers seem to agree that saving the lives of the children who lived in the cities under bombardment and improving the welfare of the generation of children born after the war were the two positive legacies of the child evacuations. Started as a short-term safety measure, the evacuations confronted the "haves" with the plight of the "have nots" and led to child welfare policies in the postwar world that considerably improved the lot of British children, especially the poor. Thus it remains a social experiment with far-reaching influences: In the midst of disaster and wartime muddle, children became for the first time a priority for such essentials as food, clothing, housing, medical treatment, and financial relief.[14]

Did the shared experiences of the child evacuees, in England and abroad, make them a "special generation"? Peter Shillingford, who was evacuated from London to Surrey during the war, is convinced that it turned out a huge variety of independent people.

> I think that the evacuation changed a whole generation of people. The expectations of the poor were raised. We had a heightened awareness of the economic differences. I don't think any of us would ever have been able to understand the level of life that some of the larger families of England had going for them in those days. We wouldn't have known it existed. [The evacuation] was the event of a lifetime for me.

The Evacuation of German Children: 1940–1945

The story of the evacuation of some 5 million children to safe places in rural Germany and to occupied countries such as Bulgaria, Czechoslovakia, Denmark, Hungary, Latvia, Poland, and Yugoslavia began on September 27, 1940 (three days after the British bombed Berlin for the first time), with a message of Reichsleiter Martin Bormann to the upper echelon of the Nazi Party. The message was labeled "strictly confidential" and began and ended with reference to an order given by the Führer: "Der Führer hat angeordnet."

It is a curious fact that there are very few published reports on the odyssey, suffering, and survival of the German child evacuees who participated in the largest evacuation of children in history. The enterprise was named "Kinderlandverschickung" (KLV)—the transport of children to the countryside. For more than four years, some 200,000 special trains carried 5 million German children, ages six to fifteen, to some 12,000 hastily erected camps—in the company of tens of thousands of teachers and (mostly female) volunteers.

As the Allied bombing of German cities intensified, especially in the north and west, the trains traveled only at night. Buses and steamboats on the Rhine, Elbe, and Danube Rivers carried cargoes of child evacuees as well. Toward the end, before the final breakdown, horse-drawn carriages were recruited to salvage whatever youngsters they could. Many of the child evacuees spent the whole war on the move—from camp to camp—as the margins of safety steadily diminished.

The silence about the extent and impact of this mass evacuation of children may reflect a dilemma that faced postwar Germany in its assessment of the Nazi period. Here was an action, based on an order by Hitler, that undoubtedly saved the lives of many children and protected them for years from the horrors of saturation bombing. But it was also an action that separated children from their parents and allowed for the mass indoctrination of millions of youngsters into the tenets of the Nazi philosophy—for the camps were run jointly by their teachers and by Hitler Youth functionaries.[15]

Three groups of individuals were the focus of the KLV:

1. Mothers with infants and preschool children, who were placed in rural areas, usually on a farm
2. Children under the age of ten, who were placed with foster parents and in local schools
3. Children above the age of ten to age fifteen, who were placed as a group in KLV camps with teachers from their hometowns

Most of the younger children grew attached to their foster parents and stayed in touch with them after the war had ended. Late in 1945, an eleven-year-old Nuremberg girl wrote an essay about her experience:

> We suffered several devastating air raids. My parents made up their mind to send me (age 9) and my brother to the countryside. My mother packed our belongings. Then . . . on September 1, 1943, we departed. There were thirty of us, varying in age from 6 to 14, from the first to eighth grade. We were accompanied by a teacher from our school. We travelled by train to Weissenburg. There we were picked up by a bus and travelled to the village of Bergen. There we all stood around, waiting to get a number. That was the number of a house. When it was called, someone from the family came to meet us. My brother and I ended up on a large farm, with strangers. But they were very friendly to us. They fed us frequently and well. We helped on the farm and stayed nearly 1 1/2 years in the village. Then our parents brought us back home.[16]

Older children who were placed in KLV camps lived their lives according to a tightly organized schedule that might look like this:

A German girl evacuee guarding her belongings.

7:00	Wake-up call
7:05–7:15	Morning exercise
7:15–8:00	Wash up and clean up rooms
8:00	Salutation of the flag
8:15–8:45	Breakfast
8:45–10:20	Lessons
10:20–10:30	Bathroom break
10:30–10:45	Midmorning snack
10:45–12:15	Lessons

12:20–13:30	Lunch
13:30–15:00	Free time
15:00–16:00	Sport
16:00–16:30	Midday snack
16:30–18:30	Homework assignments
18:30–19:00	Wash up
19:00–19:30	Supper
19:30–20:45	Time to sing, read, sew, write letters home, and listen to the news
20:45	Taps
21:00	Bedtime

Many preadolescent children liked this routine. Wrote a twelve-year-old girl from Nuremberg:

> I had the best time in my life in the KLV camp. . . . The building in which we found protection from the terror of the enemy bombs was located at the foot of a mile high mountain. Giant woods, canyons, rivers and creeks lent a romantic touch to the surroundings. . . . Together with our camp leaders we hiked to the nearest mountains and waterfalls. Our life in the camp was never boring. We had 4–6 hours of lessons each day, except for Sundays, and music and sports as well. We swam and skied. During the long winter evenings we wrote letters, and read books. In that way the horrible times around us were made more bearable.[17]

Adolescents had more ambivalent and sometimes downright negative feelings about the KLV camp experience. Wrote a German boy who was thirteen when he was evacuated:

> In 1942/43 the first bombing raid hit the city of Nuremberg. . . . When the attacks became more frequent it was impossible to have regular school lessons and we were told that we would be sent to a KLV camp. They promised us . . . paradise there. My parents believed all the PR and consented to my evacuation. Thus I ended up in Rothenburg. There we had Hitler Jugend Dienst, day in, day out, scarce and bad food, and little free time. There were nine of us boys in the same room. . . . We played a lot of tricks . . . and were often punished. We were supposed to go home after six months, but we were told that the Führer wanted protection for his youngsters and so we stayed on.[18]

A fifteen-year-old girl from the same city went to camp one year later:

Bombed out school buildings, destroyed railroad tracks, frequent air raid alarms during the day made it impossible to have regular lessons. Both parents and teachers worried about the well-being of their children. Hence we were sent to a KLV camp. On March 1944 our whole school was sent to the Riesengebirge.... There, in a small mountain village we resumed regular lessons ... and were well fed, but after a few weeks we all became homesick.... We were greatly disappointed that immediately after our arrival all our letters were censored.... Our routine of lessons, meals, play, and hiking, did not prevent us from wanting to go home as soon as possible. Our concern for our loved ones increased with the escalating frequency of the air raids on the cities.[19]

Her concerns were well justified: Halfway through the war, a teacher in a KLV camp in Carpathia made an entry into her notebook that tells of the casualties exacted at home. Margaret M. first describes the beauty of the surroundings and the security of the camp, and then she lists in her neat handwriting the names of 184 of the 250 children in her camp whose homes had been destroyed by bombs since they had been evacuated and whose parents were homeless or refugees. At the end of her list are six more names:

Margot Wolschky: Parents and little brother dead
Elly Witthaus (age 11): Mother dead
Ruth Steen (age 10): No news of the fate of her parents
Hertha Kohler (age 11): Parents dead
Ursula Bantien (age 10): Mother and siblings dead
Ursula Raithel (age 12): Mother and siblings dead

The children in the camps were usually devastated when they heard the news. Bernd M. remembered the day one of his teachers called one of his roommates, put his arms around the little boy, and took him aside to read him a letter: "We saw him only at night; pale and still. He crawled into bed, pulled his blanket over his head, and only after some hours, when I awoke, I heard him cry.... Days later, we learned that his mother and grandmother and his little sister had been killed in an air raid."[20]

And Stefanie M. recalls her reaction when one of her classmates learned that her father had been killed in action: "For days we did not want to talk to her. To be honest: We shied away from her—not to hurt her, but simply because we did not know how to deal with her loss."[21]

Christmas was a sad-sweet time for the child evacuees in the KLV camps. Their letters to Santa Claus reflected a growing awareness of the shortages at home: Children who had asked for books and games in 1943 asked for tools to fix broken toys in 1944. But they were happy with their plates of sweets and cookies, and especially with their lighted Christmas trees.

Annemarie Landenberger from Hamburg, who was a teacher in a KLV camp in Poland, reports in her diary an event that bears a striking resemblance to the experience of the child evacuees from Great Britain who spent their first Christmas in the United States: "Some 200 children walked silently [on Christmas Eve] through the deep snow to the nearby forest. It was cold and the sky was filled with stars. Suddenly they saw a tall fir tree with many candles which cast a bright glow in the darkness. They stood in a half circle around the 'Christmas tree' and sang Christmas songs. All agreed: This was the most beautiful Christmas they had ever experienced."[22]

The children had left Hamburg in June 1943 when the city was still mostly intact. They had not been told that major air raids in July, August, and September had reduced their hometown to ashes and rubble.

A fourteen-year-old boy was more aware of the grim reality. He had been evacuated in mid-October 1943 and was "content that we didn't have to endure the horrible air raids." A year later, on a gray day in November 1944, when he had been moved to a second KLV camp, he received the news that his father had been killed in action. "I was given two weeks leave [to go home]. Those were sad days. When I returned after fourteen days, it was close to Christmas—my second Christmas in the camp. We received some gifts on Christmas Eve and punch and cookies on New Year's Eve. In the evening we learned from the news that the enemy was coming closer and closer to our borders."[23]

In the months that followed, frantic attempts were made to relocate children in the KLV camps away from the approaching Allied troops, especially the Russians. On April 14, 1945, a KLV transport from Bohemia, under the leadership of a young medical student named Anneliese Schnitter, left Bad Podiebrad with sixty children. They reached the city of Prague and received another group of sick children and then went on to Furth, where they arrived on April 16 and were hooked up to a Red Cross train under the protection of anti-aircraft artillery. Early the next morning, in Schwandorf, they were attacked by low-flying enemy planes. Nineteen children perished: They ranged in age from eight to seventeen.

Thirteen-year-old Ingrid Janicke was among the survivors:

When the first bombs detonated, a nurse burst into our car and cried: "Tieffliegerangriff." The detonations came close and closer; unable to move I sat on the floor in the middle of the waggon; someone put a blanket over our head, so that our heads might be protected from splintering glass. I lost consciousness. When I woke up I looked through tattered wooden planks to the sky. An X-ray machine had landed on my right arm and I could not move my legs. There was a dreadful noise: the sound of detonations and the cries of wounded human beings. I prayed and cried for help. After some time a soldier pulled me out of the rubble and carried me to the railroad square. He asked me to close my eyes so I wouldn't see the horror around me. When I heard a woman's voice asking whether I was alive or dead I anxiously opened my eyes and saw the reassuring face of a nun.[24]

As the war in Europe neared its inevitable end, many children in KLV camps fled on their own and tried to reach home on foot. Thirteen-year-old Emil Weber left his KLV camp in the Bavarian woods, wandered on foot through southern Germany, and fetched his ten-year-old brother from another camp near Garmisch. Together the two boys wandered through the devastated countryside:

> At night we hid in barns, during the days we begged for food. . . . We looked for our aunt in Munich. We couldn't find her in the rubble, so we sat down in a corner and cried. An old woman took us home, cooked us a watery soup, and let us sleep on the floor for the night. . . . The next morning we went North. After four weeks we arrived in Düsseldorf [our hometown]. In the rubble we could barely find our street, our house was no longer there, my mother was gone. Neighbors told us that she had been evacuated to Euskirchen. When I heard the news I started to cry.

But after years of indoctrination, some children still clung to their faith in the Führer and in the final victory of the Fatherland. On April 20, 1945, a number of child evacuees were still listening to Goebbels' speech—his promise of loyalty and victory on the occasion of the Führer's birthday—in KLV camps that were surrounded by Allied troops. Gerhard M. remembered:

> Our camp leader turned the radio on—just as he had done so in previous years. We all had to line up in the yard, hoist the flag and listen to the trusted voice of Goebbels. In this moment I was immensely proud and had only one thought—to join the war and to sacrifice my life for the final victory. I lost the opportunity two days later when our camp was occupied by the Americans.

Among the documents in the archives of the KLV that survived the war is a bundle of letters that sum up what it was like to be a child evacuee in

An exhausted boy evacuee on his way home.

Hitler's Germany. The girl who wrote the letters tells an "ordinary" story set in extraordinary times:[25]

Inge L., from Hamburg, spent nearly five years in the KLV. She was first evacuated to southern Germany in October 1940 and did not return home until the fall of 1945. In the first two years of her life as an evacuee she was taken care of by kind host parents. Then she was placed into several camps (in occupied territories) where the teachers were confirmed Nazis. She worried about the safety of her mother and father and the ever lengthening separation from her family, and she witnessed in the end the total breakdown of her country and the ideology she had believed in.

On October 22, 1940, nine-year-old Inge writes her first letter from southern Germany to Hamburg: "Dear parents, I have been in Trieb for two days. I have not yet gone to an air raid shelter." Her foster mother reassures the parents: "Your daughter arrived safely on Sunday. Do not worry about her; she is safe with us and well cared for."

At Christmas, the foster mother thanks Inge's mother for the sweets and the fine soap she sent to her. She adds: "It is a beautiful Christmas for us—the feast is always more fun with children." As spring 1941 arrives, Inge asks to have her bicycle shipped to her foster home and announces: "When the war is over, I will write to Herr Hitler and ask his permission to stay here a bit longer."

In May, the foster mother asks Inge's parents: "Do you think the war will be over by fall?" Six months later, in mid-November, she puts Inge on the train to Hamburg. The girl spends the winter and spring with her family. The air raids continue. In the summer of 1942, Inge visits her foster parents again and spends several weeks with them, helping in the harvest and playing with her friend Bärbel.

In the fall, Inge turns eleven and can no longer stay with her beloved foster parents. The almighty bureaucracy decrees that she has to be evacuated to a KLV camp. On November 25, 1942, a new chapter begins in Inge's life: She travels with her class to a camp in Bohemia, in the former Czech Republic. She spends Christmas there and comes down with yellow fever. On March 10, 1943, her teacher writes to her parents in Hamburg: "Inge has come down with yellow fever for the second time. She is now with several other children in a rest camp." Inge writes to her parents from her sickbed: "I am mad at the Tommy (the British) because they do not leave you alone. In the next room, three girls have received the news that their house is totally destroyed. . . . Isn't this sad?"

The next phase of Inge's evacuation begins in June 1944—first to KLV Camp Politschka, then to Hlinsko. After the assassination attempt on Hitler on July 20, 1944, Inge writes to her mother: "When I get mail after an air raid on Hamburg, I am always worried. . . . Providence saw to it that our dear Führer escaped unharmed. We heard the story from our teacher and cried for joy."

In August, Inge tries to console her mother, who worries about the frequent air raids on Hamburg: "Do not be afraid, Mutti, and remain optimistic. Soon we will be home again. Our Führer knows well when he will strike back." But in October 1944—to their surprise—Inge's parents receive a hastily penciled letter: "I am writing this secret letter. . . . Please try as best you can to get me home. I have constant headaches and I am freezing." Another secret message arrives a day later: "The situation in the camp is awful. Every night, in bed, I get homesick." Days later, in an "official letter," supervised by her teacher, Inge writes, "We heard the announcement that the Führer is going to call up all men from 16 to 60 for the total war. I wish I was a boy so that I could fight as well."

In spite of constant air attacks on civilian trains, Inge's mother visits her daughter shortly before Christmas 1944 and then returns to Hamburg. Inge writes her parents about Christmas in camp: "On Christmas Eve, we all listened to Dr. Goebbels address. We all think of our brave soldiers . . . and especially of the Führer who cares for his people day and night."

In January 1945, the war catches up with the children. The mail to Hamburg is interrupted. In March, Inge writes to her grandmother: "I suddenly had the horrible idea that if something might happen to Mutti and Papi, I will have to take care of my little sister and brother."

The child evacuees go on another journey, this time to the west, in flight from the advancing Russians. A week before Easter, they end up barely ten miles from the town where Inge was first placed in a foster home in 1940. Her foster mother visits her on her bicycle, but Inge is not allowed to leave the camp. On Easter she writes a short letter to her parents: "This year we will not have Easter eggs. We gladly forsake them if our sacrifice helps us to bring the war to a victorious end."

That was the last piece of propaganda from her teacher, who left the camp a few days later, shortly before the Americans marched into town and distributed candy among the abandoned children. Inge was confused, for she had been taught they were devils in human form. For months she did not receive any news from her parents. At night she and the other youngsters sat in their camp, listening to radio reports of long lists of missing persons. Eventually some of the girls managed to return to Hamburg on their own.

Inge looks back at the years she spent as child evacuee: "Fate has been good to me. My family survived. . . . I had kind foster parents. . . . In the KLV camps we were well fed. But there was a steady rape of children's souls."

Not all former child evacuees share Inge L.'s assessment of the KLV camps. In 1981 Gerhard Dabel published an excellent collection from the archives of the KLV: *Die erweiterte Kinder-Land-Verschickung: KLV-Lager 1940– 1945*. The collection contains the reactions of some of the participants concerning the impact of the evacuation on their lives—seen from the vantage point of [late] middle-age.[26]

Most respondents expressed an appreciation for Dabel's efforts to write a documentary history of the KLV, so that more people would become aware that the evacuation to rural areas saved innumerable children from certain death by indiscriminate bombing. The majority agreed that such a move assured the continuation of schooling for children whose lessons had been constantly interrupted by air raids in their hometowns.

Many of the respondents also paid tribute to their teachers, who became surrogate parents for them while they were separated from home. On the whole, their classroom teachers, who taught them the basic skills necessary for survival after the war, received much higher ratings than the Hitler Youth functionaries who indoctrinated them. Many of the child evacuees still had annual reunions with their classmates and teachers from the camps.

Most former evacuees felt that the camp experience taught them flexibility and independence, and, in the case of those who were evacuated abroad, a broadening of their horizons. Most negative impressions came from the later periods of camp life, when the Hitler Youth and Party propaganda seemed to take over their lives. Most of the evacuees who were teenagers by then resented that intrusion but felt powerless to resist it.

It needs to be kept in mind that only about one half of the approximately 10 million German school children born between 1929 and 1939 were participants in the government-sponsored evacuation to the countryside. Contrary to military service, participation in the KLV was voluntary and dependent on parental permission. Many families chose to find temporary refuge on their own with friends and kinsmen in the countryside, just as they did in Great Britain. During the air raids, many parents and children preferred each other's company over the pain of separation, even if there was no extended family to fall back on.

When heavy bombing began in the area along the Rhine where I grew up, my mother had the good sense to let me stay at home. She and I were the only ones left in our immediate family, since both my father and my older brother had been drafted and were stationed in France and Russia at the time—my brother in the infantry, my father in the Luftwaffe. No doubt her decision was influenced by the specter of loneliness and by her intuition, based on past experiences with her rebellious daughter, that I would not take easily to camp life and regimentation.

When we were finally confronted with the order to evacuate in the spring of 1945, within full view of the Allied troops on the opposite side of the river Rhine, I refused to go. Like Gerhard and Ilse—who were still in KLV camps at the time—I felt that I should defend the Fatherland on my home turf until the hoped-for "miracle weapon" would turn the tide of the war! I was severely reprimanded for disobeying the Führer's order. A few days later, Patton's tanks rumbled through the narrow streets of my hometown.

4

So Far and Yet So Near

December 7, 1941: About 11:30 A.M.

As I went to the store next door to shop, a Japanese bomb fell and killed my neighbors. Soon after a fire was raging and I helped move our things as well as the neighbors' across the street to safety.... When they had it under control, the whole block, including my house, was burned down.... I was very much in grieve.

The words are those of a Japanese American Boy Scout in Troop 36, Post 1, Honolulu.[1] The boy kept a daily diary, now in the Hawaii War Records Depository, chronicling the aftermath of the attack on Pearl Harbor, which brought the reality of war to American children.

Dorinda Makanaōnalani, age seven, was having her favorite Sunday morning breakfast of papayas, Portuguese sausages, fried rice, and eggs in her house in Pearl City when the attack came. In *Pearl Harbor Child*, she writes about the events that changed her life and her country:

Suddenly we heard the sound of low flying planes, then almost immediately, loud explosions, followed by more planes passing directly over our house.... My father bolted up from the kitchen table and darted into the front yard. I was right behind him. We shielded our eyes ... and looked up into the orange-red emblem of the Rising Sun. The planes were so low, just barely above the roof tops, that we could see the pilot's faces and even the goggles that covered their eyes.... Even though we couldn't hear them, the incendiary bullets found their targets. Our kitchen was now on fire and parts of the roof were gone. The front door of our next door neighbor was so bullet-ridden from the strafing that it fell from its hinges. From our end of the peninsula we could see the old battle-wagon *Utah* as it turned on its side in the murky water. Everywhere we looked, there was smoke and fire.... One battleship was upside down and others were

61

ablaze and helpless. . . . It seemed as if the water was on fire with burning oil. Overhead, we saw a lone Japanese plane calmly make pass after pass through clouds of black smoke rising from the disabled ships. . . . Not knowing what else to do, Dad drove our black sedan up into the sugar can fields in the hills above Pearl Harbor. From the cane fields . . . we could watch the skies, and if the Japanese planes came back, we could hide ourselves in the tall sugar cane stalks. I thought of the unfinished breakfast we left on the kitchen table earlier in the morning. The bananas and papayas would really be o-no [delicious] right now. Maybe my dog "Hula Girl" had gotten so hungry that she had gotten the breakfast food. But what if she had been hit by a bomb or bullet? It was then for the first time that I began to cry.[2]

Children who lived farther away from Pearl City heard the roar of guns and saw planes diving and then soaring into the sky above the naval air base, but they thought it was merely a military exercise and went on with their usual Sunday activities. An eighth-grade boy at the Kalakau Intermediate School dashed out of his house after breakfast to play basketball with his friends in a neighboring park:

As we had just started to play, a shrieking shell passed over us. . . . Then at odd intervals more shells passed over us. . . . We thought that this was just another war maneuver. Suddenly, when I looked toward Pearl Harbor and Hickam Field, I saw great columns of black smoke and anti-aircraft shells bursting in the sky. "Look!" I shouted to my friends. No one spoke as we looked at the spectacle in sheer astonishment. Then, as we heard low flying planes above us, we saw one plane chasing another. It fired short bursts of machine gun bullets at its prey. . . . We hurried home. . . . I saw our neighbors on the rooftop viewing the spectacle with binoculars. None of them realized that they were exposed to danger. I ran into my house and turned on the radio. . . . Suddenly an excited announcer shouted, "The Japanese have attacked Pearl Harbor and a state of war now exists between the United States and Japan." . . . I sat by the radio in a daze and looked at my parents. Their faces were filled with anxiety. . . . They were natives of Japan, and no doubt, they were thinking, "What will happen to the Japanese people of these islands?"[3]

Marjorie Bond was at Punahou, a private boarding school only a few miles from the center of Honolulu. She and the other boarders had gone to church before breakfast. It was only after they returned to the third floor of their residence, Castle Hall, that they saw clouds of thick black smoke over Pearl Harbor. In a 1944 essay on "Wartime Hawaii" she wrote:

When the radio announced that it was war, everyone started going around in circles. No one knew what to do. Finally Miss Bryce called us down to the first floor and told us to get behind the furniture. This got very uncomfortable after a while, and we gradually filtered out to the fire escape, where we watched Lunalilo School burn. In the afternoon we had several air raid drills. Everyone dragged a mattress downstairs, and we lined them up along the walls in three rooms. Each girl had a pillowcase filled with what she would need in case she was bombed out, ready to grab at an instance's notice. When a shell fell on the campus in the middle of the night, the first thing I did was to grab my bag, and then I sprang up against the wall. Everyone gave up the idea of sleep after that and waited anxiously for dawn.[4]

By the time night fell on December 7, the news of the Japanese attack on Pearl Harbor had reached the U.S. mainland. In *Victory Gardens and Barrage Balloons*, Helen Jean Stubblefield, at the time a freshman at Bremerton High School in the state of Washington, remembered:

We were playing Christmas records when our neighbors . . . came running up the hill and pounded on our door. They were white as sheets and Alma was crying. Al said "Turn on your radio, Pearl Harbor has been attacked by the Japs and we are at war." My father went to the radio and my mother slumped onto the couch with her face flushed and Alma beside her. It was obvious to me that we had been notified of a dramatic blow that had been delivered not just to Pearl Harbor, but to us individually.[5]

My sister-in-law, Nancy Jacobsen, age eleven, heard the news of the attack in the late afternoon when she was listening to the radio in her Minnesota farmhouse. Nancy and her family were worried about the fate of the oldest son, Richard, who was serving in the U.S. Navy. His ship, the USS *Lexington*, was stationed in Hawaii. They learned a few days later that the *Lexington* had left Pearl Harbor hours before the attack began and that Richard was safe. Her brother, Stanley, age fifteen, vowed that evening that he, too, would go to sea and fight the "just" war. He enlisted in the navy the day he turned seventeen.

Harriet Neufeld, age fifteen, was doing her homework at the kitchen table as dusk fell on her hometown of Belmont, Massachusetts. Her dad had just turned on the radio to listen to the evening's entertainment when the news broke that the Japanese had attacked the U.S. naval base in far-away Hawaii. The next day, in a nationwide address, Franklin D. Roosevelt called December 7, 1941, a "day of infamy." The president spoke slowly, pausing frequently, and said: "I ask that the Congress declare that since this unprovoked and dastardly attack by Japan . . . a state of war has existed."

Within days after the Japanese attack and the declaration of war, Americans began to build air raid shelters. "December 9, 1941: I helped my father in digging the bomb shelter," reads an entry in one Boy Scout's diary in Honolulu. "Did home duties, built air raid shelter," reports another on December 10. "We finished an air raid shelter in our yard," writes a third boy on December 14.[6]

The girls from the Punahou School in Honolulu were getting used to total blackouts. "In the evenings, as there were no lights," wrote Marjorie Bond, "we amused ourselves by telling ghost stories." All schools were closed for the remainder of the year. Seven-year-old Dorinda Makanaōnalani spent the next few days with her dog, "Hula Girl," collecting pieces of shrapnel and small bullet casings in her neighborhood in Pearl City. Her dad removed bullets from the kitchen wall.

The military governor urged all nonessential civilians to leave Hawaii. Many military dependents boarded ships and left for the safety of the mainland. On their journey to the West Coast, the children sang a song they had just learned: "Let's remember Pearl Harbor as we go to meet the foe. Let's remember Pearl Harbor as we do the Alamo." The residents of Hawaii who stayed behind prepared themselves for an expected invasion from Japan.

"December 24, 1941: Christmas Eve and no Midnight Mass. News from the Orient very alarming," reads the diary kept by a nun at the Sacred Hearts Academy in Honolulu. "Christmas 1941: A War Christmas spent mostly in our dear Chapel, praying for the needs of all, mostly for Peace on Earth. Many of our pupils come to visit us; every one is valiant and ready to accept any sacrifice."[7]

Throughout the U.S. mainland, children feared that enemy bombs might rain down on them, too. Children on the West Coast, from California to Oregon, felt especially vulnerable. In San Francisco, children's fears were compounded by the sirens that blared on the night of the American war declaration. The local newspaper reported: "Raid alarms on the Pacific coast started at 6:45 P.M. at which time there were . . . reports [unconfirmed] of hostile aircraft. . . . In San Francisco, police sirens wailed through Market Street, and all lights went out as searchlights swept the skies. . . . The Golden Gate City abruptly became reminiscent of London and Rotterdam."[8]

In the months to come, children in the San Francisco Bay Area had to wear ID tags stamped with numbers corresponding to those on lists held by Civil Defense, in case they became evacuees or casualties. In Hawaii, where the fear of another Japanese attack persisted, even though school had reopened by early February 1942, children received gas masks and had periodic tear gas tests.

Dorinda Makanaōnalani's brother Ish was only two years old. His mask was almost as long as he was. "The infant version was really comical," wrote his sister. "It was actually a bag to slip into, with big bunny ears on top for decoration and a see-through window to look out of." Each school day, the little girl trudged to her classroom, carrying her gas mask.

An eighth-grade girl at Punahou described a drill at her school:

> If gasses were dropped every one had to leave the air raid shelter [which the boys had dug] and go to the showers in the basement of Bishop Hall. Everyone got in line and then the line walked through the double line of showers. I washed the girl's back in front of me, and the girl in back of me washed my back. . . . A man from the Chemical Engineering Department of the Army . . . prepared a tear gas chamber and everyone started through it with their gas masks on, and then half way through we took off our gas mask. . . . I came out crying and it made me realize the value of a gas mask and I wasn't so careless about mine after that.[9]

Dorinda's parents, who had remained in Pearl City, were air raid wardens and guided practice drills with make-believe bomb bursts. The little girl's favorite part was to be a make-believe "casualty," stretched out on the side of the road waiting for a volunteer ambulance crew to find her and bandage her "injuries." She found even blackouts fun—at first. "It meant taking my flashlight into the closet and looking at picture books or listening to the radio while in there," she remembered. "That was an adventure, until it also meant there was nothing else to do but go to bed when it got dark. That's when I decided it wasn't fun anymore."

On the mainland, some children panicked during air raid drills in school. "I was always afraid," remembered a young girl, "that we would get bombed when I was at school and not at home with my family"—a reaction she shared with many youngsters in England and Germany.[10] Other children enjoyed the blackouts if they could be with their parents, who might read to them by a flashlight or tell them stories. A girl from Detroit recalled: "When there would be a siren, we would turn off every light in the house, go out on the porch, and see nothing but stars, a moon and searchlights."

A more prosaic account of an air raid drill can be found in a letter written by a nine-year-old girl to the *Jack and Jill* magazine: "When the alarm goes off . . . we go down into the lower corridor [of our school] and sit on our books. We sit on our books, so we won't get tired standing."[11]

In March 1942 *Life* magazine published a picture essay with recommendations by a child psychologist, Carolyn Zachry, on how to best prepare America's children for protection from air raids. She counseled parents to "incorporate 'war's grim realities' into family life as rapidly as possible." Her prescription was part of a three-page picture essay that illustrated the civil defense preparations of the Mott family of Long Island, New York. According to Miss Zachry, seven-year-old Billy Mott and his four-year-old sister, Evelyn, were learning "to face whatever may come as a game."

In the first photo, the children wear "Churchill suits" and tin helmets, as they huddle under the dining room table to play "air raid shelter." The second picture shows Father Mott blowing a whistle, as the children run for cover. The next photo depicts both parents and children in the basement, with a flashlight and a Red Cross kit. In the next picture Billy helps his father put up blackout curtains. In the final photo, the entire Mott family huddles near the furnace as Mother Mott reads to Evelyn and Father Mott reads with Billy. Fortunately, the Motts of Long Island, New York, and Miss Zachry of *Life* magazine were spared the anxieties of a real air raid!

Ironically, the only mainland American children who died as a result of enemy action were not killed in an air raid but lost their lives in the explosion of a Japanese balloon bomb in Oregon. The tragedy occurred on May 5, 1945, two days before the surrender of Germany, and three months before the defeat of Japan. Months earlier, in late 1944, Japan had released some 6,000 balloons armed with bombs, expecting them to ride the jet stream that swings eastward across the Pacific to the United States. At speeds of up to 300 miles per hour, the bombs floated thousands of miles across the ocean in little more than a day. Built-in timers caused the balloons to drop and the bombs to explode.

On Saturday morning, May 5, Archie Mitchell, a local pastor, his pregnant wife, Elsye, and five Sunday School children from Bly, Oregon, went fishing. The children were Sherman Shoemaker, age eleven; Jay Gifford, Edward Engen, and Joan Patzke, age 13; and Joan's brother, Dick Patzke, age fourteen. At a muddy spot in the Ponderosa pine forest, Archie Mitchell stopped his car. His wife, slightly carsick, got out and wandered with the children to a nearby creek. It was about 10:20 A.M. when Elsye called her husband, "Look what I have found, dear." Her husband called back, "Just a minute; I'll come and look at it."

Archie started the car and went up the hill, followed by the foreman of a road crew who was working nearby. The men could see the woman and children about 100 yards away in the woods, staring at something. Then there were two terrible explosions. The mangled bodies of the four boys were scattered around the bomb crater; the girl survived the immediate blast, but died later, as did Elsye, the pastor's pregnant wife. To avoid panic, federal government officials prevailed upon the local coroner to conclude: "The cause of death, in my opinion, was from an explosion of an undetermined source." Their gravestones read "Killed by Enemy Balloon Bomb."[12]

By the second half of 1942, Americans felt relatively secure behind their military and civil defenses, and they worried less that their children might be bombed. Now the U.S. government—aided by the schools, voluntary organizations (like the Scouts, the Camp Fire Girls, and the Future Farmer's of America), and the mass media—called on America's children to perform a variety of patriotic tasks. Children set to work—collecting scrap, buying and selling war bonds, and tending victory gardens.[13]

The little redhead who most enthusiastically expressed the connection between volunteerism and patriotism in children was the cartoon character Little Orphan Annie. In the summer of 1942, in the daily comic strip read by millions of American children, Annie saved the East Coast of the United States from a German U-boat attack. Coincidentally, a real German U-boat was detected and sunk off the Atlantic coast some months later! (My uncle, Herbert Werner, one of the few surviving commanders of a German U-boat, wrote about its exploits in his book *Iron Coffins*.)[14]

When her comic page playmates chided Annie and her schoolmate, Loretta, because they always seemed to be too busy to play, she told them: "Loretta an I have somethin' lots more important than playin'. We're doin war work. It's our war, just as much—or maybe more—than anybody else's. We're givin all we can to help those who are givin' ever' thing for us!"

Within one month after Annie lectured her young pals about doing their bit for the war, "Junior Commando" chapters were being organized all across the country—sending thousands of youngsters scrambling through junk piles and knocking on doors to round up all the scarce raw materials needed to feed the factories that were manufacturing products. Boys and girls were eager to help the war efforts and to earn stripes. Tops in rank was Colonel Annie![15]

Meanwhile, twelve-year-old Clive Oldroyd advised the commander in chief of the Pacific war theater, General MacArthur, how to improve the weapons at his disposal. On July 22, 1942, Oldroyd wrote:[16]

> *Dear Sir:*
>   *I am sending you this idea as I thought your experts might be able to make use of it. I am very interested in planes and have built several. As I am only twelve I cannot carry out my ideas. I can only think about them and draw plans. The idea is to protect the gunner from enemy machine gun fire. While*

firing at one plane, another can attack him, but it would [be] of no use as the armor would stop the bullets. I enclose sketches. I would be thankful if you would let me know what you think of my ideas, as I want to see the Japs put in their place. My second idea is that of a quick firing gun. . . . The gun acts as a giant rifle except that the shells are loaded into the shell chute, whereas the rifle has clips. As soon as one shell has been fired, the case falls out of [the] spent shell door, which automatically is opened after the shell has been fired. The next shell falls from the chute and takes the first shell's place, and so on, until the chute is empty. The chute is then loaded with shells, one by one. The shells are obtained from the racks. The time taken to load the chute is sufficient to allow the gun to cool.

Yours Faithfully,
Clive Oldroyd

For one young girl from Lawrenceville, Virginia, the call to action was urgent. Her letter from August 9, 1942, was written some fifty years before the U.S. Army sent women into combat:[17]

Dear General D. MacArthur:
This is not a humorous letter but a letter of plea. I've asked the President, I've asked the Senator & Congressmen if they would answer my letters. I have never gotten an answer. I am asking you to at least to answer this letter. I am a girl of 12 years old (when this letter gets to you). I know this letter will sound funny to you, but I am an American and I have rights. I think I should fight for those rights. I have tried to organize clubs, but they just don't turn out, so now I'm taking more drastic steps and asking you to put me in the army. Even if it is only to be a nurses' helper (I know quite a bit about bandaging). I suppose you'll say, "you'r needed on the home front," but I'm not—I don't do anything. . . . I want to hold a gun and take orders and get down in trenches and mow these Germans down 5 by 5. Please answer this letter and tell me that I can do what I want.

Yours truly,
Patricia A. Coyle

On November 10, 1942, a girl from Wichita, Kansas, sent the general a progress report of *her* work on the home front:[18]

Dear Sir:
You may wonder why I am writing and who I am. Well to begin with I saw a piece in the paper that said a little boy of nine wrote to you. That gave me the same idea, so that is why I am writing to you. You may want to know

what I look like, so I will try my best to describe myself. I am twelve and about 5 foot 1 in. I have brown eyes and brown hair. I am in the seventh grade in school and I like all my teachers, which is quite unusual. I suppose you would like to know what we at home are doing. My mother saves grease for bullets. I also buy a war stamp every time I get a quarter. We save paper, all kinds of metal and rubber. I have a bicycle but I don't very often ride it to save rubber tires. One of the mill companies has organized a club for children called "The Junior Commandos," and they are doing a great job. We Girl Scouts are doing our bit by taking care of small children so that the parents may work in war factories. We are also running errands for people. I thought you might like to know that we here at home have a picture of you hanging on our front room wall with an American flag over it. I have five uncles in the army and one cousin in the marines. . . . I am writing this letter in hopes that you will get it, because I don't know your exact address. By the way, if you would like my school mates to write you I would be glad to tell them so. Well it is about time for taps so I had better be closing this letter.

Your Truely,
Miss Joan Dooley

P.S. If you can find a little time to answer my letter I would feel it a great honor. *We all know what a great job you are doing over there, and I know we'll all try to do our part.*

In 1942, the War Production Board (WPB) pronounced the shortage of scrap metal urgent. Children like Larry Lauerhass (age seven, from Long Beach, California) and teenagers like my future husband, Stanley Jacobsen (from Lake Benton, Minnesota), scoured their homes and neighborhoods to search for miscellaneous pieces that could be hauled in their wagons. In a nationwide scrap drive on three successive Saturdays in October 1942, youngsters all over the country tacked up posters to inform the public that one wall radiator could become seventeen .30 caliber rifles; one lawn mower could be turned into six three-inch shells; and one shovel could become four grenades. Some 30 million children brought in 1,500,000 tons of scrap metal, enough, the WPB announced, to build 425 liberty ships. On one of these, Stanley Jacobsen would be shipping out for combat duty in the Pacific in 1944.

In November 1943, *Jack and Jill*, a magazine for young children, published a six-installment story, "The Scrappers Club," that appealed to the patriotism of American boys and girls. While their father is away at war, his four children form the Scrap Happy Hiking Club. Waving an American flag, they scour the countryside, singing "We're after scrap to get a Jap." The high point of their scrap metal drive occurs in the fourth installment of "The Scrapper's Club," when the children discover an abandoned trolley car hidden in overgrown brush. They are tempted to use it as a secret clubhouse, but their patriotism prevails. They turn it over to the mayor of their home town, "so my daddy will have guns," as one of the children explains. The mayor honors the four children in a public ceremony; their father returns on a surprise furlough; their grandfather builds them a clubhouse in the family yard; and they are all served ice cream.[19]

The paper shortage became critical in 1944, as war industries at last produced sufficient amounts of material to cause a need for massive amounts of packing material. One June 7, 1944, Sammy Berman (age five, from Minneapolis, Minnesota) informed his father, who was serving as a medical officer with the U.S. Army in England: "Dear Poppy: The paper sale is not to be tooken to school. It is to be put out on the boulevard and the paper is tooken away. I hope you'r nice yet!"[20]

The war effort needed great sums of money for the production of guns, bombs, and bullets. War Bonds became special savings accounts. The people of the United States loaned money to their country, to be paid back later with interest. Children helped with bonds by buying individual savings stamps that went into a special book. In Hawaii, Dorinda Makanaōnalani went without lunch to buy ten-cent stamps that she put in her stamp book. When she had filled her book with $18.75 in stamps, she took it to the post office to trade for a war bond. She was not alone in her war effort.

On Thanksgiving 1943, Robert Puchmond, an eighth grader from Nassau County, New York, wrote a fiery essay on the topic "Why We Should Live Up to Our War Bond Pledge:"

> We should all of us live [up] to our pledge because all the soldiers in the Pacific War Theatre or on the [European] Front expect us to. We wouldn't want to let them down. If we let them down it might be the difference between [their] life or death. Who are fighting heroic battles every day. And who are unrelentingly pushing the Japanese hordes and Nazis from the oppressed countries. Back up our fighting men by buying defense stamps and Bonds so that the day of liberation [will come] and all the oppressed and dominated countries may be free once more and that victory and the shining light of hope and peace may shine [on] their happy faces. . . . So lets . . . fill that quota assigned to us by Christmas which is, we, the whole school, is to buy 9,000 dollars in Defense Stamps and Bonds and to supply or buy 375,000 rounds of ammunition. I am sure every child wants their father, brothers, and cousins to come home as quickly as possible.[21]

By Christmas 1943, the pupils from the Nassau County Schools had raised enough money to buy twenty-five fighter planes and 646,000 rounds of ammunition to honor the birthday of the Prince of Peace!

Isabel Berman—the mother of David, age ten; Betsy, age seven; and Sammy, age five—wrote to her husband, Captain Reuben Berman, in a letter on January 27, 1944, from Minneapolis, Minnesota:

Dearest Reuben:

David has almost 18.75 saved up in his bank account. He wanted to buy a bond. I gave him a check. He is supposed to pay me back out of his savings account. Actually, he can have both. He did not want to put the bond in the name of David Berman and Isabel R. Berman. He made me the beneficiary. He said the bond was all his. . . . Betsy will get a bond next. They sell war saving stamps in school. With four dollars from Rose and Dave and about fifty cents a week at school it won't be long before Betsy can have a bond. And then will come Sammy.

Dorinda Makanaōnalani in Hawaii and David Berman in Minnesota had one other thing in common: They grew victory gardens. Dorinda grew lots of vegetables and tropical fruit but hated to hoe the weeds. David had weeds, too, but also "bugs, radishes (red and white), lettuce, beets, carrots, and tomatoes. There is also a package of mixed flowers each," he wrote to his dad on a fine day in May.

Older children and teenagers took the place of adults who had gone to war: At age twelve, my future sister-in-law, Nancy Jacobsen, who had two brothers serving in the navy, became the "hired hand" on her Minnesota farm: "I was taught to milk cows. I also learned how to drive a team of horses. Then I learned to drive. Dad had bought a John Deere tractor, and I learned how to handle that."

Barbara Butler and her friends in the eighth grade at Punahou School worked one day a week in the pineapple fields and canneries because of the acute labor shortage in Hawaii. The boys in her class organized a unit of the ambulance corps and "manned" first aid stations at night. Joshua Akana, from the Kamehameha Boys School in Honolulu, wrote a letter to the *Weekly News Review* in Washington, D.C., telling the readers what "the Hawaiian boys are doing out here on the fighting front":

Our upper classmen are in school two weeks and then out on part time jobs the following two weeks. These boys . . . are able to fill skilled labor jobs at the various airfields, Electric Company, Hawaiian Airlines, Mutual Telephone Company and others. . . . We are proud of our record here and try to be worthy of our class motto: LET's TALK ABOUT IT AND THEN DO IT. Doing something here is recognized universally as of most worth. We work during vacations and holidays—this is the accepted way of life today.[22]

But there was also a darker side to patriotism. In his 1995 book *Earning Their Stripes: The Mobilization of American Children in the Second World War,*

FOLLOW THE PIED PIPER
Join the United States
School Garden Army.

Robert W. Kirk argues that although altruistic educators urged children to be circumspect in their perception of enemy peoples, government and media propaganda led many children to hate the enemy. Children learned to hate and fear Nazi brutality, but they learned to hate the Japanese on racial grounds as well.

Although American children traditionally had played cowboys and Indians, cops and robbers, war games now reached a height of popularity. One concerned mother from the American heartland complained: "It's the most ridiculous thing. My child's never seen a bomb. I doubt if he has even the vaguest notion as how to identify a Japanese, much less a German. And yet, there's real zest in killing."[23]

An illustrated article that appeared in December 1942 in *Parents' Magazine* under the heading "Toys: New and Different" presented a more relaxed adult view of war play. The writers (both women!) highly recommended the purchase of a "Super Ack Ack Gun" as a suitable Christmas gift. "It raises and lowers while a ratchet simulates anti-aircraft fire and wooden shells automatically eject." *Parents' Magazine* justified its recommendations on the grounds that "child guidance workers agree that it is best for children to be able to express freely through dramatic play what they hear and feel about war."

As members of a highly mobile population, children spread war games everywhere, from midwestern cow pastures, to the banks of the Mississippi river, to the sun drenched valleys of California. Dressed in cast-off military uniforms, decorated with patches and braids, armed with Red Ryder BB guns, boys attacked the enemy. Nobody wanted *to be* the enemy. And the enemy was *always* defeated!

*C*HILDREN'S PERCEPTIONS of the enemy were also affected by the war movies they saw. On May 5, 1944, Sammy Berman, age five, dictated a letter to his father in England:

> I'm very proud of you being a pilot. I know why the Memphis Belle *is a good show. It is about planes. . . . I would love to go up in a big plane. I have seen fighting shows before.* Guadacanal Diary—*that was very good.* Salute to the Marines—*in this one American plane shot down a lot of Jap planes. A lot of Jap planes crostet a bridge and an American blew up the bridge and the Jap tanks fell into the water.* Destination Tokyo—*that was about an American submarine. A Jap destroyer came along and they fired torpedoes at it and sunk the Jap, the destroyer. And every minute they came up to take a look.*

Two weeks earlier, the boy had confided to his poppa, "I dreamt that I made a Japanese airplane crash. . . . The pilot said to the copilot, 'I bet he doesn't know that we've got swords.' It was good because it was only a dream." And on June 7, 1944, he told his poppy: "I've got a poem for you. 'Hirohito, I hope you choke when Tokyo goes up in smoke.'"

In that same letter, Sammy offers some advice to his dad:

> I don't want you to be kind to the Germans or Japanese because they're mean. (His older sister says, "Don't you want him to be nice to the Japanese babies

and the Japanese mommas and the Japanese daddies who are not in the army?") I'll let you like the German babies and the German people who are not in the army. Because Hitler's men fight them. . . . And Hitler, you didn't know, but he is a very wicked man.

And his sister Betsy, age seven, wrote on September 20, 1944: "If i had wings like a angel(!) I would take some bombs and fli over to germany and japen and bom them, then you could come home sooner. I want you most if all."

Sometimes a thoughtful teacher helped children to see the humanity behind the stereotypes of the enemy. One of them was a grade school teacher, Inez Drummond, who taught my sister-in-law, Nancy Jacobsen, in a country school in Minnesota:

> I remember this teacher I had. . . . She would say, "Now put yourself in their place." She repeated it to keep the attention of our class: "Put yourself in their place! So many of our people are against the Germans, against the Japanese, but these people didn't make the decisions, it was their leaders."
>
> That message stayed with me all my life. She was a unique person— a very good person. She was a neighbor of ours who married a man who was killed in the war, and she still had that message for us.[24]

Other children met "the enemy" as prisoners of war and were surprised that they did not look like devils. Larry Lauerhass had cousins in Arizona. There was a German prisoner of war camp near a local air base, and Larry learned from his grandmother that "the POW's were very nice, and that they were homesick, and that they liked my cousins because they were very blond."[25] One of the Germans rescued his youngest cousin, a two-year-old boy, who had fallen into a well. What mattered, in the end, was putting a human face to the foreign names and scenes that filled the minds of American children during World War II.

One of the most endearing memories about getting to know folks "over there" comes from Lloyd Hornbostel's book *War Kids: 1941–1945: WWII Through the Eyes of Children*. Hornbostel describes a wartime Christmas in Wisconsin that was more memorable to him than all the war movies he had seen. In the fall of 1944, he and his ten-year-old classmates had collected and repaired toys that were to be sent to a far-off village in France that had been liberated in the invasion. On Christmas Eve a small miracle happened. As he sat in church, his French-speaking neighbor walked to the front, just before the end of the service, carrying a flat package:

School children reciting the pledge of allegiance, San Francisco, California.

She first translated a Christmas greeting for all of us from our French village . . . and then she opened the package. It was a phonograph record. Someone pushed the old church phonograph up in front of the altar, and for a spell our church was filled with the sound of French children's voices singing their thanks to us in traditional Christmas carols. There wasn't a dry eye in the place after the benediction. That Christmas night, as we stepped out into the cold night with our families, the joyful spirit of a small French village was with all of us. We had given so little, and had received so much in return.[26]

Three months later, in the early spring of 1945, American troops crossed the Rhine and were pushing deep into Germany. David Berman, age eleven, was eager to collect war souvenirs. On April 21, he wrote to his dad from

Minneapolis: "I showed the Nazi pin and band of cloth to the children in my room. . . . Please send me some more German stamps and other souvenirs." And ten days later: "Thank you very much for the patches, fishing knife and coins. Please send us many more souvenirs from Germany. But beware of boobytraps."

Larry Lauerhass, age ten, wrote one of his pen pals from Long Beach, California, asking for something captured from the enemy. Toward the end of the war, he received an unusual collection:

> It was all tacked onto a piece of cloth, about a foot square, on dark velvet, with a black band around it. On these were all kinds of medals and little ceramic dolls of soldiers in different uniforms. So there was the ski patrol and the Africa Corps, and all of this stuff. . . . And then there was a whole series of little photo books, with a little string at the corner. . . . They were all photo books of Hitler and of party activities and military activities. . . . I still have it today.

On May 6, 1945, the week of Germany's unconditional surrender, David Berman wrote to his "dear papa," whom he had not seen for two years:

> *At long last we have had victory over the would be destroyers of mankind. For 6 years the Nazis oppressed humanity in ways which have never been exceeded in the history of the earth. But now I want to get to the point. I believe that now that we have won victory over the Nazis, you and other men should be allowed to come back home again. I think that there are many people who would agree with me on that.*

Three months later, on August 14, 1945, the Japanese surrendered as well. Dorinda Makanaōnalani watched the V-J celebration in Pearl City, near the naval base where the war had begun. She was ten years old now, her heart full of joy and gratitude: "We could see the fireworks from the harbor, and hear the air raid sirens wailing . . . and whistles from the ships. The sky over the harbor was flashing brightly with flares, each one adding its notes in a symphony of light. . . . The war was over."

As the summer of 1945 drew to an end, most American boys had left their backyard battlefields. Mothers heard fewer and fewer shouts of "Bang! Bang! You are dead!" under their kitchen window. The boys had finally put down their Red Ryder BB guns and were busy at work in garages, sheds, and basements. On September 2, 1945, six years after the outbreak of World War II in Europe, and three weeks after Nagasaki was destroyed by a nuclear blast, the *New York Times Magazine* published an article that related the experience of a curious mother who went to see what activity had replaced the game of war. She found her son and his pals fabricating a strange contraption out of tin cans and flashbulb lights. When she inquired what project they were working on, the boys told her they were making an atomic bomb!

5

Behind Barbed Wire

O<small>N</small> D<small>ECEMBER</small> 10, 1941—three days after the Japanese air attack on Pearl Harbor—a nun at the Sacred Hearts Academy in Honolulu wrote in her diary: "Last night, the only girl left with us, Gertrude Schröder, born in Germany, has been taken away from us and kept on Sand Island. Great is our consternation as we know full well how innocent and harmless she is. Yet nothing can be done to release her."[1]

It would take seven weeks of negotiations with the Western Defense Command and the fervent prayers of the Reverend Mother Louise Henriette and her nuns before the little girl was finally released. On January 26, 1942, the nun's diary contains good news: "The schools reopen much to the delight of all. The Academy is full to capacity. Gertrude Schröder is released and arrived here today, happy, so happy! And what a loving welcome she received."

Throughout World War II, only a few hundred German- and Italian-born individuals, like Gertrude, were temporarily excluded from Hawaii and "sensitive" areas on the East and West Coasts of the United States. The brunt of American exclusion policies fell instead on some 110,000 persons of Japanese descent. Most of the Japanese Americans removed from their homes for reasons of "national security" were school-age children, infants, and teenagers too young to vote. Two-thirds had been born in the United States. None had committed crimes against their government—yet they were collectively ordered to report for internment and faced the staggering necessity of leaving all they had known, owned, and loved.[2]

My colleague, Isao Fujimoto, is one of the gentlest persons I have ever known. Born on the Yakima Indian Reservation in the state of Washington, he was in the third grade when the United States entered World War II. He remembers:

> Right after Pearl Harbor, the FBI came to our home, and my father just disappeared. I remember the last words he was saying was, "Oh, let me put my pants on." That was it. He was put in the Yakima County Jail. Then he was sent to a Detention Center in Missoula, Montana. . . . I didn't see him until about a year-and-a-half later. My mother asked me to write a letter to President Roosevelt. I wrote him about our situation. All of us were still farming, and though my fa-

Two Japanese American girls awaiting an evacuation bus.

ther disappeared in December, come Spring we put in the crops. The question is what do we do next? So I wrote to Roosevelt saying that it would be very good if my father came back because we really needed help here. My mother was only twenty-five years old at the time, and there were five kids. We were farming using horses. If was very hard if you're small, and you can't really hook up a plow. So I told the President that it would help a lot if my father could return to his family. Of course, I never got a reply. . . . I was eight years old at the time.[3]

The Fujimoto family would not be planting or harvesting any more crops for the duration of the war. On March 2, 1942, the commander of the Western Defense Command, empowered by President Roosevelt's Executive Order 9066, designated Washington, Oregon, California, and parts of Arizona "strategic military areas." He ordered all persons of Japanese descent who lived there removed from their homes. They were allowed to take with them only what they could carry.

On March 31, 1942, the evacuation began, first to assembly centers, where the average stay lasted about 100 days, then to hastily constructed relocation centers. Thirteen of the sixteen assembly centers were in California; the other three were in Washington, Oregon, and Arizona.

For many Japanese American children who were evacuated from the West Coast, the most traumatic experience was leaving behind their beloved pets, since animals were not allowed to go with them. One boy wrote about leaving his collie: "He knew something was wrong. . . . He suspected because we were carrying our suitcases with us. When we were going down our garden . . . he followed us. I told him to go home. He just sat and howled and cried. My cousin and I got mad at him but we love him almost as much as if he were a human being. . . . When we drove away from the front of the house he was sitting inside the fence looking out."[4]

GRACE NAKAMURA, testifying in 1981 to the Commission on Wartime Relocation and Internment of Civilians, recalled her trip:

On May 16, 1942 at 9:30 A.M. we departed . . . for an unknown destination. To this day I can remember vividly the plight of the elderly, some on stretchers, orphans herded on the train by caretakers, and especially a young couple with four preschool children. The mother had two frightened toddlers hanging on to her coat. In her arms, she carried two crying babies. The father had diapers and other baby paraphernalia strapped to his back. In his hands he struggled with dufflebag and suitcase. The shades were drawn on the train for our entire trip. Military police patrolled the aisles.[5]

*A mother and three child evacuees on a train to
the Manzanar Relocation Center, California.*

To this day, child evacuees often recall two images of their arrival at the assembly centers: a cordon of armed guards and the barbed wire and search-lights, symbols of a prison. Many families arrived at the assembly centers in-complete. In some cases, as was true for Isao Fujimoto, fathers had earlier been taken into custody by the FBI. Peter Ota, sixteen, and his thirteen-year-old sister traveled by themselves. Their father had been detained and their mother was in a tuberculosis sanitorium, where they were allowed to visit her only once in four and a half months.

One of the most severe discomforts of the assembly centers was the lack of privacy. Eight-person families were placed in 20-by-20-foot rooms; six persons, like Isao's family, in 12-by-20-foot rooms; and four persons in 8-by-20-foot rooms. Within the confines of the assembly centers, the Japanese American evacuees tried to create a community. They organized schools, sport programs, talent shows. Yet even the youngest knew they were no longer free.

A young girl wrote about her life in the shadows of the guard towers at the Tanforan Assembly Center in California:

> We have roll call about 6:30 every day. I'm at the rec hall every day before roll call we are playing basketball or swinging on the bars. When the siren rings I get so scared that I sometimes scream, some people gets scared of me instead of the siren. We run home as fast as I could then we wait about 5 minutes, when the inspectors come to check that we are all home. . . . After the camp roll call finish the siren rings again. . . . I hate roll call because it scares you too much.[6]

Ironically, Independence Day was cause for elaborate celebrations among the children. Sachi Kajiwara described her preparation for the Fourth of July at Tanforan:

> I worked as a recreation leader in our block of 7–10 year-old girls. Perhaps one of the highlights was the yards and yards of paper chains we (my 7–10 year-old girls) made from cut-up strips of newspapers which we colored red, white and blue for the big Fourth of July dance. . . . These paper chains were the decoration that festooned the walls of the Recreation Hall. It was our Independence Day celebration, though we were behind barbed wire, military police all around us, and we could see the big sign of "South San Francisco" on the hill just outside of the Tanforan Assembly Center.[7]

In the late summer and fall of 1942, the assembly centers were emptied and their tenants were loaded onto trains and sent to relocation centers in Manzanar and Tule Lake, California; Poston and Gila, Arizona; Topaz, Utah; Minidoka, Idaho; Heart Mountain, Wyoming; Granada, Colorado; and Jerome and Rohwer, Arkansas. Like the assembly centers, the relocation centers were inadequate in size, sanitation, and protection from the elements.

They were located in the most God-forsaken regions of the United States, exposing the evacuees to windblown deserts, blistering summers, and freezing winters. At Poston, Arizona, summer temperatures reached 115 degrees; at Minidoka, Idaho, they averaged 110 degrees. In the relocation centers in Wyoming and Colorado, winter temperatures fell to minus 30 degrees. The centers in Arkansas were in damp, swampy lowlands where poisonous snakes made their home.[8]

A young girl, Itsuko Taniguchi, described in a poem her journey to "the land with lots of sand":

> *My Mom, Pop, & me*
> *Us living three*
> *Dreaded the day*
> *When we rode away,*
> *Away to the land*
> *With lots of sand*
> *My mom, pop, & me*
> *The day of evacuation*
> *We left our little station*
> *Leaving our friends*
> *And my tree that bends*
> *Away to the land*
> *With lots of sand*
> *My mom, pop, & me.*[9]

In August 1942, Isao Fujimoto's mother and her five children, ranging in age from eight years to ten months, made the trip from the Portland Assembly Center to the Heart Mountain Relocation Center on a rickety train accompanied by armed guards. Isao recalls:

> Once we got to Heart Mountain, I remember how traumatic it was because we got separated again. My youngest sister Keiko had measles, so she was quarantined. My mother had to be with her. When we got taken to the barracks, I didn't know where my mother was. I wandered all over the camp looking for her. I found her. I don't know how. . . . I discovered her in an empty barrack sitting all by herself with my [baby] sister.

Keiko was not the only infant who would spend years of her life in a concentration camp. One hundred and one Japanese American orphans and foster children—some as young as six months—were quietly rounded up by the U.S. Army during the summer of 1942. These children, some with only one-eighth Japanese ancestry, were sent to a hastily built children's village at the Manzanar Relocation Center in southern California. A number of them had been in the care of Catholic nuns in the Maryknoll Home for Japanese Children in Los Angeles. Father Hugh T. Lavery of the Catholic Maryknoll Center was so taken back by the harshness of the commandant presiding over the uprooting of the orphans that he wrote a letter to President Truman

Nursery school at Heart Mountain Relocation Center, Wyoming.

after the war, protesting the man's confirmation as undersecretary of the army: "Colonel Bendetsen showed himself to be a little Hitler. I mentioned that we had an orphanage with children of Japanese ancestry, and that some of these children were half Japanese, others one fourth or less. I asked which children should we send. . . . Bendetsen said: 'I am determined that if they have *one* drop of Japanese blood in them, they must go to camp'"[10]

Bendetsen was true to his word. He gave the first order to evacuate an orphanage—the Shonien, or Japanese, Children's Home of Los Angeles—in a telegram on April 28, 1942, ignoring the frantic pleas of mercy from the board's chairman. Twenty-four children from the Shonien were evacuated to Manzanar. The Catholic nuns at the Maryknoll Home for Japanese Children did not wait for the army orders. They tried to whisk away thirty-three orphans to foster homes outside the West Coast evacuation zone. Eventually only seven of their orphans were sent to Manzanar.

Supervisors from the Salvation Army's Japanese children's home in San Francisco also fought hard to keep their nineteen children—but to no avail. Army officials also sent to Manzanar seven Japanese American children who lived with white or Latino foster families and a blond and fair-skinned six-year-old boy by the name of Dennis Bambauer who had been placed in a Los Angeles orphanage for white children; officials did not know that his mother was Japanese American until someone checked his records.

On June 21, the first forty orphans arrived at Manzanar. On the army bus that transported them to the center, a social worker named Matsumoto tried to keep the children entertained. She encouraged a four-year-old girl to sing. A young military policeman listened to her sing "God Bless America" and wept. In the next two and a half years, sixty-one more youngsters were admitted to the children's village at Manzanar. Among these "orphans" were babies born to unmarried teenage mothers in other relocation centers. Others were classified as orphans when the FBI arrested their fathers and when their mothers were dead or had been hospitalized for tuberculosis or mental illness.[11]

Manzanar

The children's village at Manzanar included three one-story frame buildings, next to a pear apple orchard. They were bigger than the other barracks in Manzanar and included a wrap-around porch and broad lawn. Unlike the rest of Manzanar, each building also had running water, baths, and toilets. The Matsumotos, a husband and wife team of social workers from the Japanese Children's Home of Los Angeles, served as professional administrators, supported by two Maryknoll nuns, three members of the staff of the Salvation Army home, and some of the older girls from the main center who worked as part-time "helpers" at the village.

Francis L. Honda was seven years old when he was moved to the children's village and remembered it as "a very lonely place with babies crying and nothing to do. It was like the end of the world for me."[12] Without families of their own, the orphans relied on each other for support. At night, the teenager Sohei Hohri told bedtime stories to the fourteen small boys in pajamas who slept on metal folding cots in his dormitory. Since there were few books around, he told his stories from memory and acted out scenes from his favorite play, *Les Misérables*. There was a nursery school and kindergarten in the children's village, but most of the children attended school and recreational facilities in the main center at Manzanar. Jeanne Wakatsuki—who was seven years old at the time—observed that the other evacuee children treated the orphans "as if a lack of parents put them somehow beneath everyone else."[13]

On Thanksgiving Day 1942, the director of the Manzanar Relocation Center, Ralph P. Merritt, visited the orphans and was greatly moved by the youngsters' fate. He wrote in his daily notes: "The morning was spent at the Children's Village with the 90 orphans [to date] who had been evacuated from Alaska to San Diego and sent to Manzanar because they might be a threat to national security. What a travesty of justice!"[14]

Located some 210 miles northeast of Los Angeles in the California desert, surrounded by sand, sage, and Joshua trees, Manzanar was the first of the relocation centers to which Japanese American evacuees were sent. It was also the largest center—holding, at its peak, over ten thousand men, women, and children. Surrounded by barbed wire, it was guarded by eight towers with machine guns. No area within the center was beyond the reach of a soldier's bullet, not even at night, when searchlights continually scanned the brush.

The center covered one square mile and was divided into thirty-six blocks, with twenty-four barracks to each block. Each barrack was 20 feet wide and 120 feet long. Laundry and bathroom facilities were located in the center of each block, each of which had an open mess hall. Soldiers marched the new arrivals to the mess hall, where their numbers were recorded. Guards searched them, seizing anything they considered dangerous— kitchen knives, knitting needles, even hot plates for warming babies' milk.

Each internee was issued a cot, an army blanket, and a sack to be filled with straw for a mattress; then families were assigned to a barrack according to size and number of children. A family of four lived in a 20-by-25-foot space; two couples without children shared one space, with only sheets hung as partitions to separate them. Soon, lids from tin cans became items highly valued by all Japanese American families in the center. They nailed them over knotholes in the floor and walls to repel the desert winds. No one ever completely overcame the relentless onslaught of desert grit.[15]

The 250 people living in a block shared common bathroom facilities. On a concrete slab, down the center of the room, toilet bowls were arranged in pairs, back-to-back, with no partitions. Teenagers, especially, resented this loss of privacy and identity. Only after many complaints were the toilets partitioned.

Kinya Noguchi described the routine in his testimony to the Commission on Wartime Relocation and Internment of Civilians in San Francisco:

> Life began each day with a siren blast at 7:00 A.M., with breakfast served cafeteria style. Work began at 8:00 A.M. for the adults, school at 8:30 or 9:00 for the children. Camp life was highly regimented and it was rushing to the wash basin to beat the other groups, rushing to the mess hall for breakfast, lunch, and dinner. When a human being is

placed in captivity, survival is the key. We spent countless hours to defy or beat the system.[16]

In *Farewell to Manzanar,* Jeanne Wakatsuki described how her brothers would make a game of seeing how many mess halls they could hit in one meal period: "Be the first in line at Block 16, gobble down your food, run to 17 by the middle of the dinner hour, gulp another helping, and hurry to 18 to make the end of the chow line and stuff in the third meal of the evening. . . . No matter how bad the food might be, you could always eat till you were full."[17]

Getting to the mess hall on time; finding an empty shower; keeping the baby's diapers clean; and coping with the heat, dust, and insects were major tasks. Holding the family together without privacy required a full-time commitment. So did the evacuees' determination to get an education for their children.

At Manzanar, the elementary school opened on September 15, 1942, in un-partitioned recreational barracks, without lining on the wall or heat of any kind. Within two days a cold wave combined with dust storms forced the school out of operation until the barracks could be lined and stoves could be installed. Such problems were common to all the relocation centers where schools opened that fall, in spite of lack of buildings, lack of teaching staff, furniture, and textbooks. In the first few weeks, many of the children had no desks or chairs and were—for the most part—obliged to sit on the floor or to stand up.

But in a few months there were improvements. The War Relocation Administration (WRA) reported: "By the end of 1942 . . . it was no longer necessary for many pupils to sit on the floor, but seating was frequently of a rudimentary character. Text books and other supplies were gradually arriving. Laboratory and shop equipment and facilities, however, were still lacking. No center had been able to obtain its full quota of teachers."[18]

The shortage of textbooks and supplies was mitigated by donations through the American Friends Service Committee. Many of the Caucasians who came to the center to teach and do volunteer work were Quakers. They were held in high esteem by the children. Remembered Jeanne Wakatsuki: "What I see clearly is the face of my fourth grade teacher—a pleasant face, but completely invulnerable, it seemed to me at the time, with sharp commanding eyes. . . . She was probably the best teacher I've ever had—strict, fair-minded, dedicated to her job."

By the spring 1943, two blocks of the center had been turned into Manzanar High, and a third block of fifteen barracks was set up to house the elementary grades. The children had new desks, blackboards, reference books, lab supplies, and a school newspaper, the *Manzanar Whirlwind.*

As the months turned into years, the center began to resemble an American small town, with schools, churches, fire and police departments, Boy Scouts, baseball leagues, and glee clubs. Outside the regular school sessions and the recreation programs sponsored by the WRA, classes of every kind were being offered: singing, acting, trumpet playing, tap-dancing. Observed Jeanne Wakatsuki: "The fact that America had accused us, or excluded us, or imprisoned us, or whatever it might be called, did not change the kind of world we wanted. Most of us were born in this country; we had no other models."

One of Jeanne's favorite songs that she sang in the Glee Club, made up of girls from the fourth, fifth, and sixth grades, was the "Battle Hymn of the Republic." She also learned baton twirling, a trick that was thoroughly, unmistakably American—spinning the silvery stick to the tune of a Philip Sousa march. Her brother Ray played in a six-man touch football league. Her sister Lillian, who was in high school, sang with a hillbilly band, called the Sierra Stars—wearing jeans and cowboy hats. Her oldest brother, Jim, led a dance band, called the Jive Bombers. He played trumpet and took vocals from Glenn Miller arrangements. But there was *one* song he refused to sing—out of protest—"Don't Fence Me In."

The younger boys, including those from the children's village, played marbles, sandlot baseball, and a war game called "Capture the Flag," the same game that other boys played throughout the nation. They yelled enthusiastically, "Kill the Jap," as many a "Jap" was slaughtered by seven- and eight-year-old Americans with Japanese faces. But whatever games they chose, there was one thing that made their playgrounds different from the rest of America: Between the children and the highway, there was always a fence and a guarded gate!

A fourth grader's comments on the Statue of Liberty, printed in the *Manzanar Whirlwind*, eloquently sums up the mixture of innocent pleasure and pain that was part of the children's daily existence in the relocation centers: "The statue of liberty is big and tall, the light in the torch is very bright. It can be seen far out at sea. People say it is very beautiful. I wish I could see it."

John Tateishi, in his "Remembrances of Manzanar," sums up the paradoxical experience of growing up as an American-born child of Japanese descent within the confines of a detention camp:

> In some ways, I suppose, my life was not too different from a lot of kids in America between the years 1942 and 1945. I spent a good part of my time playing with my brothers and friends, learned to shoot marbles, watched sandlot baseball and envied the older kids who wore

A baseball game in the firebreak between barracks at the Manzanar Relocation Center, California.

Boy Scout uniforms. . . . We imported much of America into the camps, because, after all, we *were* Americans. Through imitation of my brothers, who attended grade school in the camp, I learned to salute the flag by the time I was five years old. I was learning, as best one could learn in Manzanar, what it meant to live in America. But, I was also learning the sometimes bitter price one has to pay for it.[19]

Minidoka

Among Ella C. Evanson's students at Washington Junior High School in Seattle were many Japanese Americans who were sent off to Camp Harmony and later to Minidoka, Idaho. Students wrote short messages in her scrapbook prior to evacuation and later wrote letters from camp.[20] One of them, dated March 20, 1942, reads:

> *I will start out my letter by writing about the worst thing. I do not want to go away but the government says we all have to go so we have to mind him. It said in the Japanese paper that we have to go east of the Cascade Mountains . . . to Idaho. . . . If I go there I hope I will have a teacher just like you. And rather more I hope that the war will be strighten out very soon so that I would be able to attend Washington school again.*

And on May 10, Miss Evanson's class received a letter from camp:

> *I wish to say hello in a short way. Now to begin with our room, we have one room shared among 7 pupils [people?] and the walls are full of holes and cracks in which cold and chile air struck us in a funny way that I could not sleep at all last night. . . . Our beds are on loose by the U.S. Army and our mattress is a cloth bag strawed with hay. Now is a nice place to end my letter, so "good bye" until next time and please write to me, all.*

Another Seattle teacher, Mrs. Elizabeth Bayley Willis, taught at Garfield High School. One of her seniors wrote from Minidoka in November 1942, frustrated and angry: "Barbed fences are going up, and there are eight watch towers. . . . I just can't see why the government must coop us up after throwing us in the middle of sage country. . . . If this is democracy, I think I'd rather be under a stern dictatorship. At least I wouldn't be winding up behind barbed wire fences every time."[21]

Topaz

The Japanese American children from the San Francisco Bay Area were sent to Topaz, a three-day trip by train from San Bruno, California, to a harsh windblown desert near the town of Delta in Utah. There they would live till the evacuation orders were rescinded. During the spring and summer of 1943, the High Third Grade class of Mountainview School at Topaz kept a class diary that reflects the children's fervent desire to contribute *their* part to the war effort.[22]

The March 11, 1943, entry into *Our Daily Diary* read: "Today we started to join the American Junior Red Cross. Please remember to put 10% of your pay into war bonds and stamps. We should not kill spiders because Uncle Sam needs them for the war." The next day, March 12, the children wrote: "There are many people ill in Topaz with mumps, pneumonia, appendicitis and cold, so we must take very good care of ourselves. We shall save rubber, money, spiders, paper, and lots of other things to help Uncle Sam."

Two months later, on May 18, 1943, the third graders drew two American flags in their diary and reported proudly: "We have a large box filled with nails. Every day we bring more and more nails for Uncle Sam." Three days later, on May 21, the children drew planes and tanks under the announcement: "This afternoon the second group of the Japanese American Combat Team left Topaz to join Uncle Sam's army. Edwin's uncle is a volunteer."

And on July 5, their diary entry displayed an American flag, proudly waving from a flagpole. The children reported: "There was a camp-wide 4th of July carnival on the weekend. . . . It was lots of fun." Two weeks later, they resolved, "The girls of our class will knit small squares of yarn. . . . We shall put them all together and make a blanket for the American Red Cross."

Donald Nakahata, born in San Francisco, was twelve years old when he and his mother were transferred from the Tanforan Assembly Center to the relocation center in Topaz, Utah. He remembers learning to drive a tractor and going out to work on the center's poultry ranch. The most distressing part of his experience was the absence of his father, who was arrested by the FBI and spent years in justice department internment camps from Santa Fe, New Mexico, to Bismarck, North Dakota. There he died from a stroke. Remembered the boy:

> Occasionally we would get a letter from him, and there would be sections . . . cut out. He never really said anything much about his health. . . . We got a telegram one night after dinner saying that he'd died and that we should advise the authorities by eight o'clock the following morning as to the disposition of the remains. So my aunt who worked for the welfare department in camp in Topaz, went and beat on her supervisor's door and managed to get them to send a wire saying they should send the remains back. He was cremated in Delta, Utah, and my mother carried his remains around for a long time. . . . My mother, as I learned after she died, had been a missionary to Japan, and she was really a very devout Christian. And that's how she made it.[23]

Yoshiko Uchida, a young student from the University of California at Berkeley, worked as prison camp teacher, both at the Tanforan Assembly Center and the Topaz Relocation Center. In her book *The Invisible Thread*, Uchida chronicled her experiences teaching Japanese American children in barracks cold as a refrigerator with wailing winds that poured buckets full of

A classroom at the Topaz Relocation Center, Utah.

sand through the holes of the roof of her classroom. She also remembered happier times, especially her "Concentration Camp Christmas," when there were decorated trees, special food, and presents donated by the Quakers.

> The day before Christmas a large carton of greens arrived for my mother from her friends in Connecticut. Opening it was like opening a door to an evergreen forest. It smelled glorious. It was the smell of Christmas. . . . That night, as I lay on my cot, surrounded by the fragrance of the fir sprays, listening to Christmas carols on the radio, I thought about how we would spend Christmas Day in a concentration camp. We would go to church, we would visit friends, and we would have a special turkey dinner at the mess hall without having to stand in line. As they had on Thanksgiving, the mess hall crew would serve us at our tables as a special treat.[24]

Poston

Christmas was also on the minds of the children in the Poston Relocation Center in Arizona. In 1943, Emiko Kamiya, a seventh grader, wrote about her "First Christmas in Poston":

> Have you ever lain awake on Christmas Eve with everything about you strange, quiet and still as death?. . . . As Christmas drew nearer, we older children knew that this year there wouldn't be gifts and much fun for the little children, for out here in a concentration camp we thought no one would think of us. So we tried extra hard to make Christmas as happy as possible for the tots. Christmas was ushered in with cold, howling winds. . . . Refusing to be discouraged, we planned a party for which everyone gladly donated some money. We decorated the Mess Hall with red and green crepe papers and wreaths made of desert holly. . . . As if with the waving of a magic wand the bare cold mess hall was changed into an enchanting place.[25]

On New Year's Day 1944, the teenager Kazue Tsuchiyama wrote an essay that was printed in a high school album entitled "Out of the Desert" and distributed by the Junior Red Cross to their chapters throughout the United States.

> Even though we are far out in the desert, we were not forgotten at Christmas time. Gifts from long unforgotten Caucasian friends were received. . . . My gratefulness cannot be expressed, except, that I will always remember that I had a friend outside even in this serious time. New Year's came with a lot of resolutions to be followed—to bring comfort and joy to young and old and bring courage to each and everyone of us to show the outside world that we are *not* cowards. There will be happy days in days to come, and there will be sad ones, but we'll always face them with smiling faces.[26]

Tule Lake

For Isao Fujimoto and his family, 1944 would bring another move—this time from Heart Mountain, Wyoming, to Tule Lake in northern California, near the Oregon border. Isao's fate had been determined by his parents' answers to a WRA loyalty questionnaire. If the evacuees answered "Yes" to the questions "Will you stop pledging allegiance to Japan?" and "Would you serve in the Armed Forces of the United States?" they were considered loyal;

Fishing in a canal at the Poston Relocation Center, Arizona.

if they answered "No," they were considered "disloyal." The questions were posed to anybody over eighteen. Isao, then ten years old, remembered:

> My mother and father did not want our family separated again. My father had been confined in [the Justice Department internment camp in] Missoula, Montana, and joined us at Heart Mountain about a year-and-a-half afterwards. So when the questionnaire was administered my parents decided [to answer] "No," "No." As a result we were among the segregated families and sent to Tule Lake. . . . It was

a very different kind of camp, because now you were not among people you knew. You were among people who had voted similarly on the
loyalty test. The atmosphere was quite charged. . . . There were many
kinds of organizations that were very pro-Japan. In fact, that became
not only a dominating but a divisive force within Tule Lake. It set up
an atmosphere of tension and intimidation.

Tule Lake was being transformed from a resettlement to a segregation
center. A double eight-foot fence was erected; the guard was increased to a
battalion; and six tanks were lined up conspicuously. Within the camp, potential troublemakers were isolated in a detention center that was known as
"the stockade."

One of the evacuees later testified at the public hearings of the Commission on Wartime Relocation and Internment of Civilians about the aftermath of a food riot:

> I was thirteen-years-old when we were at Tule Lake. . . . The most
> upsetting experience happened to me when martial law was declared
> throughout the camp because of a food riot. We were told that the
> military police would come to search each one of our families in the
> barracks. The two MP's looked formidable as they walked in with
> guns at their side and asked roughly if we had any weapons, liquor or
> cameras. To be forced to let the MP's in our small humble quarters
> seemed like such invasion of personal privacy that the emotional effect
> of the search still haunts me.[27]

Ben Takeshita, fourteen at the time, remembered what happened to his
older brother, a teacher, who sponsored a sports tournament for the children
that was considered too militaristic by the center's authorities. After days of
questioning about what was going on, he was brought in front of a group of
MPs ready with rifles:

> He was asked if he wanted a cigarette; he said no. . . . You want a
> blindfold?. . . . No. They said, "Stand up here," and they went as far as
> saying, "Ready, aim fire," and pulling the trigger, but the rifles had no
> bullets. They just went click. . . . I really got mad listening to it, be-
> cause of the torture that he must have gone through, and the MPs al-
> lowing it to happen. I mean it's like the German camps: Torturing the
> people for the sake of trying to get them to break down.[28]

At Tule Lake, Isao Fujimoto found himself in a relocation center that was
not oriented toward the American mainstream, as had been the case at

A young boy on the day of departure at the end of internment, Tule Lake Relocation Center, California.

Heart Mountain. Now he was placed in a setting where there was much more emphasis on the Japanese culture and martial arts. "The pro-Japanese people were very well organized," he remembered. "They even organized young kids but my family was not into that." Instead the eleven-year-old boy learned to live with contradictions in his daily life. In the morning he would go to the Japanese school, where he and his classmates assembled outside and started the day off by bowing to the east—toward Japan. In the afternoon, he would attend the American school, where he and the other children would pledge allegiance to the American flag.

"We thought nothing of it," he recalls. "For kids growing up, you just go along. There were more important things [for me], like baseball, collecting and trading stamps, and hunting for Indian arrowheads." When he came home from school or play, he found the grown-ups in his block listening attentively to the Japanese war news over a shortwave radio. "The propaganda came from the Japanese Ministry of War which was broadcasting all the victories. People took this all very seriously. They thought the war was going well."

Isao gained a different perspective from the teaching staff of the American school, who were his only contact with the outside world. And he discovered that his Japanese American compatriots were not the only ones who were behind barbed wire. On his way home from school one day he saw a group of Caucasians working alongside a ditch. "The strange part of it was that they were being bossed around [by MPs]. I asked, 'Who are these people?' They turned out to be prisoners of war (POWs). I learned later on that they were Italians captured in North Africa."

Even as the interns lived behind barbed wire, young Japanese American men served their country on battlefields in the Pacific and in Europe, and as interpreters, providing probably the most important link in American Intelligence. The 442nd Combat Team, an all Japanese American unit fighting in Italy and France, emerged with more casualties and more decorations for bravery than any other unit of comparable size and length of service in the army's history. One member of this unit was the teenager John Kanda, who had finished high school in Tule Lake.

On December 17, 1944, more than three years after the attack on Pearl Harbor, Japanese Americans finally regained their freedom to come and go to any part of the United States. The *San Francisco Chronicle* of Monday, December 19, 1944, announced the end of exclusion with these words: "The Western Defense Command yesterday lifted restrictions prohibiting the return of approximately 100,000 persons of Japanese ancestry excluded from California, Washington and Oregon in 1942 for reasons of military necessity. Exclusion has now been placed on a basis of individual loyalty instead of race."

Two fifth-grade girls who had been interned for a quarter of their lives celebrated the news in the poem "Our Flag," published in the Manzanar school newspaper:

> *Our flag is waving high*
> *Against the light blue sky.*

We salute to you.
We sing to our Banner
In a gallent manner
Dear Red, White and Blue
We stand up for you.
We all sing
While Liberty reigns
Dear Red, White and Blue
We remove our hat for you.[29]

Erica Harth, the six-year-old daughter of a WRA worker at Manzanar, was the only Caucasian child in the first grade at the elementary school in the last year of the center's existence. She met no resentment among her Japanese American classmates. "I felt accepted in a way perhaps unique in my life," she wrote later.[30] She revisited Manzanar on the fiftieth anniversary of President Roosevelt's Executive Order 9006, on the day when it was designated a National Historic Site!

A chalk-white funeral monument to Manzanar's dead now dominates the scene. Along with the former auditorium and two small stone guardhouses that flank the entrance, the monument is all that remains of the center today. Erica found the site much smaller than she had remembered: "This shrinkage in dimension, so common to adult's perceptions of childhood scenes revisited, applies inversely to the place of Manzanar in history. On the flimsiest of pretexts, ten thousand people were jammed into the small plot of land that made such a puny prison cell for them and such a large playground for me. The meanness of the space measures the enormity of the injustice."

— 6 —

The Schoolgirl and the General

I N THE DWIGHT D. EISENHOWER LIBRARY in Abilene, Kansas, a special folder of correspondence sits right next to the letters Ike exchanged with the king of England, President Roosevelt, foreign dignitaries, and the generals under his command. But the letters in this folder are different. They are letters written over a period of sixteen months—from April 8, 1942, to August 2, 1943—between Mary Louise Koehnen, a schoolgirl in Dayton, Ohio, and Major General Eisenhower—her favorite soldier.

Mary Louise was in the seventh grade at Corpus Christi School in Dayton when she sent Eisenhower the first of her letters, together with a miraculous medal and a copy of the Crusader's Prayer. It was the second week in April 1942, and Eisenhower was in the midst of preparations for the Allied landings in North Africa.[1] By the time he wrote his last letter to Mary Louise in August 1943, she had graduated from the eighth grade, the Axis forces had capitulated in North Africa, and the Allied forces had gained a foothold in Sicily.[2] It was, as his son John would later write, "a time of great stress" for the Supreme Commander of the Allied Forces in Europe.

The twenty-two letters that traveled across the Atlantic and along the shores of the Mediterranean show the human side of World War II—a child's enthusiasm and a general's gentle longing for an ordinary, peaceful life, a peace that he and his soldiers fought for in distant lands.

> *2441 Auburn Avenue*
> *Dayton, Ohio*
> *April 8, 1942*

Dear Sir:

I am sending to you a Miraculous Medal and a copy of the Crusade Prayer, which you are supposed to say every day. I will go to Mass and Holy Communion once a week, and offer it up for you. I am sure your prayers will be answered.

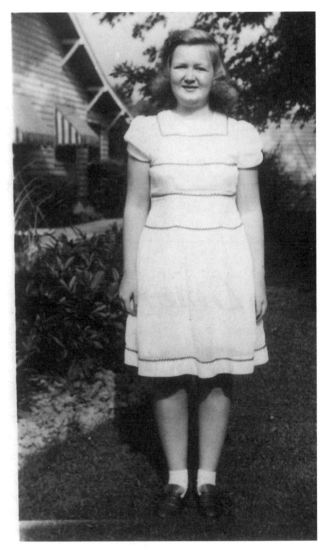

Mary Louise Koehnen.

I am in the seventh grade at Corpus Christi School and I like it a lot. My Daddy just received his commission as first Lieutenant, and he will be stationed at Patterson Field, here in Dayton. We are very happy because he will be home with us, and we hope he will stay with us during the duration. I hope you are happy and contented where you are stationed. I know you are a very busy man, but I would love to have you answer my letter.

Monday was Army Day, and they had a big parade downtown, it was very interesting. There were many different kinds of trucks from Wright and Patterson Field and there were also many "beeps" if you know what I mean. They had a German plane which was made in Germany, finished in England and Post Mortem in Dayton, and two Japanese planes which were made in Japan, finished at Pearl Harbor, and Post Mortem in Dayton. They also had many High School Bands. After the parade we went out to Wright Field which had open house, and saw many different planes including a few English and British planes.

Well I guess I will have to say good-bye now, for I have to go to bed.

As ever—*Your unknown little friend,*
Mary Louise Koehnen

P.S. If you want to write to me, my address is on the other sheet of paper.

————————

April 15, 1942

Dear Mary Louise:

My sincere thanks for your thoughtfulness in sending the Miraculous Medal and the Prayer. It is generous of you to think of this for me and I am deeply appreciative. But wouldn't it be better to say them all for the boys that will take part in this great struggle? Not all of them are fortunate enough to have a friend like you.

I am glad you enjoyed the Army Day parade and display at Wright Field. Your description was so vivid that I could almost see them myself. I hope that you will not have to move from Dayton, since you like it so well.

One again my thanks and good wishes for your happiness.

Sincerely yours,
Dwight D. Eisenhower
Major General, U.S.A.

————————

A SOLDIER's PRAYER

At Taps and Reveille

O God of power and love, behold me before Thee this night (morning) to add my faltering prayers to those which a little child daily brings to Thee in my behalf.

Make me a soldier (sailor, Marine) worthy of the great cause for which we fight.

Give me strength when the going is hard

Give me courage when danger is near.

In Thee I place my trust. Lead me through the perils of this war to the peace of that better world to which I have dedicated my life. But if the service of Thee and my Country calls for the sacrifice of my life, I only ask, dear God, that Thou be with me at that moment, confident that Thy peace awaits me in eternity.

AMEN.

May 21, 1942

Dear Mary Louise:

Thank you so much for your letter and for the card with the daily prayer. I truly appreciate your thoughtfulness, especially because I know that you would have much more fun playing in the garden or riding a bike than writing to me.

I am happy to be your adopted soldier—I am quite sure that no other soldier has such an interesting and conscientious adopted mother.

Military business will take me out of town for the next few days, so I hope that if you should write in the meantime and fail to get a proper reply, you will understand that it is not due to thoughtlessness or indifference on my part. I will be looking forward to your next letter.

Cordially,
Dwight D. Eisenhower

P.S. I hope that your daily prayers include a petition for the quick and complete victory for the United Nations in this terrible war.

————

2441 Auburn Avenue
Dayton, Ohio
June 26, 1942

Dear General,

I can never tell you how happy I was when I received your telegram. I think I have the best adopted soldier boy ever in the world. My little brother said he got gypped because his adopted soldier doesn't write any more, but I told him that he was in Australia. You have been so much honored and praised in the paper and on the radio, that I am almost afraid to write, but Mother said I should just write and tell you the news.

We are now on our vacation. I go swimming and play tennis and help around the house. I helped mow the lawn the other day, that sure was a job. I don't like it very well, but Daddy pays us for it. Are you happy in England? I hope you are. I pray for you every day and go to Holy Communion for you, so I know you will be all right and will be home soon.

I cut the picture of you out of the paper and all the news, so when you come home, I'll send it to you. I wonder if you will like this, I hope you won't be angry, but every one thought it was so grand of you to let me know about your going away, that there was something in the paper about you being my adopted soldier, and what a lucky little girl I was. I think I am, but please don't be angry about it.

I would be happy to hear from you but if I don't I will write to you anyway.

> *Always your little friend and adopted mother*
> *Mary Louise Koehnen*

> *7 July, 1942*

Dear Mary Louise,

While I have had no letter from you for some time, I thought I should write to tell you my new address. It is

> Force Headquarters,
> A.P.O. 887
> New York, N.Y.

We arrived here two weeks ago and we have been very busy ever since.

I constantly wear the miraculous medal you sent me. I have fastened it to my identification disk, which all soldiers keep on their persons at all times.

Last week I went to Ireland for a short visit. That is a beautiful countryside: green fields, big trees, many lakes and quaint villages. Here and there, especially in the country, are old castles and estates. I can understand why the song writers have written so much about Ireland. I hope you are in good health and having a lot of fun. Faithfully,

> *Your soldier*
> *Dwight D. Eisenhower*

> *2441 Auburn Avenue*
> *Dayton, Ohio*
> *July 17, 1942*

Dear General,

I hope you received my last letter. I know you are very busy but I just thought you would like to hear from me. It is very hot here to-day so I guess we will go swimming. We usually go out to the pool at Patterson Field, it sure is a swell pool.

Wright Field is sponsoring a horse show for the benefit of the Army Relief. I hope I get to go. I went to camp last summer and went horse back riding a lot. I didn't get to go this year, but maybe I will next year. I hope so anyway. I am cutting pictures and all the news of you and making a scrap book, so when you come back I will send it to you, but I want it back.

We had a complete black-out the other night. I hope we never have to have a real one, because Daddy is in the Army, and Mother was a nurse, so she would have to help out, and my brother and I would be alone. My brother said he would hide and forget to come out.

I guess I will close this letter now, and I want to remain your
little adopted mother,
Mary Louise Koehnen

P.S. Please excuse my writing but it was just so hot today that I could
hardly sit still to write.

———————

2441 Auburn Avenue
Dayton, Ohio
August 18, 1942

Dear General,

How are you? I am fine. I wonder if you are receiving all of my letters, this
is my fourth so far.

I have had a real swell time since I last wrote you. Last Saturday, August 8,
my girl friend and her father took another girl and I down to the baseball game
in Cincinnati. The "Reds" played the Chicago "Cubs," the first game went to
twelve innings, and the score was 3 to 1 in favor of the good old "Reds," and the
second game they lost. Then I have gone swimming a lot of times. Wednesday
night Mother and Daddy took my brother and I to the park, and of course we
rode everything we could, and then Friday night we all went to the Circus. Oh!
It was thrilling, and I laughed so hard at the clowns, and my brother laughed so
hard that the next day he had a pain in his side.

You know I would like to send you some cookies. But I guess it would be sorta
far, don't you think. I can make good peanut butter cookies, do you like them?

Well, its lunch time, we are going to have Hamburgers and do I like them,
but I guess I'll have to go on a diet because everyone says I am getting fat.

I am anxious for another letter from you real soon, and take good care of
yourself.

Sincerely,
Your friend
Mary Louise Koehnen

P.S. I am still praying for you every morning and night.

———————

21 August, 1942

Dear Mary Louise:

Thank you so much for your letter. I always enjoy hearing from you.

The summer here is very comfortable and we usually sleep under a blanket
at night. It's not really warm enough for swimming, so I imagine you would
prefer Dayton. It would be impossible to meet a finer or more courageous
people than the English. Their homes and their cupboards have been opened
generously to all, and I know you can understand how much that means to
us—especially when they sacrifice many of their own comforts for our united

effort. I hope that some day you can see these things for yourself and understand the close relationship between our two great peoples.

I shall look forward to seeing your scrap book when I return, and I am enclosing one or two clipping you might like to include.

All of us here hope and trust that the lights in America need never be dimmed, and that the people at home will welcome us back in the best of health and spirits.

I hope you will soon have a chance to ride and continue to enjoy yourself. Faithfully,

> *Your soldier*
> *Dwight D. Eisenhower*

> *27 August, 1942*

Dear Mary Louise:

You will be surprised to know that your letter, written last June 26th, reached me only today—just two months later. I can't account for the delay but I am happy that your message finally arrived safely.

Please don't hesitate to write to me when you have the time and with nothing better to do. I like your notes because it is pleasant indeed to know that a fine little girl, like yourself, will take time off from her regular play and duties to write to a soldier. I am certainly glad that your paper knows you are my adopted mother—I am very proud of it.

By the time this reaches you, I suppose you will have started school once more. I don't think you have ever told me what grade you are in but you write such a nice letter that I am perfectly sure you are a fine student.

Good-by for this time and with best wishes. From—

> *Dwight D. Eisenhower*

> *2441 Auburn Avenue*
> *Dayton, Ohio*
> *August 29, 1942*

Dear General,

I received your letter yesterday, and I was as always happy to hear from you and glad every one is so nice to you.

The clippings you sent me for my scrapbook are swell, just think to have a piece of news-paper from London, well I was just thrilled that's all I can say and thanks again. In the "Look Magazine" (September 8 issue) there is a big page of pictures and lots of news about you, but I would still write to you every week even if you were just a Pvt.

Gee—I hate to think of just one more week of vacation, and then back to school we go. I wish I was a boy I would join the Air Corp and be a pilot if I could. Did you every fly?

It was too bad about the Duke of Kent. I read about it in the paper. I feel so sorry for his children, don't you?

Well take care of yourself, and if you see the Princess Rose Marie, or Elizabeth, or the King and Queen about London be sure and tell me and write to me again when you can.

Always your friend and adopted Mother
Mary Louise Koehnen

P.S. Eddie (my brother) said to tell you hello. I am still praying for you every morning and evening, and I hope you are receiving all my letters.

Mary Louise

---

21 September, 1942

Dear Mary Louise:

Your last letter reached me very quickly, and, as always, I enjoyed reading it.

When I was in school I was always disappointed, just as you are, to see vacation end. Looking back now, though, I realize that while "reading, riting, and rithmetic" were occasionally tiresome, I always had time for a lot of fun. Be sure to tell me what you are studying and how you like your teacher.

Yes, we fly a great deal and, during my year in the Philippines, I learned to pilot an airplane. That was great sport, and I flew by myself a lot for two or three years. During these busy days, however, I have to use different pilots, and have given up piloting a plane myself.

The Duke of Kent was a fine man and everyone will miss his presence. I met the King shortly after arriving here and you would like him. He is quiet and unassuming, and interested only in serving his people.

Thank Eddie for his greetings, and write again, soon!

As ever,
Dwight D. Eisenhower

2441 Auburn Avenue
Dayton, Ohio
October 7, 1942

Dear General,

I received your most welcome letter last week, and it was very interesting. I just read them over and over again, and then I put them in my scrap-book. I hope you received all of my letters and also the box of candy I sent to you for your birthday. I sent it several weeks ago.

The Cardinals won the World Series. I got home from school just in time to hear the end of the 9th inning. Gee, I bet they are thrilled, we all wanted them to win at our house.

I went to the Football game Sunday afternoon, it was a swell game to see. Our side won 14 to 0. Do you like football? I just love it. Mother and Daddy went to a game Saturday night to see the Patterson-Wright Fields team play the Navy at Hamilton, Ohio. They said it was a punky game, but during halves they did a lot of drilling. They said the drilling was swell, and sorry to say, we lost.

I have to prepare a talk at our Civics Club for Friday, and I don't know what to talk about. The eighth-graders in all the Catholic schools have the Civic Club. I am trying out for the girls' Kick-ball team at school, but I suppose I won't be able to kick the ball good enough or run fast enough, but I sure would like to get on it, for I just love to play it.

My Daddy was promoted to a Captain, and I was so proud, just so he stays in Dayton. So many men have to go away, and we pray every day in school that the war ends. That old Hitler and those old Japs simply make me sick.

My brother Eddie was sort of swelled in the head when you told him "hello." It was his birthday the other day, and he was eleven years old. We are having a birthday dinner tonight for him. Mother lets us order our favorite dish on our birthdays. Eddie ordered roast chicken for his.

Last night we had a lot of fun. Daddy took us all out to the field to see quite a lot of soldiers go away, and then later, some Major came up and asked if Eddie and me would like to take a ride in a Jeep, and we said yes, so we took one, it was a lot of fun, but boy, oh boy, they sure do throw you around.

Well I guess I will have to start signing off now, because it is getting late and we have to get up early in the morning.

"Your little adopted Mother"
Mary Louise Koehnen

P.S. I am still praying for you, morning and night, and I hope you are still wearing the Miraculous Medal.

Mother, Daddy, and Eddie all said to tell you "hello."

Mary Louise

---

21 October, 1942

Dear Mary Louise:

What a pleasant surprise! I appreciate your thoughtfulness in remembering my birthday and the candy is delicious.

Just returned from a trip to Scotland, and regret that I have not had time to write you lately. You would have enjoyed the trip—the country is lovely with the changing leaves, and the lakes are all the poets claim. I would like to spend more time among the people, who are most hospitable.

Hope you are well and happy and enjoying school again. Take care of yourself this winter and know that I look forward to your letters.

As ever,
Dwight D. Eisenhower

————

2441 Auburn Avenue
Dayton, Ohio
November 10, 1942

Dear General,

I do hope some day or other you will receive this letter, I will send it to the same address. There has been so much news about you in the paper, and you have taken such a big responsibility now, I'll just have to pray that much harder for you and I promise I will.

Enclosed you will find this spiritual bouquet for you and I thought it was the nicest thing I could send you, for right now.

School is getting better every day, though I do have lots of home work every night, but my report was swell last month, so I guess I'll keep on studying hard. I got a 100% in my arithmetic test today. I study the maps and sometimes I just imagine I know where you are.

I just love to receive your letters but if you don't write I know you are too busy, but take care of yourself and remember I want you to get the best honor out of this old war, and come out with the best of health that any General ever had.

My scrap book is filling up fast.

As always, Your "adopted Mother"
Mary Louise Koehnen

————

20 November, 1942

Dear Mary Louise:

Your last letter took over a month to reach me but I was glad to hear from you. The box of candy was received before I left London and I have it here— in fact, it is in my office where I can enjoy it daily.

I like football very much and played it as West Point. I have not attended a game for several seasons, so the next time you go let out a cheer for me!

This is a very interesting part of the world we are now occupying. My impression of Africa was all wrong. It is not all barren and sandy waste as I imagined. The ground is covered with green grass and flowers, brilliant in their colors, are everywhere. The people are very interesting and the costumes of the Arabs remind me of Jacob's coat of many colors. The cities in their white stucco covering, and the rustle of palm trees is audible on every side. It would be truly enjoyable but for the war.

Thanks again for you nice letter, and I extend to you and all your loved ones my best wishes for a Merry Christmas and a Happy New Year!

Cordially,
Dwight D. Eisenhower

———————

2441 Auburn Avenue
Dayton, Ohio
December 22, 1942

Dear General,

You will never know how glad I was to hear from you. I thought maybe you would be so busy that you wouldn't have time to write to me anymore. I am always thrilled when your letters arrive.

We get out of school tomorrow for our Christmas Vacation. Just think two more days until Christmas, I can hardly wait. There are so many things that I want this year, that I can't begin to explain.

We had a play at school today and I was in it. We had a lot of fun. We were pretty wild in school today, but I guess you couldn't really blame us. I think Sister was so nervous that she could of screamed out loud.

Your last letter taught me a lot of interesting things, why I thought Africa would be as ugly as anything, no flowers, or anything else; as you described [it] in your letter it was really very interesting. I imagine now since I've heard so much about it, that it is a beautiful place.

I will have to be signing off pretty soon. I have to help Mother. I will write to you again real soon, and tell you what "Santa Claus" brought me. I imagine when this letter reaches you, it will be way past Christmas, but anyway I hope you have a very "Merry Christmas" and a "Happy New Year."

Sincerely yours,
Mary Louise Koehnen

P.S. I am still praying for you daily, and also that we will see victory real soon.

I forgot to tell you that my Scrapbook is filling up very rapidly with pictures and news about you.

1 February, 1943

Dear Mary Louise:

Your letter written November 10, enclosing the spiritual bouquet, has finally reached me. You have been very kind to write to me so regularly.

It's nice to know that your school life is pleasant, and I am glad arithmetic is one of your best subjects. I always liked it. However, by the time this war is over, I imagine geography will be my strong point—even believe that I could qualify as a teacher.

Here the air is full of the scent of mimosas and the fruit trees are beginning to bloom. The Mediterranean is as blue as the sky, and is almost warm enough for swimming.

Again many thanks for your nice letter and thoughts of me.

Sincerely,
Dwight D. Eisenhower

———————

1 March, 1943

Dear Mary Louise:

Your letter of January 25th reached me only today, and I regret that so much time passes before our letters arrive at their destination.

I am glad to hear that you indulge in many activities, and feel certain that your school play will be a success. I would like to know the name and the part you play.

Your prayers are appreciated, and be sure that all of us are looking forward to returning home after this war is won.

Sincerely,
Dwight D. Eisenhower

———————

2441 Auburn Avenue
Dayton, Ohio
May 22, 1943

Dear General,

It has been some time since I have written to you, so I thought I would sit right down, while I had time, and write you a letter. I've been pretty busy lately, you see we graduate from the eighth grade, June 6, and I have been studying a lot, and we had to write our Class History, Prophecy, and Class Song. My Class History was chosen to be read at the Graduation, so I had to write it all over. I was also chosen as one of the attendants to the May Queen.

Well, I guess that's enough about myself. How have you been? O.K. I hope. My Scrapbook is almost filled, there is something about you every night in the paper. I heard you on the radio, couple of Saturdays ago. You have a very good voice.

I also hope you will excuse this messy letter, but I am trying to write and take care of some little boy, if that isn't a job, I don't know what is. He's a cute little thing, but, oh boy, is he a pest. This is the second time I've started this letter, the last time the phone rang, and I went to answer it, leaving the pen on the desk, and when I came back, the letter was so scribbled up, I couldn't begin to read it.

Some weather we are having it has been raining the whole week. I am so sick of rain, I don't know what to do. I hope the weather is nice Monday night, because the crowning of the May Queen takes place outside. I saw in the paper where your niece, Peggy Eisenhower, was May Queen. I think she is awfully pretty, so does my brother.

Well I guess I will have to say good-bye now. I have to help Mother get dinner, because I am going to a party. We are celebrating five girls' birthday, and it is also a graduation party. So good-bye till later.

As ever
Mary Louise Koehnen

----

12 June, 1943

Dear Mary Louise:

Thank you very much for your letter of May 22nd, which reached me today. I send my heartiest congratulations to your graduation, and I hope that you will enjoy your high school studies.

I trust that the rain and floods that have been prevalent throughout the Middle West did not affect your May Day celebration.

I look forward to the day when all of us can return to our homes and enjoy such events.

Cordially,
Dwight D. Eisenhower

2441 Auburn Avenue
Dayton, Ohio
June 22, 1943

Dear General,

I haven't heard from you for some time, but I guess you are pretty busy trying to mow all those old Japs down.

Well school is out, and I am a graduate of the eighth grade, just think next year I will be a Freshman. Our graduation exercises were lovely, first we went to Mass and Holy Communion and then we had a Breakfast in the School Cafeteria. During the Breakfast we had the reading of the Class Prophecy and the Class History. I was chosen to read the Class History, and then we had the Tribute to the Priest, Sisters and Parents, and a Farewell

Address to the School. In one way I am glad I am leaving, and in another way I wish I was going back. After all that, we presented our gift to the school, the gift was two American flags. We had our Class Picnic last Monday. The eighth grade was the best of all the grades put together. We had a lot of fun. We had the Civics Club, and the meetings were held every Friday afternoon, and at stated times members of the Club would go on excursions. We had a Variety Show, and we established a Defense Stamp Campaign. We sold enough War Bonds and Stamps to purchase ten Jeeps in two months' time. I think that's pretty good, don't you? All together we sold about $10,000 worth of Bonds and Stamps in that short time.

Last week my brother and I had our tonsils taken out, and boy, oh boy were we sick. I was the worse, my brother was up and about four days before I even thought of getting up. Did you ever take ether? Isn't it terrible. I hope I never have to take the old stuff again.

You and your son's picture was in the paper last Sunday, my girl friend and I think you are both very good looking. There has been an awful lot about you in the paper lately. I cut it all out and put it in my Scrapbook. We have a book about your life, and it tells how you wanted to go to Annapolis, but ended up at West Point. If I was a boy, I would like to go to West Point, but I guess I would never get there. My Daddy is still a Major out at Patterson Field, he has been in the Army a year and two months yesterday. I hope he gets to stay at Patterson Field the rest of the duration.

Well I guess I will have to say good-bye, because I have to get dressed. I am going to a party this evening. Write to me when you have a chance, because I love hearing from you, and feel honored to have a man of your importance to bother to write to me.

Sincerely yours,
Mary Louise Koehnen

August 2, 1943

Dear Mary Louise:

Your account of your graduation exercises was very interesting. The past year will always be a bright spot in your memory and I am sure you have left a good record behind you.

I am pleased to hear of the amount of War Bonds and Stamps your school purchased. We need the support of everyone at home to help us complete our mission.

I thank you for writing and hope you enjoy your summer vacation.

Cordially
Your soldier
Dwight D. Eisenhower

In the months to come, Mary Louise went on to a busy life as a teenager, and Eisenhower went on to the Allied invasions of Italy and Normandy. Finally, seven years after the war ended, in 1952, Mary Louise Koehnen met her pen pal during a whistle-stop in his presidential campaign in Dayton, Ohio.

7

In Harm's Way

I N T H E A R M A D A O F S H I P S that crossed the English Channel on D-Day, June
6, 1944, were two fifteen-year-old American sailors: Seaman Gene Sizemore
from Tennessee and Coxswain Joseph E. McCann Jr. from Everett, Washington.
Both had lied about their age when they enlisted in the U.S. Navy. Eddie McCann
was already a battle-hardened veteran who had signed up at age thirteen and seen action in the North Atlantic, North Africa, Sicily, and Salerno when he was fourteen.
Gene Sizemore had never before been in harm's way.

Just before departing England on the LST 530, the seaman had gone to his commanding officer, Captain Anthony Duke, and told him: "I'm only fifteen . . . and I
don't want to go on this trip. . . . I am scared, and I want to get off, NOW." Captain
Duke felt sorry for him, but since his ship was already sealed, he could only encour-
age the boy to report to him at least once every watch. "That way I'll be able to see
how you are doing, and you'll be able to see how I am doing," he told him.[1] So Sizemore reported faithfully to the captain for the next several days. By D-Day + 2 he
was doing fine.

At 5 A.M. on June 6, Coxswain Eddie McCann picked up thirty men from the First
Infantry Division in a small LCVP (Landing Craft Vehicle) from a transport ship in
the English Channel. He had trained with troops from the same division in North
Africa, but this was his first experience with a daytime landing. By the time they left
the line of departure—just before daybreak—the men had become so seasick from
the rocking and rolling of his small boat that McCann could only wonder how they
would be able to take care of themselves when they hit the beach.

About four hundred yards before they reached Omaha Beach all hell broke loose.
An LCVP to the right of Eddie was hit by German artillery fire and his boat was
showered with parts of human bodies. The water was crowded with disabled craft
and mines. "I felt as if I was fighting my own private little war trying to find a hole
or shelter for my troops," he remembered. "I got them in as close as possible. The water was not above their knees. . . . The scene was mass destruction. . . . The wounded
on the beach and in the water [were] crying for someone to help them."[2]

*An Italian girl cries because she cannot find her doll in
the ruins of her house near Solerno, September 24, 1943.*

During the next forty-eight hours, there was no rest for Eddie and his
small crew. They made run after run, picking up Allied troops and ammunition from the transport ships and returning with the wounded to the
LSTs (Landing Ship Tanks) that became hospital ships after unloading. On
D-Day + 3, he picked up nineteen wounded Germans, among them a father
and a son, who had been wounded together and captured at the same time.

About a quarter of the distance between the beach and the hospital ship,
Eddie's LCVP was hit by an explosion that had taken place on the port side,
where he was steering his boat. The shattered plywood and splinters stuck to
the inside of his right leg, but he made a run for the hospital ship. Everything
in his small LCVP was floating now and the wounded were wet and scared.
By the time they were picked up by the hospital ship, his boat was sinking
very fast. "I felt that I had lost one of my best friends," he remembered.

A French boy hugs his dog as American shells fly overhead.

A French refugee girl on her way home after U.S. soldiers liberated her town during the Normandy invasion.

On D-Day + 4, Eddie was assigned to a new LCVP and to a heartbreaking task: He and his crew had to remove the dog tags from the bodies of their drowned comrades that had risen to the surface in the waters near the Utah and Omaha beaches. After that, armed with bow hooks, they sent the dead back to the sea.

On June 7, 1944, German newspapers relayed a short message from the headquarters of the supreme commander of the armed forces: "In der vergangenen Nacht hat der Feind seinen seit langem vorbereiteten und von uns erwarteten Angriff auf West Europa begonnen" (During the past night, the enemy began his attack on Western Europe, an attack that had been planned for a long time and that we have expected).[3]

On D-Day, the Allies had put some 175,000 men ashore in Normandy. Hundred of thousands more in reinforcements from Britain and the United States crossed the channel in the weeks to come. In the summer and fall of 1944, they overran Normandy, liberated Paris, and began their drive to the German border. On October 21, 1944, Allied troops captured the first German city, Aachen, near the Belgian border. That same month, an order from the Führer created the German Volkssturm—all men from sixteen to sixty would be drafted to defend the Fatherland. SS Reichsführer Himmler told the people: "Wie die Werwölfe werden todesmütige Freiwillige unseren verfluchten Feinden schaden" (Unafraid of death, like wolves, our death-defying volunteers will put the cursed enemy in harm's way).

To provide the will to resist the inexorable onslaught of the Allied forces, Hitler counted on young boys. The German soldiers who carried the brunt of the last desperate fighting—from the Battle of the Bulge to the Battle of Berlin—were mostly born between 1925 and 1928. At the end, some "volunteers" were only twelve years old. They had the fanatical bravery the Führer counted on. They truly believed that they could still win the war and that the deaths of their fathers, uncles, cousins, and older brothers—and of countless civilians in their bombed-out hometowns—had not been in vain.

In mid-December, German troops launched an all-out counterattack in the Ardennes. The Battle of the Bulge would be the costliest battle—in terms of casualties—for the Allied invasion troops on their way to Germany. There was a brief lull in the fighting around Christmastime. Allied troops and German soldiers alike put up Christmas trees. For decoration, they used the tinfoil dropped by bombers to fool radar, just as we civilians did, sitting in the cellars of our bombed-out cities on the Rhine. "Lametta from Heaven," we children used to call the glittering silver bands.

On Christmas Eve, the soldiers in the Ardennes, friend and foe alike—and the civilians on the home front—sang the same Christmas carols. The favorite on *both* sides was "Stille Nacht, Heilige Nacht" (Silent Night, Holy Night). The scenery was like a Christmas card. The rolling hills, fields, and forests of the Ardennes and the ruins of the bombed-out houses on the Rhine were covered with thick snow. The weather had turned very cold.

Private Herbert Meier, a teenager, was in a German tank division that had suffered nearly 70 percent casualties since the Allied invasion had begun. On Christmas Eve his weary unit stopped in a Belgian village near Bastogne. The men of his squad took refuge in a partially destroyed house. The

A Minnesota GI gives an apple to
Dutch children on Santa Claus Day, 1944.

boy cut down a small fir tree and brought it into the cold house. Then the soldiers proceeded to have an impromptu party. They drank coffee—captured from the Americans—and a bottle of schnapps shared by seven men. One soldier wrote Christmas cards. Another, a lieutenant, opened his mail from home and learned that evening that his brother had been killed in action on the Russian front. Herbert Meier took his place at the watch that night. The celebration was over.[4]

Three weeks later, on January 14, 1945, the Russian army entered East Prussia. Days later, Soviet tanks entered Upper Silesia as well. Opposing them were batteries of sixteen-year-olds who had been drafted into the Volkssturm and even younger members of the FLAK, the anti-aircraft artillery. German newspapers hailed the heroic fighting of the German youths and their courage, persistence, and willingness to sacrifice their lives in the face of overwhelming odds.

In February, a war correspondent for the *Völkischer Beobachter*, the official mouthpiece of the German Propaganda Ministry, filed a report on the fighting spirit of a battery of anti-aircraft artillery, manned by the Hitler Youth, which successfully fended off the Russian onslaught for a period of six days—at the cost of innumerable lives:

> Faithful to their orders, they kept their position . . . three days entirely surrounded by the Bolshevics and without any connection to the outside world. . . . With unparalleled heroism, they were able to incapacitate 1,200 Soviets, and to delay the progress of the enemy across the ice of the frozen Oder River. . . . They destroyed four T34's, three with their Panzerfausts, many grenade throwers and dozens of vehicles. When they were ordered to break through to their own lines, after six days of incessant fighting, they had no more ammunition left. They managed to escape late at night under the cover of darkness, across the icy Oder—but not until they had destroyed their cannons and their maps. Some did not make it back. We salute these youngsters who held out against the odds for six days that must have seemed like eternity to them. They did it with faithfulness and loyalty, with persistence and stubbornness, in spite of the constant presence of death. They pledged their lives for the Fatherland.[5]

On both the Eastern and the Western front, the replacements for the German troops were now frightfully young. Sgt. Ewald Becker, a member of the Panzer Grenadier Regiment 111, told a squad of youngsters who reported to him that the war wasn't just about them individually, but that it also mattered what happened to the men fighting to the right and left of them. "They had a difficult time understanding that it wasn't an individual effort," he remembered. "They still believed in the war and our chances of winning."[6]

Those chances became slimmer and slimmer when the Allied forces were able to capture the bridge at Remagen on March 7, 1945, and gained a foothold on the east bank of the Rhine. Sixteen-year-old Private Heinz Schwartz was present at the abortive attempt by the Germans to blow up the bridge. He heard the order ring out, "Everybody down!" and then an explosion. "We thought it had been destroyed, and we were saved." But as the smoke cleared up, he saw that the bridge, though damaged, was still standing. An American unit was coming across. The boy escaped through the rear entrance of the tunnel and ran home to his mother as fast as he could.

He made it back to his village, a short distance upstream on the east bank of the river, without being captured.

A group of sixteen-year-old high school students in the Ruhr area were not so lucky. Their anti-aircraft artillery battery had dispersed when the U.S. Ninth Army reached the Rhine south of Düsseldorf. Eight of the surviving students had been ordered to hold up any tanks that might be rolling up a hill on which they had found temporary refuge. They heard the noise of the battle in the Rhine Valley, but no one approached their hill. The Americans had passed them by. One of the boys who had hoped to be a hero lay in the grass, staring at the sky. Tears ran down his face.

In the afternoon, when no enemy soldiers had shown up, the boys took a chance and went down to the valley—after having abandoned their guns in the bushes. The star pupil of their class who was good in English composed a letter: "To an officer of the U.S. Army! Eight German soldiers will surrender. They are disarmed and beg for safe conduct. The man, who brings the letter, will lead you to the place where we await you." Waving a white handkerchief, the tallest of the eight boys went to the village. After half an hour he came back, visibly disappointed. The American jeeps were riding around in the village streets, but no one had paid any attention to his surrender offer.

The eight decided to go down to the village and hide in the school. A woman brought them some sweet milk and bread. Then they covered themselves with their tattered coats and slept through the night. The next morning they tried again to surrender. This time they were in luck. Within minutes, three American jeeps rolled into the courtyard of the school. An MP shouted, "Alle rauskommen!" (Everybody come out!) and then, laughing, "Look, the babies!"[7]

The eight teenagers would become prisoners of war in the largest Allied camp for underage soldiers, located in the French village of Attichy, not far from Compiègne, where the French had surrendered to the Germans in 1940. The camp earned the nickname "Kinder Käfig" (Children's Cage). Eventually, it would house some ten thousand boys, ages fourteen to sixteen—in tents that accommodated thirty boys at a time. They would not be released until the first week of September, after the Japanese had surrendered.

On March 8, German newspapers printed a statement from the headquarters of the Führer, the supreme commander of the Wehrmacht: "Das OKW gibt bekannt: An der Oderfront führt der Feind nördlich Frankfurt . . . zahlreiche Angriffe an. . . . In Köln sind heftige Strassenkämpfe entbrannt. . . . Britische Terrorflieger griffen am Tage und in den Abendstunden west-

German boy soldiers taken prisoner by an American GI.

deutsches Gebiet an" (The enemy conducted numerous attacks along the Oder, north of Frankfurt. . . . In Cologne there is heavy fighting in the streets. . . . British planes terrorized western Germany during the day and in the evening hours").[8]

By the first week of spring 1945, Eisenhower's troops had reached the Rhine River along its length, with a major crossing north of Düsseldorf and additional crossings in the center and south. On March 21, the Americans occupied Mainz, at the intersection of the Rhine and Main Rivers. Mainz, like Cologne, was the site of a magnificent cathedral that towered like a ship over the ruins of the bombed-out city. The weather had turned warm; the apple and almond trees were in full bloom.

A week later, on March 28, my hometown, across the river, came under heavy bombardment. A shell ripped into our house and left gaping holes in the bedroom and living room. German troops had left our town—the last group, a company of fifteen-year-olds with their lieutenant, had done so reluctantly. A delegation of citizens, including the mayor and the Catholic priest, crossed the river in a small boat and reassured the Americans that there was no need for further heavy bombardment. We had no defensive forces left. The next day in the early afternoon, on Good Friday, when in ordinary times people would be in church praying at the Stations of the Cross, the first contingent of American tanks rolled into town. With few exceptions, the citizens had hung out white bedsheets from their windows to indicate their surrender. There were no white sheets in our windows: As a stubborn fifteen-year-old with strong convictions, I had pleaded with my mother that it would be a disgrace to surrender. And so we didn't.

Our small act of defiance led to an edict by the occupation forces that any weapons held by the citizens of our town would have to be turned over immediately to the MP. I owned a BB gun that once belonged to my brother, who had been killed in action in Russia. This time my mother won the argument: Dirty, bedraggled, but with a last shred of dignity left, I turned over my BB gun to an American sergeant whose tank stood on our street. When I approached him I saw he was black. I had never seen a black person in my life, except for the statue of one of the three wise men, Balthazar—the king from the Orient—that stood in the local Catholic church.

As I approached, the infantrymen surrounding the tank laughed and the sergeant smiled at me. I didn't think that surrendering my BB gun was funny, but what took me by complete surprise was that he held out his hand in a friendly gesture. I noticed that he held an orange, a fruit I hadn't seen or tasted throughout the long years of the war. He offered it to me—and I refused. I was too proud in my first encounter with the enemy to accept this simple act of kindness. Fifty-five years later, I still wonder how life turned out for him when the war was over. As Germans would learn in the months to come, the black soldiers in the U.S. Army (which was still segregated at the time) were especially kind to children. Everywhere in the American occupation zone, from the Rhine to Berlin, these soldiers would offer children, unasked, a bit of chocolate, chewing gum, or a handful of raisins—they were like magi from afar.

On the day my hometown was occupied, the Ninetieth Division, on Patton's left flank, headed east toward Hanau on the Main River. Stephen E. Ambrose, in *Citizen Soldiers*, tells the story of Major John Cochran's encounter with a group of Hitler Youth officer candidates. The boys had set up a roadblock. As Cochran's men advanced toward it, the German teenagers attacked with their machine guns, killing one American. Cochran ordered his artillery to fire on the roadblock. They destroyed it, killing three of the defenders. One sixteen-year-old survivor held up his hands. Cochran, who was upset over the loss of a good soldier, grabbed the boy and took off his cartridge belt.

"I asked him if there were more like him in the town," Cochran recalled. "He stared at me and said, 'I'd rather die than tell you anything.' I told him to pray, because he was going to die." The major hit him across the face with his thick, heavy belt and was about to strike the boy again when he was grabbed from behind by his army chaplain. He said, "Don't!" Then he took the crying child away. The chaplain had not only saved a life but prevented a murder.[9]

On Easter Sunday, April 1, 1945, the Twenty-first and the Twelfth Army Group linked up near Paderborn, completing the encirclement of the Ruhr area. Nearly a half million German soldiers were trapped; the remainder of Germany was cut off from its weapons and ammunition supply. Eisenhower issued a proclamation, in leaflets and radio messages, urging the German soldiers to surrender and the people to begin planting their spring crops.

Most Germans agreed with his assessment of the hopelessness of the situation. But a core of fighting men remained, most of them mere boys. They had little experience with making war, but they were still armed and could cause considerable harm. One of them, Al Ptak, from Essen, was fourteen years old at the time. In his book *Firestorm*, he remembers going with some youngsters to the top of a lightly wooded hill that overlooked the nearest town the Americans had taken. They saw artillery on the main street, lots of weapons and vehicles, and many American soldiers. Suddenly, there was artillery and machine gun fire directed toward the boys. He and his comrades disappeared as fast as their legs could carry them. But Al Ptak was angry! Hours later, he went back to the hill, without the children, armed with a discarded German machine gun that was in perfect shape. Years later, he remembered: "I let a burst fly and seemed to have . . . aimed correctly, for suddenly the street was empty of American soldiers. I have no knowledge of hitting anyone, and I will never know. At the time I was angry enough to hit as many as possible. . . . I then went home, leaving the machine gun atop the hill, satisfied that I had done the right thing."[10]

Al Ptak survived unharmed, unlike a half dozen Hitler Youth who had dug themselves in at a hunting cabin and fired at the American vehicles passing by the road below. They had no machine guns, only a couple of rifles. Al's father went up to the cabin to convince the boys to give themselves up, but he arrived too late. "All were dead, and practically turned into sieves. Their I.D.s told us that the oldest of the boys was sixteen, and the youngest fourteen. . . . My father took their I.D.s and wrote letters to their parents to

Fourteen-year-old boys from the Volkssturm,
captured on April 24, 1945.

inform them of the death of the boys. Other men went out and buried the
boys on the spot."

THE SIXTEEN-YEAR-OLD BOYS from the Gymnasium in Osnabrück
who were trying to stem the tide of American invaders south of the
city of Münster were better equipped, but their resistance was equally futile.
Knut S., their forward observer, kept a diary of their last engagement and
subsequent captivity:

> *April 1:*
> Sixty American tanks are visible. Our battery shoots at an assembly of
> American infantry men. At night all is quiet.

April 2:
Observe many more American tanks. Our battery shoots at enemy troops and is observed by American reconnaissance planes. At night we receive heavy artillery fire. Some of our cannons are destroyed.

April 3:
We are preparing to make a break-through since we are surrounded by Americans. All of our cannons have been destroyed by heavy artillery fire. We are unable to break through at night.

April 4:
This morning we tried to break through, but were surprised by an attack of American infantry men. We were captured and marched off to Münster. . . . We spent the night behind barbed wire, heavily guarded, in rain, wind and cold.

April 5:
We are now knee-deep in mud.

April 6:
We are loaded in a truck and driven across the pontoon bridge at Wesel. At midnight we are loaded into a train where we are at least protected from the rain.

April 7:
The train rolls through Holland and Belgium. We get no food.

April 8:
At noon, we are unloaded in a train station near Namur and spent the night there.

April 9:
We are loaded into locked railroad cars. At night we begin our trip to France.

April 10:
Still on the trip through France. For forty men, there are only two canisters of water. It was very hot.

April 11:
Still on the trip through France. No food, only a canister of water in the afternoon. During the day it was again very hot.

Members of the Volkssturm in a POW camp.

April 12:
We unload in the afternoon at the train station of Chef du Pont and march ten kilometers to the main prison camp at Foucarville. Few are able to complete the march on foot. Many fell by the wayside and had to be transported by wagon. We survived the march, in spite of great heat and thirst. There are fifty-seven men in one tent.[11]

By April 16, American troops had reached Nuremberg. A fourteen-year-old boy who had left the town with his mother and younger siblings to find safety in a nearby village wrote in a school essay later that year about his first encounter with the enemy.[12] On April 18, the first American tanks rolled through his village, after German troops had abandoned it the day before. His family looked for safety in a nearby air raid shelter where they spent the night.

An injured German boy screams in pain.

Suddenly they heard a knock on the door. His sister opened it. A black soldier told the frightened family in broken German, "Kommen alle mit mir in das Dorf, wir nichts tuen Euch" (Come back to the village with me, we will do you no harm). The boy and his sister picked up their suitcases and headed for home, followed by their two younger siblings. Just as they entered the house, they were stunned by a terrible noise. German artillery batteries were shooting at the town. The American soldiers herded the smaller children into the house to get them out of harm's way.

The boy ran back to the air raid shelter nearby, but then there was a second explosion. He noticed that blood was running down his arm. He had been wounded by shrapnel. An American soldier bandaged him. His mother wept when she saw her wounded son. Suddenly, a third barrage hit the house and it collapsed. The younger children were buried under the debris. Mother and son, together with the American soldier, dug the young-sters out of the rubble. Miraculously, the children had survived without any bodily harm. But the house was totally destroyed. "We had nothing left but our lives," remembered the boy. "That was a terrible experience."

Elsewhere, teenage soldiers from the German Volkssturm continued to cause mischief wherever they could. Twenty-year-old Pvt. Erich Womels-dorf of the Eleventh Panzer Division, who had fought in Russia and France, found himself in charge of two truckloads of fifteen- and sixteen-year-old boys who had arrived as replacements. "Each of them had a brand new Panzerfaust," he recalled. "They went out hunting, climbing a switchback road up into the Harz Mountains, hiding—waiting for the next American tank to come along. When it came, they hit from the side, then ran away, to play the game again. They could not be pinned down. It held the Americans up some, but it really did not accomplish much."[13]

The game between the daredevil children and the weary American GIs would continue as Eisenhower's troops slogged their way across central and southern Germany. On April 27, just ten days before the final surrender of Germany, an American company came to the town of Deggendorf, north-east of Munich. The Hitler Youth had barricaded themselves in the center of the town; they had no artillery or mortar support and no tanks but a few machine guns and Panzerfausts, and they let go in a last desperate effort to defend the Fatherland. "Their bullets sounded like angry bees overhead," wrote one American officer, who ordered an artillery assault that destroyed the hive and their lives.

Altogether, the campaign to defend the western part of Germany had been ruinous. The Germans suffered some 300,000 casualties and lost vast amounts of irreplaceable equipment. In territories that were not yet occu-pied by the Allied forces, the German newspapers informed their readers that the Anglo-American spring offensive had been successful. But they still held out the hope that German troops in the east could hold off the Russians from conquering the nation's capital. That hope would prove in vain. The boy soldiers could not save Berlin.

Sixteen-year-old Dieter Borkowski served in one of the FLAK battalions that defended Berlin during the last months of the war. His diary, *Wer Weiss, Ob Wir Uns Wiedersehen* (Who knows if we will meet again), gives a graphic description of the state of mind of the young soldiers who were still hoping for a miracle weapon that would save them from dis-aster and ruin.[14] On February 14, 1945, Dieter learned from the newspapers of the Anglo-American offensive on the Rhine and of the invasion of the

German children surrender to the
U.S. Seventh Army near Oberammergau.

Russians in the neighboring provinces of Silesia, Pommerania, and East Prussia. He noted in his diary:

> During the evening watch with Max . . . we can see in the clear weather the bursts of Russian artillery along the Oder [which is only 70 kilometers from Berlin]. When the East wind blows, we can hear the noise of their cannons. Both of us feel dejected, nearly hopeless. . . . Max carries a pistol which is strictly forbidden! He tells me quietly that he will commit suicide, together with his father and his sister, if the Bolshevics reach Berlin. I cannot imagine that this will happen. That would mean that the Führer and his government have lied to us for years.

The next days brought more bad news: Rations were drastically reduced. The boys were now constantly hungry. In his diary Dieter lists a litany of Ger-

The last photograph of Hitler, decorating a boy soldier with the Iron Cross, April 1945.

man towns that had been lost to the Russians: Liegnitz, Glogau, Graudenz, Schneidemühl, Posen, Guben, and Först on the river Neisse. On February 26, 1945, he noted: "Our city looks horrible. In the area that we are supposed to protect from air raids, many houses are on fire. What sense does it make to continue to fight? And the miracle weapons . . . where are they?"

By the end of March, Dieter and his classmates were practicing with Panzerfausts and rifles, together with some old men from the Volkssturm. The reports from the supreme commander of the Wehrmacht did not reassure him:

> The Russians are near Frankfurt on the Oder: Silesia, Pomerania, and East Prussia are now completely in their hands. In the West, the Americans have reached beyond Koblenz and Mainz. . . . The destroyed streets of Berlin are filled with soldiers who have been separated from their companies. Something will have to change drastically

in this war, or will the Führer die a hero's death in Berlin, together
with the rest of us?

The answer to that question came one month later, on April 30, when the
sixteen-year-old met one of his lieutenants who had escaped from Hitler's
bunker. "Adolf Hitler shot himself today," he told the young soldiers, "after
marrying a young woman named Eva Braun. Goebbels is dead as well . . .
and there are *no* miracle weapons and *no* armistice with the Americans.
. . . The war has not yet ended. We need to break out of the city and go
north." Dispirited, Dieter wrote in his diary that night:

> I believe my life has no more meaning. Why do we engage in a last
> battle? Why did so many human beings die? Life is worthless, for if
> Hitler committed suicide, the Russians will be victorious in the end.
> . . . I remember the last speech of Goebbels, on the occasion of
> Hitler's birthday [April 20]: Never will the people betray their Führer
> or the Führer betray his people. But now the Führer *has* betrayed his
> people. Who will take the responsibility for everything that happened
> in this war?

Dieter's last diary entry was made in the late afternoon of May 2, 1945,
the day the Red Army had entered Berlin. At dawn, his artillery group had
made a desperate effort to break out of the city. It did not succeed. All hell
broke loose when Russian tanks opened fire. Dieter's sixteen-year-old classmate, Karl-Heinz, was severely wounded and died without gaining consciousness. A drunken SS officer tried to prevent the retreat of the surviving
boys by pointing his pistol at them and urging them forward. A battle-
hardened German soldier shot the officer on the spot. The boys escaped and
slept a fitful sleep in an abandoned store. Hours later, Dieter woke up when
he heard a sound:

> A young Russian soldier . . . is about to collect our weapons which we
> had laid down under the shelves of the store. I do not feel well. . . . For
> a moment I do not know where I am. Peter looks at me with a crooked
> smile. Manfred curses under his breath and glares at the young soldier
> from the Red Army. But the Russian seems unaware of our combative
> mood. He laughs and informs us with considerable pride: "Woyna ka-
> puut, Hitler kapuut. . . . Ihr gehen nach Hause zu Babuschka" (The war
> is over, Hitler is dead. . . . It's time you go home to Grandma).

One week later, on May 9, sixteen-year-old Klaus Granzow found himself
with the remnants of his artillery battery south of Dresden. His company

German boy soldier discharged from captivity.

commander informed him that the war was over—lost. He wrote in his diary: "We were brought up to believe in the national-socialist Germany that no longer exists. I still have a strong faith in Christianity. Will I lose that one day as well? What then?"[15]

That evening he met his first Russian soldier and thought, instinctively, that he would be shot. To his surprise, the young soldier in his dirty uniform, with a machine gun slung over his shoulder, ran toward the young German—and embraced him. "He was no older than I. He laughed and laughed and said I was free to go home. . . . Please, dear God, help me to find my way home."

HALFWAY AROUND THE WORLD, seven-year-old Tomiko Higa was caught in one of the last bloody battles in the Pacific theater—the battle of Okinawa. On April 1, 1945, Easter Sunday, a fleet of about 1,300

Allied ships had assembled in the East China Sea, on the southwestern coast of the main island of Okinawa. They carried out a two-and-a-half-hour sea and air bombardment. An invasion force of some 60,000 troops proceeded to come ashore from early morning until late afternoon. In the weeks to come, some 200,000 people would be killed, half of them civilians caught in the cross fire.

Tomiko Higa lived with her brother Chokuyo (age nine) and her sisters, Hatsuko (age thirteen) and Yoshiko (age seventeen), in Shuri, a town that came under heavy assault by the American forces in mid-April. The four children were on their own. Their mother had died one year earlier; their father had gone south to Makabe, to get food for the Japanese Signal Corps unit that was stationed nearby. Yoshiko decided to escape with her brother and sisters to the south. She and Hatsuko carried two bundles on their heads that contained some cooked rice and a few cherished belongings. The nine-year-old boy followed behind, holding Tomiko's hand.

In her book *The Girl with the White Flag*, Tomiko Higa remembered: "We could walk only at night, for in the daytime, the enemy . . . offensive was so heavy that we had to take cover in air raid shelters and caves. Even at night we did not walk very far because flares would begin to make everything as light as day, followed by explosive shells. It was eerie and terrible, and thinking about it even now makes cold shivers go down my spine."[16]

When they got to Makabe, the children were half starved and thirsty. Their possessions had been reduced to one bundle, since they had eaten all their rice. Tomiko and her brother found a temporary shelter in a cave—the older sisters went looking for their father. Their search was in vain. In the meantime, the fighting was getting closer, so the children started walking south again, stumbling over bodies in the dark, not knowing whether they were dead or alive. Tomiko would never forget a scene she encountered along the way—a scene that still gave her nightmares forty-five years later:

> A woman was lying on the ground, hit by a shrapnel from a bomb, with blood streaming from her chest, and at her breast an infant about a year old lay sucking up the blood. . . . When the baby saw us it lifted its face, whose features were just a mass of blood, and stretched out its arms toward us as if to say "Carry me!" Its arms, too, were covered with its mother's blood. . . . It was a scene straight out of hell.

Days later, the children found their way to the shore. They dug out shallow holes in the sand to sleep in—the two older sisters huddled together in one hole; Tomiko and her brother rested in another. Soon she was asleep with her head on her brother's shoulder. When she woke up her brother sat beside her, seemingly asleep with his eyes open. She tried to shake him awake, but couldn't. Her older sister removed the cloth that covered his head and found a hole at the back of his head. A stray bullet had killed the boy. Tomiko, whose head was less than eight inches apart from her brother's, was unhurt. They buried him in the hollow by the sea, at Komesu Beach, at the southernmost tip of Okinawa. The children were only nine miles away from home!

It was about May 20 when they joined crowds of refugees who had been driven away from Komesu Beach by the shelling. They had been on the road for weeks. Tomiko clutched tightly to the clothes of her older sister Hatsuko, almost running to keep up, for fear of being separated from her sisters. When she looked up at night at her protector, whose face was barely visible in the starlight, the seven-year-old girl discovered to her horror that she had clutched the garment of a total stranger. She had nothing left to eat and no change of clothes, and she was now utterly alone.

She spent the next days sleeping in caves and looking for shelter in empty houses, fleeing from American machine gun fire. She was unwittingly going toward the action instead of away from it, wandering around in the very center of the battle. Some days later, toward the end of May, she recognized a road she had traveled with her brother and sisters much earlier in their flight. A day later, she found refuge in a cave, with an old couple: a nearly blind woman and a man with a limbless torso. Together they heard the blare of a loudspeaker with a funny sounding voice that announced over and over again: "People of Okinawa, I am a Nisei. My father and mother are Okinawans. Please believe what I am telling you. Come out of there quickly. The American Army does not kill civilians. There is no time to lose. It is dangerous to remain in the caves. . . . Please come out quickly. People of Okinawa, the war is over."

Armed with a white flag, torn from the loincloth of the old man and fastened to a bamboo stick, seven-year-old Tomiko Higa walked out of the cave into the sunlight, hitching up her torn pants with her left hand and supporting the branch with the white flag with her right hand and shoulder. When she saw the first American soldiers, her heart missed a beat. One of them was holding something in front of his face, with a hole in it, pointed directly at her. It did not look at all like the rifles and machine guns that Japanese soldiers carried. "This is the end," she thought, "I'm going to be killed." Then she remembered her father's admonition: "If you come face to face with the enemy, don't let him see you cry. Die with a smile."

So the seven-year-old girl let go of her pants and waved with her left hand, palm outstretched, as if she was offering a greeting of peace. With her right hand, she gripped the white flag that had been resting on her shoulder

Tomiko Higa approaches U.S. lines with a white flag, Okinawa.

and held it high. There were no tears in her eyes as she faced the American GI who took her picture. It was June 12, 1945. Days later she met her two sisters among a crowd of refugees on the beach. Thirteen-year-old Hatsuko had been hit by a shrapnel from a bomb and carried her left arm in a white sling. Seventeen-year-old Yoshiko took Tomiko's face in both hands, examined it carefully, and then burst into tears. Between sobs, she gently chided the little girl, who was the only one of the sisters not to cry: "You act as if nothing had happened at all. But I suppose that's why you have managed to survive." Then the three girls were loaded into a truck and driven to an internment center.

I discovered Tomiko Higa's picture among World War II photos from the U.S. Army Signal Corps that have found a home in the National Archives in College Park, Maryland. I wept when I saw it for the first time.

— 8 —

Surviving the Firestorm

*I*N JANUARY 1941, Alice Brady had visited Coventry after the big raid. She was overwhelmed by the devastation that had been wrought by the German planes. "The place was a mass of twisted steel and debris," she wrote in her diary, "and when one looked around and saw the thousands of devastated homes, it made one sad to think of man's inhumanity to man."[1]

Two years later, it was the turn of German children to ponder the lessons learned by the British. After sporadic air attacks that had begun in 1940, the combined might of the bombs of British planes by night and of American planes by day brought the horror of war to German doorsteps—day after day, night after night. From 1943 to 1945, the Allied forces dropped almost 2 million bombs on German cities. About half were dropped on residential areas, making some 13 million people homeless.

During the latter part of the war, bombing became a daily and nightly occurrence, especially for families who lived in the northern and western part of the country, in the Rhine and Ruhr areas, and in cities like Hamburg and Berlin. Bombs were either high explosives that exploded on impact, or delayed explosives that would go off hours later when rescue efforts were under way. Bombs also took the form of air mines, creating vacuums that imploded buildings. Some of the incendiary bombs contained a mixture of gasoline, rubber, and vicose, the forerunner of future napalm bombs; other were phosphorous canisters that burned everything in their paths, including human flesh, and kept fires smoldering for hours. I have been acquainted with them all.

High explosive bombs, incendiaries, and liquid phosphorous bombs could create an inferno that sent a firestorm howling and raging through the cities, notably in Hamburg and Berlin and, toward the end of the war, in Darmstadt, Kassel, and Dresden, where over a half million fire bombs created a firestorm that was visible for several hundred miles.

No one who lived through this relentless terror will forget the sounds of the high-pitched air raid sirens that warned of the approaching bombers. Even today, such a sound, common to fire engines and ambulances in peaceful American cities, makes

Two children climb out of the cellar into their gutted home.

me jump. My first thought is to duck under a table—a reaction that comes in handy in earthquake-prone northern California. The race to the shelter, whether a humble wine cellar at home or a makeshift shelter in the basement of the school, involved grabbing a small suitcase or satchel in an instant and getting into temporary safety before the anti-aircraft guns, manned by fifteen-year-old boys, many of them classmates, would shower us with fragments of exploding shells.

A classroom air raid shelter, Düsseldorf.

Then we sat, and listened, and prayed, knowing that the whistles of the bombs would draw nearer and nearer, and hoping that our house or school would not receive a full hit. When it did, we hoped that someone would find us alive in the rubble and that we would not suffocate from lack of oxygen. Yet in the midst of this daily and nightly routine, children managed to get snatches of sleep, to read or tell stories that would keep their anxiety at bay, and in my case, even to learn some rudiments of Latin, for our teachers managed to instruct us in the air raid shelters in the few short hours in which we still attended school. "Gallia omnia divisa est in partes tres" rings in my ears as clearly as the rumble of the air mine that fell into the school yard and buried my best friend in the rubble.

The crumbling walls killed my Latin and English teacher as well. We never could find my best friend. For weeks, I would sit on a pile of rubble—

which was all that was left from the three-story school building that had collapsed on her and the other children—and wonder why fate had saved me and allowed her to perish. Each school day she had sat beside me in class and played with me in the courtyard, and now she was gone. And I was still there.

Not everyone among the Allies approved of the "area bombing" that began in 1943 and whose main victims were women and children under the age of sixteen. On the British side, the archbishop of Canterbury and other high officials of the Church of England and Scotland had condemned the "blanket bombing" of large population centers in the European war theater. So did members of Parliament. After the devastating raids on Dresden, even Churchill was alarmed and sent a memo to his chiefs of staff, among them General Arthur Harris, the chief of the Royal Air Force Bomber Command: "It seems to me that the moment has come when the question of bombing German cities, simply for increasing the terror, though under other pretexts, should be reviewed. Otherwise, we shall come into control of an utterly ruined land."[2] His predictions would prove true.

Meanwhile, the German people, especially the women and children, endured the full brunt of the air warfare as stoically and bravely as the British people had done. But the air strikes in 1943–1945 were far more devastating than those the Luftwaffe had dealt to the populace of London in 1940–1941. Allied bombing of Germany caused ten times as many civilian casualties. And unlike the English king and queen, the Führer, who had unleashed these furies, never visited a bombed-out city. It was a duty that seemed simply too painful for him to endure—until he committed suicide in his "bomb-proof" Bunker in the rubble of Berlin—in the final Götterdämmerung.[3]

Our defenders were fourteen-, fifteen-, and sixteen-year-old high school students—boys who were *Luftwaffenhelfer* (air force aids). In February 1943, the first of these student-soldiers were drafted to "man" the anti-aircraft artillery guns surrounding the German cities. The first to be called up were the boys who were born in 1926 and 1927; by March 1945, they were calling youngsters of my age, born in 1929. Some 200,000 of these *Schüler-Soldaten* (mainly seventh and eighth graders) received military training with the anti-aircraft cannons and observation equipment of the FLAK *(Flieger-Abwehr-Kommando)*.

In the beginning, the boys served in units near their hometowns but later were moved wherever a desperate last stand was called for. They were stationed in barracks, separated from their families. Under the best of circumstances, they were allowed to go home twice a year on a short leave, if their homes were nearby—and still standing! They received a modicum of schooling—when it was possible—that included German, Latin, history, geography, mathematics, chemistry, and physics.

In their commitment to defend the Fatherland, they maintained a remarkable esprit de corps wherever they served. They considered themselves soldiers rather than students, and they found themselves often in conditions more dangerous than their elders on the Eastern and Western front. Thousands of these boys died from wounds received by strafing planes or direct bomb hits on their cannons, or they were burned to death by exposure to phosphor. They are buried under the Iron Cross in cemeteries scattered from France to Germany and Austria. Their eyewitness accounts of the firestorms of Hamburg, Berlin, and Dresden are among the most dramatic first-person accounts of what it is like to live under conditions of "Total War."[4]

The city of Hamburg, home to some one million inhabitants, had experienced 137 air attacks before the fateful days of July 25–28, 1943, in which it was almost totally destroyed by some 800 to 1,000 Allied bombers. The first major attack came around midnight on July 25 and lasted about three hours. The second and third attacks came soon afterwards, on the afternoon of July 25 and the morning of July 26. The three-hour attack on the night of July 27–28 caused a firestorm that raged through the inner city. The next day, the survivors couldn't see the sun, only a red ball, which was almost completely hidden behind giant clouds of smoke. It remained dark till late afternoon.

Half of the teenage *Luftwaffenhelfer* who had been assigned to defend the city with their anti-aircraft artillery had been on midsummer leave when the Allied attacks began. The others were new at their jobs. Many had been called up only ten days earlier and had little training and no gas masks or helmets. A steady shower of tinfoil dropped by the Allied bombers made it impossible for them to target the attacking planes correctly. Most batteries shot blindly into the dark—occasionally they downed a hapless plane that was caught in their searchlights. When it was over, the young defenders of Hamburg had no homes or parents to go back to. Eight hundred thousand residents were homeless, "wandering up and down the streets, not knowing what to do," as Goebbels wrote in his diary.

In a moving collection of interviews, entitled *Aber Wir Müssen Zusammen Bleiben: Mütter und Kinder im Bombenkrieg* (But we must stay together: Mothers and daughters during the bombing), Rita Bake evokes some of the scenes that the children witnessed during those fateful midsummer nights.[5]

Ursula Corinth was twelve years old at the time. She lived in Hamburg with her parents, her six-year-old sister, and two younger brothers (ages two years, and eight weeks). When the sirens first rang, around midnight, her family, who lived on the fifth floor of a large apartment house, did not want to get up. The baby had the mumps, and her mother did not want to wake the feverish child. But then the noise of detonating bombs was so deafening that she barely had time to pick up the children and run to the cellar in their basement. They carried only a small suitcase with family papers. Soon after they had settled in the cellar, incendiaries fell on the roof of their house, and the fire, slowly but surely, worked its way from the top floor to the basement.

Only after the third try were they able to leave their cellar and reach an air raid shelter nearby. As she ran to safety, Ursula saw the burning houses in her neighborhood collapse, one by one. She clutched her celluloid doll with both arms, but her horrified mother urged her to throw it away for fear it would ignite. The next morning, they could not see the sun—the air was filled with smoke. Laid out on a canvass, under the sky, were babies who had been badly burned by phosphor. Some were still alive. The girl called for her mother, "Mutti! Mutti!" (Mommy! Mommy!). She was afraid she would be left behind to die like the babies.

Eight-year-old Margret Kaufmann spent the second night of the attack with her thirteen-year-old brother and her mother in the cellar. When the air mines fell, she felt as if she was experiencing an earthquake. She put her head under a pillow in her mother's lap, so she would not be able to hear the constant explosions. Her brother bravely ventured on the roof to get rid of the incendiaries that had fallen on the house. The next night, loud explosions ripped their neighborhood apart.

Another girl, who was seven at the time, still remembers the fear that gripped her when her house collapsed and she sat in their cellar stunned, unable to move. Whey they recovered from their panic, she, her sister, and her mother managed to crawl, like rats, out of the narrow window of the cellar. They were lucky—all the others who had been with them were buried in the rubble. Outside, the lone mother and her two dazed children wandered aimlessly in the burning streets. Suddenly, one of the little girls was swept away like a piece of paper by the sheer force of the firestorm. The desperate mother held on to her other daughter. Eventually, someone found the missing child and brought her back to her mother. They slept that night near the railroad station, together with thousands of others, in the ruins of their city.

Today, the only reminders of the firestorm are the ruins of a church in which some had sought shelter and a monument to the 55,000 people who were killed in the area-bombing of Hamburg. The inscription below the sculpted figures of old men, women, and children reads:

> *May the people who come after us be saved*
> *From the destruction of the innocent.*
> *May this memorial exhort us*
> *To love all mankind.*

There would be thousands of other children killed or maimed in other firestorms, in other cities, before the survivors would finally heed that advice.

Throughout the war, Berlin was one of the most heavily bombed cities in Germany. Regina Schwenke, who experienced her first air raid as a five-year-old in late August 1940, was by the beginning of 1945 a battle-hardened survivor.[6] One of the favorite playgrounds of the children in her neighborhood was a giant bomb crater in which they built sand castles and streets, threw sand at each other, and where, for a few hours, they would forget what explosive force had created their favorite playground in the first place.

One day, they found a pair of glasses and a set of false teeth in their "sand-hole." Every one of her companions tried on the glasses and, after some hesitation, even the false teeth. Then they played a game, in which each of the twelve assembled children had to declaim a sentence from a favorite poem—decked out with glasses and teeth, like actors on the Berlin stage. Eight-year-old Regina couldn't think of any poems, so she sang her favorite hymn: "Maria zu lieben" (Mary, I love you). But when lunchtime came, the children realized that they were stuck in the bomb crater. Eventually, a neighbor discovered them and threw a clothesline down. One by one, a dozen children scrambled up—the last one wearing glasses and false teeth!

The next day a Party official knocked at the door and inquired about the articles the children had found. A member of the Party had lost them during the last air raid and offered three bonbons as a reward. The children threw dice four times—the first three could suck on the candy for ten seconds. Then it was the turn of the next three lucky ones, and then the next three, and finally the last three. There was nothing left anymore for the last three after the count of six.

Their game was a happy interlude before the most devastating bombing attacks on Berlin in the waning days of the war. Between February 3 and February 5, some 1,000 Allied bombers created an inferno in the German capital. American bombers attacked in broad daylight, first dropping explo-

sive bombs, then phosphor canisters, then explosives again. Regina's mother had a difficult time reaching a shelter with her five children: Regina; her older brother, Jürgen; her two younger sisters, Angela and Rita; and baby Michael.

Jürgen pulled Rita by the hand, but she dragged behind. She had lost her new doll, a Christmas gift, and was trying to find her favorite toy in the light of the exploding incendiaries. Her mother pushed the baby carriage with the infant as fast as she could, while bombs fell to her right and left. The five minutes that it took the children to get to the shelter of the Nicodemus Church seemed like an eternity.

They made it to the shelter, but only after the carriage and the baby tipped over on the crowded stairs and a fierce argument erupted between the anxiously waiting crowd and the mother intent to rescue her infant from being trampled. During the night, there was no chance for anyone to sleep. In the early morning, the church received several hits and began to burn. In the cellar the children listened to the crash of the roof that descended down to the basement. They scrambled up the staircase and saw a brightly lit sky that was illuminated by the burning nave of the church. There were lifeless bodies everywhere, and burning pieces of the roof had fallen in the church-yard.

Regina's mother urged her children to run to Saint Christophorus, the nearby Catholic church, without paying heed to the destruction on their right and left. So they did. The planes were now flying so low that Regina could see the pilots and hear the ak-ak-ak of their machine gun fire. Regina dragged her younger sister Angela by the hand and ran as fast as she could. The little girl's shoelaces had opened up and she stumbled every few feet. But they made it safely to the church, where they found Jürgen and Rita on the stairs to the basement. After an agonizing wait, her mother arrived as well, with the baby in her arms. Silently, a priest took the infant out of the arms of the exhausted mother and found a place for the children. They slumped on the floor of the basement and fell asleep—their dreams were filled with fire and lifeless corpses.

In the morning, as if by sheer magic, the priest had found some tea and a few pieces of dry bread for the hungry little family. Then they made their way back to their bombed-out home, rescuing what little they could. At night they went back to the shelter of the Catholic church. The next nights were relatively quiet. There was nothing more left to destroy in their neighborhood.

SIXTEEN-YEAR-OLD Dieter Borkowski served in a FLAK company that was to defend Berlin from air attacks. By chance he had a dental ap-

Children play in ruins

pointment in the neighborhood of the zoo when his battery was destroyed by the surprise attack. One of the bombs fell on the munitions chamber of their main cannon. Four hundred rounds of ammunition exploded and killed all of his classmates. On the evening of February 3, 1945, he wrote in his diary:

> The nine boys gave their lives for Germany and the Führer. But we could not find any traces of them, except for some helmets and watches. . . . In the inner city there are firestorms everywhere. . . . There are heaps of burnt corpses which have shrunk in the heat to the size of children's bodies. The ruins are saturated with the sweet smell of burned flesh. . . . It is said that some ten thousand people have died in the firestorm.[7]

Ten days later, on February 13–14, 1945, Allied planes conducted a massive bombing raid against Dresden, a commercial city with numerous hospitals but without any military targets. During the night, some 873 British bombers dropped thousands of incendiaries and high explosives on Germany's most beautiful city. The bombs started an immense firestorm, as the rising columns of heat sucked up oxygen, creating hurricane-like winds and temperatures up to 1,000 degrees Fahrenheit or higher. At noon, 311 American B-17s released 771 tons on the flaming city, with the aim of destroying firemen and rescue workers when they were out on the streets. The following day, 210 B-17s dropped another 461 tons of high explosives.

A violent firestorm raged for four days and could be seen for hundreds of miles. Dresden, a city of 650,000 permanent residents, had swollen to one million people by the end of the war. Hundreds of thousands of refugees who had fled from the approach of the Soviet armies in the east had come with small children and with carts and hand wagons packed with some household goods. Every park on the riverbank was filled with refugees. In the railroad stations were trains with children who had been evacuated from the bombings of cities in western Germany.

The people in the air raid shelters and city parks were either suffocated in the inferno or were baked alive. Many people who made it out of the city and reached the Elbe River were killed by machine guns from Allied planes. Kurt Vonnegut, the author of *Slaughterhouse Five*, was one of several thousand American POWs in Dresden at the time.[8] He described the scene in a letter to his parents shortly after the war:

> *On February 14th, the Americans and the R.A.F. came over. Their combined labor killed 250,000 people in twenty-four hours and destroyed all of Dresden—possibly the world's most beautiful city. But not me. After that we*

Children sit on the threshold of ruins they call home.

were put to work carrying corpses from air raid shelters: Women, children, old men; dead from concussion, fire or suffocation. Civilians cursed us and threw rocks as we carried bodies to huge funeral pyres in the city.[9]

The bombing had started at the railroad station, where two trains carrying evacuated children between ages twelve and fourteen were hit. In an instant, most of the children were turned into corpses. In one of the passenger trains were seventy-eight children from Oppeln, Upper Silesia. Johanna Mittmann, who now lives in the United States, was one of the survivors.

When the bombs began to hit the Dresden station, she and the other children prayed fervently, "Hilf, Maria, es ist Zeit, Mutter der Barmherzgkeit!" (Help, Mary, it is time, Mother of Mercy!)[10] As the flames began to engulf their passenger coach, the children continued praying. Exhausted from the heat caused by the fires, they fell asleep. Johanna and the children in her care were the only survivors at the station.

Five-year-old Uta Wutherich, a native of Dresden, had spent the night in the cellar. The sirens and the droning planes woke her up. Her eight-year-old brother and her three-year-old sister were next to her, but her mother was missing. Anxiously the children cried, "Mutti! Mutti!" There was no answer. Uta climbed up the staircase and cried again and again: "Mutti, wo bist du?" (Mommy, where are you?). She looked in every room in the house. Her mother was not there. She opened the door to the children's bedroom and saw that it was bright red. Two figures stood by the window—her mother and her nanny. They looked silently down on the burning city. When they noticed the little girl, they motioned her back to the cellar. Uta saw the tears in their eyes. Decades later, she was still afraid to sleep alone at night and would dream periodically of the glowing red fire that had destroyed her hometown.[11]

Fifteen-year-old Willy A. Schauss, a member of the Volkssturm at the time, escaped with a seriously wounded friend from the burning hotel in which they were stationed. Draped in two wet blankets to keep themselves from burning to death, the boys struggled to reach their homes. During their odyssey through the inferno of Dresden, they met up with five POWs, two British and three American pilots, who tended to their wounds. "I thought to myself, what a screwed up world we live in," Willy wrote later in *My Side of the War*. "Here are prisoners of war who dropped bombs to kill, then they risk their lives to save two boys who should be the enemy."[12]

When they came to the *Grosser Garten,* the great city park, where many had sought refuge, they found crater after crater, filled with dead people and dead animals who had escaped from the zoo. The British officers had tears in their eyes when they saw the women and children. "I think 20,000 feet up in the air, killing people is not the same as seeing somebody dying," mused Willy. He made it to the apartment complex in which his parents lived and collapsed at their doorstep. Days later, he and his father went to look for his grandmother in Friedrichstadt, a part of Dresden that was totally destroyed.

His grandmother's house was a pile of rubble. People were digging to get to the basement. There was still smoke coming out of the rubble. Armed with a gas mask, Willy's father entered the cellar. He found the charred body of his mother on a small foot bench. He wrapped her in his coat. "We took the remains of Grandma to our nearby cemetery," Willy remembered. "There was no use for a large coffin, a few boards and nails that was all we had. We dug the grave ourselves."

Among the bodies discovered by weary rescue workers in the days to come were the remains of a mother and child. They had shriveled and charred into one piece and had been stuck to the asphalt of the street. The mother must have covered her child with her own body because one could recognize its shape with the mother's arms clasped around it. Nobody would ever be able to identify or separate the mother and child. They were bound for eternity.

One of the boys whose anti-aircraft battery was called up to dig the mass graves around Dresden's inner city was sixteen-year-old Klaus Granzow. On February 18, 1945, four days after the firestorm, he wrote in his diary: "Is this war or murder? Where is the front? What the civilians suffer seems much worse than what the soldiers must endure. And the worst is, not being able to help."[13]

No one will ever know the *real* number of those who perished in Dresden. The memorial inscription to the firestorm victims reads:

> *How many died? Who knows their number?*
> *From the wounds, one can see the agony of the nameless,*
> *Who were burnt in the fire from human hand.*

In March and May 1945, it was Tokyo's turn to be destroyed by firestorms. Katherine Kaoru Morooka, a California-born Nisei, and her family were among hundreds of thousands of civilians who bore the brunt of the attacks by American planes based in Saipan. Katherine had come to Tokyo as a teenager, with dual American and Japanese citizenship, and found herself now among people whose country was at war with the United States. When air raid bombing had become a fact of life in Japan, her widowed mother and her three daughters had built an air raid shelter in the yard of their home. Together, they dug out a rectangular trench with sitting areas on the side, then placed a heavy board on top and covered it with two feet of dirt. The shelter would save their lives in the firebombings.[14]

On the night of March 10, 1945, Katherine was awakened abruptly by air raid sirens. When she turned on the radio, she heard that a large flotilla of B-29s was headed toward Tokyo. In pitch darkness, she put on her clothes hurriedly and scrambled into the bomb shelter with her mother and sisters. As she looked toward the northeast, she saw that the entire sky was crimson from raging fires. The night was as light as day—the central city had be-

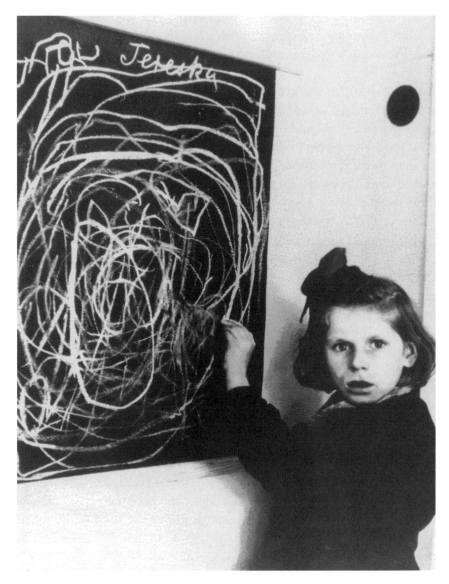

Eyewitness to the death of her family, this child can only trace chaotic lines to describe her bombed-out home.

come an inferno. The massive firebombing that night wiped out a quarter of Tokyo and killed thousands of civilians. But Katherine's home was untouched by the flames.

She was not so lucky during the next air raid, which came on the night of May 23, 1945. When the sirens blasted, Katherine, her mother, and two of her sisters made it to the shelter. Her sister Mayme was sick with pleurisy and could not get out of bed. Soon Katherine heard the rustling sounds of incendiaries and saw their yard ablaze. Hundreds of flames were shooting out from the rooftop. Katherine dragged her sick sister out of the house and to a clearing nearby. Her mother cried helplessly as she saw their house go up in flames.

That night, Katherine, her mother, and her two sisters slept in a vacant house behind their lot that had miraculously escaped the bombs. The next morning, they hosed down the smoldering embers in their compound. They had lost everything except for the clothes in two suitcases. Their family photos and memorabilia from their old home in the United States were gone forever. But worse was yet to come.

Two nights later, on May 25, 1945, they were again awakened by the shrill sound of sirens. Hurriedly, they carried Katherine's sick sister into the shelter they had built. They could hear the drone of the planes right above their heads and then heard, again and again, the sound of falling bombs. They looked back toward the house where they had sought refuge and saw that the flames were rapidly turning it into ashes. In two days, they had been burned out twice. They spent the rest of the night in a neighbor's home. The next day, Katherine's mother and sisters went to stay in the mountain village where her father had been born before he emigrated to America.

Katherine stayed in Tokyo and saw firsthand the destruction the firestorms had wrought. Thousands had died from lack of oxygen in the bomb shelters. The injured lay on the streets and sidewalks. There were smoldering ruins everywhere. Dazed and homeless women and children were wandering about aimlessly. But others who lost their homes in the bombings chose to remain on their property. They built shacks of corrugated tin, wood, and cardboard next to the bomb shelters that had saved their lives. By the summer of 1945, the capital city of Japan was in total ruins.

Among the primary-school students who had been ordered out of Tokyo to keep them safe from the devastating air raids was Shinsuke Tani, who was sent with her class to a Buddhist temple in the countryside. In *Seasons Unforgotten* she wrote about the way she and other third through sixth graders spent their nights in the waning days of the war. When the attack warnings came over the radio, the children would get up, change their clothes, sling the bag in which they kept their hoods and underwear over their shoulders, and then march single file out in the temple compound where they sought shelter.[15]

Around midnight on May 24, 1945, the children were awakened by their housemother, who kept repeating in a high-pitched voice: "Tokyo is burning. Have a good look at it, Tokyo is burning." Shinsuke rubbed her sleepy eyes and dashed out of the main hall, racing to get ahead of the other children: "Then I saw it—the faraway sky in the East was dyed an intense red as if a crimson sash were being stretched out across it. . . . I was shivering. I stared at it while my teeth chattered. The yellow fire blew up now and then like flashes of fireworks. That night . . . our city was completely destroyed in a crimson sash."

When the little girl returned to Tokyo after the end of the war, she could not recognize her house. Beneath a stairway that vanished midway in the air, she found a *daruma* doll—also chairs with some legs missing and a half-melted sofa. And suddenly, incongruously, there stood in the bushes an un-broken urinal. She felt as if she was still in a dream. Then she went into the empty city to search out the secrets of her new playground. The three major air raids on her hometown in March and May 1945 had destroyed 233,000 houses and killed 211,400 persons.

TEN WEEKS AFTER the May raids on Tokyo, an American B-29 named *Enola Gay* dropped the first atomic bomb on the city of Hiroshima. The bomb wiped out the center of the city. American estimates were of about 80,000 dead; another 20,000 died within two weeks from the effects of radiation. Japanese estimates of the total casualties from the blast and radiation ran as high as 250,000. Many people were evaporated. Their shapes remained as shadows, like negatives from exposed film, on the stone walls and steps of the city. No one counted the shadows.

Six years after the event that ushered in the atomic age, a group of school children from Hiroshima wrote a series of essays that were dedicated to the memory of those who perished. In *Children of the A-Bomb: The Testament of the Boys and Girls of Hiroshima,* the children spoke about the impact of the A-bomb on their lives.[16] One ninth grade boy, Shigeru Tasaka, who had been in the third grade that fateful day, wrote:

> For the first time I came to understand what a detestable, frightful thing war is. . . . I think it would have been a good thing if, in the course of this war, atom bombs had fallen on every country. . . . This is because I believe that by experiencing atom bombs people will understand how barbaric, how tragic, how uncivilized, how hateful a thing war is, and we could have an end of the revolting wars we have now.

On the morning of August 6, 1945, at 8:15 A.M., some six thousand school children were working or playing in the epicenter of the blast. Not even shreds of clothing remain of them, except for a white eyelet petticoat with brown-rimmed burn holes, stained with black rain, worn by a school-girl named Oshita-chan, which is displayed in a museum that commemo-rates the A-bomb victims.

Setsuko Yamamato, a first grader in grammar school, was having breakfast with her mother that morning when "from no particular place there was a bright flash." Then she heard a tremendous explosion, and everything became pitch dark. The girl couldn't even see the face of her mother. Seconds later, a heavy object fell on the child, but she managed to crawl out. With a heavy beam across her right arm and back, Setsuko's mother was pinned to the floor. The little girl tried to pull her out—without success. Around her, flames were beginning to spread, and her clothes were already on fire.

Screaming "Mommy, Mommy!" Setsuko ran outside and jumped into the water tank next to her house. The water was hot like a bath. Everything seemed like a dream—then she lost consciousness. She awoke when someone lifted her out of the tank. Her mother had perished in the fire, just as Setsuko had left her. Five days later, after the child had found refuge in her grandmother's home in the countryside, her uncle brought her mother's ashes. "Holding the urn in my arms, I lifted up my voice and wailed," she wrote. "The tears kept on and on."

Yasushi Haraki had gone to school about eight o'clock in the morning. He was doing a second grade assignment when, suddenly, there was an enormous flash, and it got dark in his classroom. A moment later, the ceiling came falling down on the children. Yasushi managed to crawl out of the room under a row of desks and into the school yard. By that time, the whole school building was a sea of flames. Limping along with an injured foot, he went back to his home. It was burning fiercely. His little sister, who had stayed alone at home while their mother had gone to work, was nowhere to be found.

He *did* find his injured mother. Together they went to a hospital, where they stayed for nearly two weeks. After that, they continued their search for his missing sister and found her finally in the care of some kind strangers who had rescued her after her home had collapsed on her. She had been pinned under the house, her legs broken, and was suffering from severe radiation poisoning. She died one hour after she was reunited with her brother and mother.

Kiyoka Tanaka was in the third grade on August 6, 1945. On that day she went to play with some of her friends in the neighborhood. When the flash of the atomic bomb came, she was pinned under the house where they were staying. She pushed some boards out of her way and crawled out. Once outside, she found to her astonishment that every house in sight had collapsed and was burning. She managed to reach her burning home. Her mother had put her one-year-old baby on top of a pile of bundles and was carrying things out into the street. The baby was unconscious.

Taking the bundles on her back and the baby in her arms, the mother started off with Kiyoka. They were heading toward a hill where people were jumping into water tanks and ponds because their burns hurt badly. Others were sitting beside the road, asking everybody who passed, "Please give me water." Some were drinking the dirty water by the roadside.

When they reached the river, they boarded a boat to get to a suburb of Hiroshima. There they met a lone girl whose whole body was covered with burns and wounds. She seemed to be in great pain and kept calling her mother. Then she held out something to Kiyoka's mother. It was her lunch box that her mother had fixed for her that morning when she left for school. "I am going to die. Give it to your daughter," she said. And then she died.

Ten-year-old Yoshihiro Kimura attended school in a temple near his home. Their teacher was late for class, so the children were talking about the war. Pretty soon they heard a hum and saw an airplane in the sky to the southeast. Suddenly it dropped something that looked like a white parachute. Seconds later everything turned yellow in an instant. Yoshihiro felt as if he was staring straight into the sun. Then there was a tremendous crash. Everything became dark, and stones and roof tiles came pouring down on the boy's head. For a while he was unconscious, pinned down by a heap of fallen lumber.

When he came to again, seared by pain, he crawled outside to the street. Lots of people were lying around there, with their faces so charred that he could not recognize them. Then he discovered that the skin of his right arm was peeled off from his elbow to his fingers, and it was all red. His sister was calling for him, "Sumi-chan!" Her clothes were torn to rags and her face was so bloated that he could not recognize her.

Together they walked toward their home. But the house was no longer standing. His mother, with a five-inch nail stuck in her head, had died instantly. Together with their father, the children set out for the river. From upstream a great many black and burned corpses came floating down the river. But the boy was so thirsty that he pushed them away and drank the water. At the riverbank people were lying all over the place. Some were not dead yet, and among them were some children who were screaming, "Mother! Mother."

The next day, relatives pulled the two children on a cart to the country-side, to their grandmother's home. There, on August 15, Yoshihiro's sister died. "Your mother and your sister are with Buddha now," his grandmother told the grieving boy.

*A*T TWO MINUTES AFTER eleven o'clock on the morning of August 9, 1945, an American plane dropped a second atomic bomb on the city of Nagasaki. Again the city center and thousands of lives disappeared in an instant. But there were children who survived and remembered. *Living Beneath the Atomic Cloud: The Testimonies of the Children of Nagasaki* is a riveting account of their encounter with Armageddon.[17]

Eleven-year-old Toshihiro Fukahori was going to confession that day. In a week, he and his family would celebrate the feast of the Ascension of the Virgin Mary. Just then, the bell of the air defense position behind the church rang furiously. He jumped into a nearby air raid shelter. There was a strange light, then a terrific boom. Then something that looked like blue gas seeped into the shelter. The boy could hardly breathe. Putting his hands on his chest, he called to his favorite saint, "Mother Mary! Mother Mary!" He thought he was going to die.

After a while, somebody called from outside the shelter, "Are you alive? Are you all right?" It was his uncle with a hoe, ready to dig him out. When the boy crawled outside the shelter everything had changed. The surrounding houses had collapsed; trees had fallen; tiles, stones, and trash were scattered everywhere. Nagasaki was a sea of fire. The Catholic church was on fire, too. Everyone watched helplessly.

That night, people slept in the shelter. It was so crowded that people slept sitting up. Somebody found a mosquito net, so Toshihiro put his mat on a vacant spot in front of the air raid shelter. Suddenly a woman whose hair was disheveled like a madman's and whose face was swollen up like a balloon tottered toward the entrance of the shelter. When she came closer, the boy recognized his aunt, who had been severely injured by the blast. There was no place left for her to rest, so she laid down on the road, like a fallen stone.

Ten-year-old Michiko Ogino was playing house with her sisters when the clock struck eleven. Her mother had gone to the fields that morning to pick some eggplants. Just then, the girl was glancing at the window and saw a lightning-like flash. The next thing she knew, she was pinned under the house. Her oldest sister, who had been outside, ran for help. She found five sailors, who pulled Michiko out of the rubble. Standing outside, Michiko was astonished that what had been a beautiful clear day had changed completely: Black clouds were writhing all over the sky. Then they heard the voice of her younger brother and the cry of her two-year-old sister. Both were trapped under the house.

The two girls were able to pull their brother out after removing a pile of roof tiles, but they were unable to move the toddler, whose legs had been pinned down under a huge cross beam. Then they saw someone dashing to-

Boys in the rubble of Nagasaki.

ward them—a woman with disheveled hair and a purple-colored body. When she called out, the girls recognized their mother's voice. She had been hit by the blast when she was picking eggplants. Her coat and trousers were burnt and torn to pieces. He hair had turned to reddish brown and was frizzled and torn. She was burnt all over her body.

She looked down on her youngest child, studying the beams that were piled up on her. Then she got into an opening under the cross beam and put her right shoulder under it. Straining with all her might, she was able to lift the beam a little. The little girl's legs were freed. The oldest sister pulled her out. The mother hugged the child tightly to her breast. The skin on her right shoulder, where she had lifted the beam, was gone, revealing raw flesh and red blood that was oozing out. Michiko's mother died that night, knowing that all her children had survived.

Nine-year-old Mitsuyuki Nishada was playing marbles at a neighbor's house when he saw a blinding flash. From that moment on, he could not see anything more. He *did* hear voices. His father called his name and so did his mother. Someone had picked him up and carried him to an air raid shelter. Someone else took his badly burned mother to the hospital. But then they seemed to have forgotten about the blind boy and his father who lay beside him, badly injured. They waited for help. They waited and waited for two days, without water and food. But then help did come.

The boy and his father were brought to the navy hospital, where they shared the same room. Mitsuyuki was the lucky one—his eyes got better and better. But his father's radiation disease got worse and worse. He died weeks later, lying on the bed next to his son. "I wished I had remained blind," wrote the boy later. "Then I wouldn't have seen him die. I didn't know what to do."

Three weeks later, on September 2, 1945, the Japanese surrender was signed in Tokyo Bay aboard the USS *Missouri*. World War II had officially ended. But it was still very much in the minds and memories of the children of the A-bomb when they wrote their essays in honor of the dead. One of the most moving accounts was written by Fuiji Tsujimoto, who lost his whole family—mother, father, brother, and two sisters—in the atomic blast of Nagasaki. He was five years old at the time. He and his grandmother were the only survivors in their family. The air raid shelter in which they had found refuge was dug deep in a cliff at the corner of the playground of the Yamazato Primary School, and, miraculously, the little boy and the old woman escaped the effects of the blast and the radiation.

In *The Testimony of the Children of Nagasaki*, Fuiji wrote:

> I am now in the fourth grade of the Yamazato Primary School. The playground of terrible memories is now completely cleared and many friends play there happily. They don't know that so many children were killed and cremated in that place. I play with my friends there, too, but sometimes I remember that awful day. When I do, I squat on the spot where we cremated our mother and touch the earth with my fingers. When I dig deep in the ground with a piece of bamboo, several pieces of charcoal appear. Looking at the spot for a while, I can dimly see my mother's image in the earth. . . . The ground is dear to me, but at the same time it makes me very sad. . . . Grandmother goes to church every morning to hear Mass. She often prays with a rosary, and says to me, "Everything is in God's will. Everything is all right." I wish I had as pure a heart as Grandma.[18]

— 9 —

We Regret to Inform You

$\mathcal{W}$HEN WORLD WAR II ENDED, some 40 million civilians and some 15 million soldiers had lost their lives. The immense task of grieving would not be over by the time the fighting stopped. For my family, like for many others, it continued for years to come. All the men in my family, except for my father, had perished in the war.

My adopted brother was killed in action in Russia. Two of my uncles died on the Eastern front; a third succumbed to a painful illness he contracted as a prisoner of war in Siberia. My cousins became "half orphans." Their fathers were killed near war's end. I recite this litany of loss just as the Russian boy N. P. Dovbenko did in *No Longer Silent*: "At the end of September, 1941, we learned from an eyewitness that father had been killed in action near Kanev. . . . In the fall of 1943 . . . a sniper's bullet killed Uncle Serafirm. . . . Then, in 1944, Uncle Misha, who was a participant in the defense of Leningrad, perished in Estonia."[1]

The Russian boy and I were young teenagers at the time. Our two countries suffered the largest number of casualties, both military and civilian, in World War II. In all likelihood, my brother was in the same battle as Uncle Misha—he was killed near Leningrad (Saint Petersburg). Both soldiers, according to the rhetoric of their time, died a "hero's death": Misha gave his life for Mother Russia; my brother gave his for the German Fatherland. None of us saw the remains of our kinfolk—we do not know where we could find their graves.

Would it have made a difference in our acceptance of their deaths? The Russian boy could console himself that his country was among the victors of World War II, and that his father and uncles did not "die in vain." My kinfolk belong to the vanquished invaders. Perhaps it is the senselessness of their "ultimate sacrifice" that has made it so hard for me to mourn their loss. What I *did* mourn were my classmates who died in the saturation bombing of our cities. My closest friend was buried in the rubble of a three-story schoolhouse that collapsed after a particularly ferocious air attack. She was in the sixth grade.

There was a special poignancy when families received the news of death around Christmastime. Seven-year-old Elsbeth Emmerich had made a special greeting card for her dad, who was fighting near Leningrad in the winter of 1941–1942. Two weeks before the holiday, she wrote: "Dear Daddy, many thousand Christmas greetings from your Elsbeth, Margret, and Elfielein. I have made the card [especially] for you. It was the best in our class. We have been waiting for a long time for your visit. When can you be with us again? Now I wish you all the best and an early holiday."[2]

Christmas came and went without any news from her father. Elsbeth's mother was very worried. Years later, Elsbeth still remembered the day the postman came:

> He was usually a very jovial man, but he hesitated when he asked my mother for her signature for the registered letter he had. It was a blue envelope with official stamps on the back. My mother took the letter trembling. She opened it, read it with an ashen face, threw the letter on the table, and left crying for our bedroom. My sister Marget and I stood bewildered. . . . I shook with every limb as I read that my father had been wounded in the right shoulder. . . . I didn't read any further. I could not bear it. I could not bear my daddy being hurt and being so far away from us. I burst into tears and followed my mother into our room. She lay on the bed crying. . . . I remember crying for a very long time. . . . It was much later that I saw the letter again and learned of the circumstances of his death. [After he was wounded] he had to be taken by dog sleigh, in the freezing cold, to an ambulance station. It took three days and three nights, and he was so exhausted and had lost so much blood that he died of heart failure the day of his arrival, twelve days after his 28th birthday.

Elsbeth's Christmas card was returned to her family. Her dad had kept it in his wallet.

A year later and half a world away, a five-year-old girl in Florida missed her favorite uncle on another Christmas Day. Six days earlier, on December 19, 1942, her father had received a telegram from the War Department:

> *MR BRADFORD:*
> *THE SECRETARY OF WAR DESIRES ME TO EXPRESS HIS DEEP*
> *REGRET THAT YOUR BROTHER, SECOND LIEUTENANT*
> *WILLIAM HOWARD BRADFORD WAS KILLED IN ACTION IN*
> *DEFENSE OF HIS COUNTRY IN NORTH AFRICA NOVEMBER 8.*
> *LETTER FOLLOWS ULIO THE ADJUTANT GENERAL*

*A grieving mother
holding her daughter
in her arms.*

My dear Mr. Bradford:
    *It is with deep regret that I learned of the death of your brother in North
Africa. I realize that there is little that can be said to alleviate your grief, but
I hope that you will derive some consolation in the knowledge that Howard
Bradford served with honor in the United States Army and died in the best
traditions of the service. To men like your brother who have died that the
American way of life can continue, the nation owes an everlasting debt of*

gratitude. Again, my deepest sympathy to you and to the other members of the family.

> *Faithfully yours,*
> *George C. Marshall*
> *Chief of Staff*

"We went through the motions of Christmas," Elizabeth Shelfer Morgan remembered in *Uncertain Seasons*, "but it felt like everything had been shut down. . . . Mama insisted we all keep busy and keep involved in the spiritual meaning of Christmas."[3] Meanwhile, in a faraway country a true Christmas miracle came to pass:

> *DECEMBER 29, 1942*
>
> *MR. BRADFORD*
> *REFERENCE MY TELEGRAM DECEMBER 19 REPORTING*
> *YOUR BROTHER SECOND LIEUT WILLIAM H BRADFORD*
> *INFANTRY KILLED IN ACTION. REPORT NOW RECEIVED*
> *FROM AFRICAN AREA STATES YOUR BROTHER IS SLIGHTLY*
> *WOUNDED NOVEMBER 19 ULIO THE ADJT GENERAL*

His little niece rejoiced: "Uncle Howard had survived, . . . turning the grief of uncertainty of the Christmas season into a finish not unlike that of the serials of the Saturday afternoon picture show. I continued to believe in hope and trust." But her favorite uncle would live only twenty more months and be killed in action during the Allied invasion in France. Decades later, his niece would remember the echo of the words in the postscript of his last letter, written from a muddy place in France: "I am beginning to wonder if I have a right to live."

On January 12, 1943, Lorraine Fader from Glenwood, Iowa, wrote a letter to the commander in chief of the Allied forces in the southwest Pacific area:[4]

> *Dear Gen. MacArthur:*
> *I am a girl 14 years old. I have a twin brother, Lloyd. . . . I also have 8 other brothers. I am the only girl in the bunch. . . . The brother I am writing you about went to the Philippines in November before the Pearl Harbor tragedy. I know you were there at that time. I was wondering if you knew if he was all right before you left there. He was with the Quarter Master 2nd when he left Fort Douglas, Utah where he was stationed for a year before he sailed for P.I. His name was Walter D. Fader. He was short and sorta fat and*

he was just a wonderful brother and we miss him so very much. The War Department wrote that he was Missing in Action but said he might have been taken prisoner by the Japs. If you knew him and you get this letter will you just write me a few lines and tell me. I think your little boy is very sweet and Mrs. MacArthur is very nice looking and we all back here think you are very wonderful too. . . . May God Bless you all and keep you safe. We all buy every stamp and bond we possibly can and I only hope it will in some way help my Dear Brother who is there in the P.I. at the mercy of those rats. Maybe he is killed. Maybe a prisoner. O God, which is worse I am sure I don't know. Well, God Bless You again Gen. MacArthur and little family and Every Mother's Son in the Service.

'Amen'

On December 29, 1943, thirteen-year-old Charmaine Leavitt of Kalamazoo, Michigan, sent a note to Private Justin J. Slager, a family friend and neighbor, stationed in North Africa:[5]

Dear Justin,
   I don't know whether you will get this letter or not, but I hope that you do. This morning your mother got a telegram saying that you were Missing in Action. I sure hope that you are O.K. and I also would like to know where you are. Everybody is worried about you around here and so am I.

Charmaine

Months later, Private Slager's family and friends were informed that he had been killed in action.

John Nichols Jr. was nine years old when the news arrived of his father's death. He had died from a Japanese sniper's bullet in late June 1944, during the American assault on Saipan. John was playing on the streets outside his home in upstate New York when the news arrived. His maternal grandmother opened the door to a Western Union messenger who handed her a telegram and then took off, without saying a word. His grandmother opened the telegram and started screaming. His mother had not yet come home from work. When she did, in the evening, the boy remembered: "She just went out of it. It seemed like days that all she did was lay on the couch and cry."[6]

Three months later an officer brought his father's medals: A Silver Star, a Bronze Star, and a Purple Heart. There was a short memorial service in honor of his father when the flag and the medals were presented to John's mother. That was all!

In August 1944, twelve-year-old Robert Raymond learned from his sister that a telegram had arrived at the railroad depot in Rapid City, South Dakota, and that it was about a death in the family. His brother Jack, who had served with the 109th Engineers, had been killed in Italy. Robert wrote:

> My anger at God that night was very real and intense and I regaled him long and hard about permitting wars and especially about letting one's brother be killed. Suddenly I was very lonesome for my Mom [who had died six years earlier]. . . . The family all gathered together except [my brothers] Murphy and Billy. Murphy was in Infantry Officer Candidate School at Fort Benning, and Billy was somewhere in the South Pacific.[7]

They received Jack's last letter about the same time he was killed: "Have been quite busy lately. Sure did enjoy the packages you sent an awful lot. Can't use the baseball shoes and glove for awhile but probably will be able to later. When I wrote and asked for them we were still at the Anzio Beach head. . . . It has been such a long time since I've written I don't know where I left off."

Two months later came another message, this time from the chief of staff, War Department: "General Marshall extends his deep sympathy in the loss of your brother. He died in the honorable service of his country to preserve the freedom under which he lived."

Jack's body was returned to the states in the spring of 1949. He was buried on a hill above the Keya Paha River Valley, South Dakota, among the members of his family and tribe, the Rosebud Sioux.

On Christmas Eve 1944, eight-year-old Ulla Ellersdorfer was listening to her favorite Christmas songs. Her mother was playing the piano. Her grandparents had brought gifts for her and her two little brothers. Only her dad was missing. She had written a Christmas card to him and decorated it with the drawing of a fir branch. There was no greeting from him on Christmas Day, but everyone said he would be home soon from the front. Meanwhile they waited patiently for a letter.

Early in January 1945, on a cold and sunny Sunday, Ulla's mother took her three children for a sleigh ride. When they came back, their grandparents were in the living room, their eyes red with tears. Grandfather gave his daughter a letter that had come in the mail. Ulla's mother cried and fled from the living room. Remembered the little girl:

> Grandfather told me to be very good to Mommy—my daddy would not be coming back from the war. That was it! Later we sat in the living

room. Darkness fell, but no one turned on the lights. My mother and grandmother wept incessantly. My grandfather stroked my arms—"he cries inside," I thought. He told me that my dad had been killed in action before Christmas—*before* I had written my Christmas letter. Something got stuck in my throat.

"You are now a half orphan," said my teacher. "Your dad gave his life for the Fatherland. You should be proud." I felt nothing and I did not cry.[8]

Annie Bennett's father was killed in a small northern Italian village in mid-April 1945 by a sniper's bullet. When the family received word that he had died, her mother took her three children to her sister's house. Everybody—aunts, uncles, grandmother—was crying:

> There is no crying in the world like that of someone who has just received such terrible news. It's an ocean. My brothers and I were surrounded and swept up in this ocean of grief. . . . Sidney was six and a half, I was four and a half, and my younger brother Tom, born after my father left, was only four months old. Sidney took me by the hand and led me away to take care of me as he had been told to do. He was now the man in the house. He explained to me that my father died for his country, that he was a hero. His was the only explanation I ever had. Shortly after that I remember telling someone who came to the house that my dad killed Hitler.[9]

Nancy Rougvie's father had served with the U.S. Army Air Force in China. He died there on July 17, 1945. The end of the fighting in the Pacific theater was less than one month away. Nancy, who was twelve and a half years old at the time, remembered that his letters from China continued to arrive after the family had been notified of his death. For years she watched the newsreels of returning servicemen looking for his face in the crowd, hoping, against the odds, he would return alive.[10]

SOME OF THE MOST POIGNANT comments on the deaths of their fathers on the front come from essays of German school children written at the end of 1945.[11] Wrote a ten-year-old girl: "When the first air attacks happened in Nuremberg and we could see the damage, we knew that the war was for real. My dad was drafted . . . and sent to Russia. He was seriously wounded and came back home. . . . But as soon as his wounds had healed, he was sent back. . . . He was 30 km before Moscow when they had to retreat. . . . He was hit by a bullet and died."

This essay was written by an eleven-year-old girl:

My father was a carpenter. I was often in his workshop. He made beautiful furniture. . . . My dad was very good to us. We always went on walks together. . . . When the war began, he like many other men, became a soldier. He was in the infantry. . . . He was gone for a long time and then came once on leave. How happy we were, my mother and I. . . . But time went by too fast and soon he had to go back to the war. Then it was lonely and sad. . . . One day a letter came, written in a strange hand. My dad was killed in action in Russia. He was 31 years old when he died. I will never forget him. May God grant him eternal rest.

And a twelve-year-old wrote: "I entered school in 1940. My father was drafted that year. When he came on leave he always brought something for me, and he sent me packages with sweets. . . . My father was in France for two years, and then he went to Russia. . . . He became very ill . . . and died after a short time. He worried about me until the end."

THE CHILDREN OF World War II learned to mourn the loss of civilian lives as well. Among the first to lose close family members were Polish children who had been deported from their homes between the spring of 1940 and the summer of 1941. Some 140,000 youngsters were sent with their families by truck and train to the Taiga, a 1,000-mile belt of forests stretching right across Europe and Asia, from the White Sea to the Pacific Ocean. There they were forcibly settled in labor camps. After a short, scorching hot summer, they experienced nine months of winter, with temperatures as low as 90 degrees below zero. They were constantly hungry and cold.

Here is a Polish child's account of the death of her mother and brother:

We would go around the Soviet villages exchanging clothing for food. One day mama . . . took sleigh with her; on the sleigh she put a big pot, a pillow and a fabric she still had from Poland. . . . Mama with brother went on Monday and said good-bye and went. . . . One day passed and another its cold outside. . . . We worry why Mamma isn't coming back. On Friday this woman comes over and says that one woman with a boy froze to death. We all cried at once dad walks around barracks like crazy. . . . Older sister fainted. . . . They found her two kilometers away from the village. Mama was sitting on the sleigh and holding my brother in her arms. They took them on the wagon and brought them to the kolhoz. . . . Dad and dad's friend started carrying Mama and Tadzik from the sleigh and they put them on the table . . . and then one woman started warming bricks and warming up the body and started taking mama's clothes off and washed her and dressed her in a new dress and dressed brother in his travel suit. . . . Dad went to a carpenter

French boys honoring soldiers who died in the war.

to make coffins. . . . In the evening we led mommie and Tadzik from the barracks . . . to the cemetery. We buried mommie in one grave with the brother. We covered it with sand and prayed over the grave and [when] we came to the barracks my sister was lying on the bed sick. That was my worst day in Russia.[12]

For children who were not deported, the "home front" was fraught with danger. Bombing of major cities, by both Allied and Axis planes, brought death to the streets where children lived and played, to the pantry under the stairs or the cellars where they sought shelter, and to the schools where they huddled in the basements—with the constant wailing of air raid sirens in their ears. Some were speechless when they learned of the loss of their loved ones after an air raid attack.

Alice Brady, a member of the U.S. committee that shepherded hundreds of British children to safety across the Atlantic, was in Coventry after the German air raid in January 1941. She wrote in her diary:

> Many children were found wandering around dazed. . . . Sometimes . . . [they] waited in vain for Mummy and Daddy. One little girl who had not spoken to anyone since she had been injured in the blitz was in the hospital and her parents were killed. A kindly neighbor . . . searched through the debris of the child's home and found her doll, mended it and took it to the hospital and put it in the child's arms. The child said, "You naughty girl, don't you know I have been looking for you for weeks. Where have you been?" These were the first words she had spoken since she was injured.[13]

Laurencia Abatayo was seven years old when the Japanese bombed Pearl Harbor in December 1941. She remembered the newsreels that were shown at the movies after the United States entered the war. "We saw the Americans bomb Germany," she recalled, "and everyone in the theatre would clap."

Four months after the outbreak of the war, an accident ripped her family apart. One day in March 1942, her father was in the cane fields where he worked as a foreman when one of his coworkers found an unexploded bomb that the Japanese had dropped on December 7 but that had lain dormant in the field. The man picked up the bomb to show it to Laurencia's dad. It slipped out of his hands and exploded. Both men died instantly.

Laurencia remembered:

> I was at school when the accident occurred. My mother, who was pregnant . . . at the time, was informed at home and she and one of her friends came and picked me up. . . . My mother was crying, but I didn't understand why. It wasn't until my father's body was brought to the house . . . that I realized he had died. . . . I began to understand better what happened during World War II a few years after its conclusion. Sometimes I would reflect upon Hiroshima . . . and hope that the Japanese and Russians would never do the same thing to us.[14]

Thirteen-year-old Hans Sester lost his parents and his two-year-old sister in a firestorm that enveloped the German city of Cologne after a ferocious air attack around midnight, June 29, 1943. They perished in a cloud of

A British war orphan, adopted by the U.S. Air Force, gives a salute.

phosphor that enveloped their street and liquefied the asphalt of the side-walk. Hans found refuge in an air raid shelter, where he discovered his six-year-old brother in the arms of a stranger. The next morning, nearly blinded by the smoke of the burning buildings in their neighborhood, the two boys managed to find refuge with an aunt in a suburb of the city. Here they waited, in vain, for the return of their parents. Hans describes the funeral of his mother in the first week of July:

> They did not show us her remains which had been partially inciner-ated. . . . I consoled myself with the thought that she had lost con-

sciousness from lack of oxygen before she died. . . . For the funeral, I wore a used dark brown suit given to me by a compassionate soul and hoped, against all odds, that my father might re-appear at any moment. The remains of my dad and my little sister Karin were never found. It is highly likely that they were interred in a mass grave in the South Cemetery of Cologne—complete with military honors and great pomp. My brother and I now had to come to terms with the fact that we had become orphans during that horrible night and that we could only hope for a reunion with my parents and my little sister in a realm "where there is no death, no sadness, no grief, and no sorrow" (as the New Testament says). We were grateful that we had our aunt who gave us a refuge in her home and who cared for us. Our life continued, and, sadly, so did the war.[15]

A fourteen-year-old German girl remembered a night in 1944 that changed her life forever:

> The sirens wailed, and my mother, brother and I went with our luggage to an air raid shelter that had been our refuge throughout the war. . . . As soon as we were in the cellar, bombs were crashing down on us. . . . My father joined us when the houses next doors went up in flames. When he tried to get out, he discovered that all exits had collapsed. There was hardly any oxygen to breathe for the fifty people in the shelter. Not even a candle would burn. We sat in the dark, hoping that we would be excavated when daylight came. I soon fell asleep in my mother's lap. Everyone lost consciousness. When I awoke . . . I was in the shelter of a [neighboring] school. Two days later they transported me to the children's hospital. I stayed there for one and half months, and then I finally learned from my grandparents that my parents and my brother had not survived the attack. I will never forget that experience.[16]

In the waning months of the war, the number of civilian casualties became staggering! During a major air raid on Nuremberg on January 2, 1945, a twelve-year-old girl was visiting with friends in a neighboring suburb. She wrote a few months later: "We all huddled together in a corner. Each explosion made us jump. . . . A few days later I learned that our house [in the city] had been hit by an explosive. My father and twenty-five other people were in the cellar below. They were all killed. Now I am alone in the world, for I lost my dear mother when I was eight years old."

One of the last major attacks on the city of Ingolstadt was on March 1, 1945. A fourteen-year-old girl wrote about her experience of being separated from her parents during the bombing:

A terrorized orphan seeks protection and consolation from an adult friend.

I had just arrived at school when the air raid sirens alerted us to an air attack. . . . Scarcely had I closed the cellar doors when the bombs fell. . . . After a while it was silent, and I ventured out, but then came an attack by low flying planes. I went right back to the cellar. Finally, it was quiet. When I got out, half of the city was in flames. I went home. . . . Something terrible had happened—my mother had been killed—she had stayed inside our house. My dad was at work. I ran to him and told him that my mother had died. His eyes were full of tears. He went home with me. My mother was buried the next day.

Two weeks later the war in Europe was over. It would continue in the Pacific theater until August 15, 1945, when Emperor Hirohito announced Japan's unconditional surrender.

On that day, six-year-old Keiko Sasaki was looking forward to her mother's return from Hiroshima. Keiko was staying with her grandparents in the countryside. After the atomic bomb attack, her grandmother had gone to the city to look for her daughter. When she returned a week later the little girl asked her eagerly, "Where is mother?" Her grandmother answered, "I brought her on my back." When she said that, Keiko was happy and shouted, "Mamma!" But then she saw that her grandmother only had a rucksack on her back. Her heart sank. Her grandmother and the neighbors who had come to her home burst out crying:

> I thought, why are they crying? I didn't realize. Grandmother took the little box out of the rucksack and showed it to them all. What she showed them was only mother's gold tooth and the bone of her elbow. Even then I didn't understand. Even when one year passed and then two years passed, Mother didn't come back. After three years passed, I was in the third grade; then for the first time I finally understood that Mamma had died. After that I missed Mamma badly and almost every day I went to her grave.[17]

Picking Up the Pieces

IN ALL THE COUNTRIES OF EUROPE—except for vanquished Germany—the church bells began to ring in May 1945. People in England, France, Russia, and all the other liberated countries gathered in the streets, singing and dancing, weeping for joy. Three months later, in August, the war in the Pacific was over as well. It was the end of the most massive destruction in human history. There were big victory parades in the United States.

The children of Europe and Asia who had survived the war now had to survive the peace. Millions of them had no homes; millions were orphans; and many whose parents were still alive had no idea where they were. In Europe, children roamed the streets and countrysides in "wolf-packs." They begged or stole the food they ate, the sticks to make fire, old rags for clothes. They sought shelter in the ruins of bombed-out buildings in cellars and basements. With the German capitulation came the liberation of occupied Europe but also the beginning of a long period of misery for her children.[1]

There was not enough food. Expelled Germans and refugees from the east poured into the country until its population had increased above its prewar level by one-fifth. Refugee children, many of whom were lost or abandoned, passed through Berlin at the rate of about three thousand a day. A camp was set up for 300,000 of them in Bavaria. There were all sorts of diseases among them, including scurvy and rickets, but very little could be given to them except gruel and oatmeal soup.

Before the end of 1945 the food shortage became alarming. For a time the official ration fell to 900 calories a day—2,000 less than is requisite, normally, for health. (Two years later, in the winter of 1947, it dropped to 600–750 calories per day.) Food stocks had run out in many towns during the fall, and shattered communication made the labor of replacing them slow. Babies were abandoned by mothers who could not feed them. The infant mortality rose to 107 per 1,000 live births, double that of the prewar period. By the end of 1945, more than half of the children in Germany were showing signs of malnutrition, and teenage girls, like myself, ceased to menstruate.

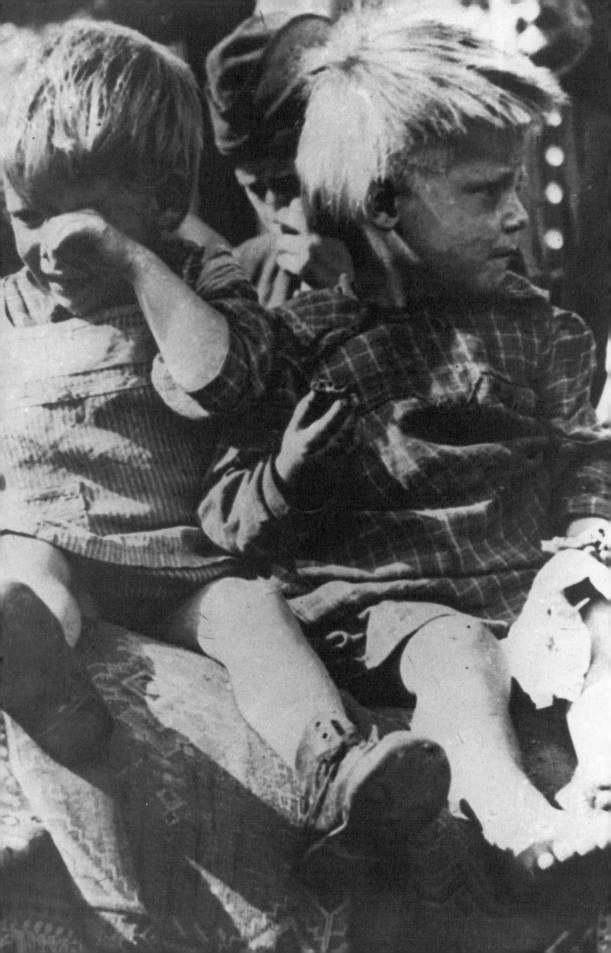

Children stole scraps of food from Allied depots and scavenged in refuse bins. I became an expert scavenger of scraps and sticks, of beets, turnips, and potatoes gleaned from the fields near our house. I was also good at stealing coal from the railroad tracks and wood from the nearby forest—at night, in the dark, after the Allied curfew had descended on our town. In the summer and fall, before the schools were reopened, I worked on a farm and got paid each day with a leftover crust of bread and a small pail of milk that fed the two of us who were left in our family—my mother and myself. But when the farmer slaughtered "Hector," a gentle white dray horse on whose back I used to ride, I couldn't eat a bit of the horse goulash. I had loved "Hector" as much as my dog "Lux" who had sat beside me, patiently, in our cellar during the air raids.

When the schools reopened in the fall of 1945, they were filled with ragged, half-naked children who usually came barefoot, for they lacked shoes, and who sat in a stupor, for lack of a breakfast. Most school buildings were partially destroyed and unheated, and there was a general lack of pencils and writing material. So it came to pass that my first essay on the virtues of democracy was written in a torn scrapbook in which, years earlier, I had reported on the excitement of a summer camp on top of the Lorelei. I had received an "A" for my essay on camp life but could muster only a barely passing grade for my essay about democracy. I expressed too many doubts about it! I was ready to drop out of school after that experience, for I knew I could do better as a scavenger or smuggler of goods for the thriving black market. I was small, wiry, and good at running fast when chased by border guards or military police. My mother pleaded for me to stay in school. So I did!

My experience was not unique. Two boys from Nuremberg, about my age, wrote essays in school toward the end of 1945 that were entitled "Wie ich jetzt lebe" (How I live today). A fourteen-year-old wrote:

> Our apartment was partially destroyed by a bombing attack in January. Our bedroom is wet when it rains, because the roof leaks, and we have no windows in our kitchen. At night, when my father comes home from work, we sit mostly in the dark—we have only a small kerosene lamp to light one corner of a room. We go to bed early. . . . I have no suit, only one patched pair of trousers, three pair of socks, and one pair of shoes in need of repair. When the weather is bad, I stay out of school because I lack decent footwear.

A thirteen-year-old boy wrote:

Hungry German children in Frankfurt.

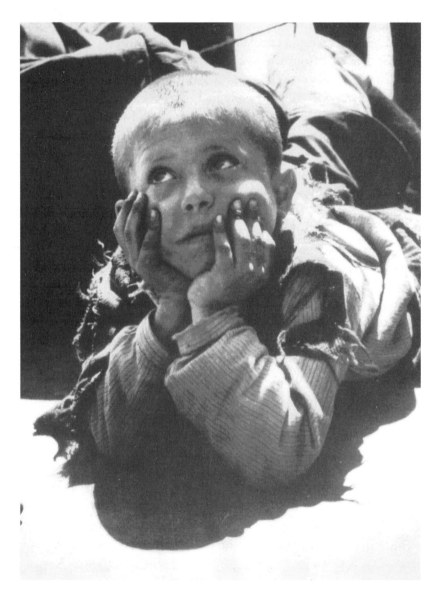

An enterprising street urchin listens to a conversation between adults, hoping to catch something that will help him survive.

When the Americans came and the artillery attacks began, our roof was damaged and all the windows fell out. At night, when it rains, my bed is always wet. . . . I had no trousers for a while, but my dad finally gave me one of his old trousers which were much too big. My grandmother shortened them for me. . . . My shoes are totally ruined. My uncle gave me a pair of his own to exchange at the shoemakers. He found one to fit me. . . . Now I have at least a pair of shoes [and can go to school].[2]

But in spite of the seemingly hopeless conditions, many children showed an amazing amount of resilience. Many half-grown sons took on the responsibilities of absent fathers and became quite adept in the game of survival, displaying the skills and independence of seasoned adults. The mother of an eleven-year-old boy whose father still languished in a Russian POW camp had a special survival pact with her son:

> I went to the farmers in the countryside and asked them what they needed—for example nails, or yarn, or candles. Then my son would scrounge up cigarettes and exchange them on the Black Market for the things the farmers needed. He was a good little businessman—I was not used to these complicated transactions, but I could rely totally on my son. Somehow, he would always manage to find the nails and the yarn and the candles, and I would exchange them for potatoes and vegetables. I became a good hoarder. . . . We always had more food than we could get on our [meager] ration cards in Berlin.[3]

In spite of the cold, the hunger, and the cramped circumstances in which they lived, many children found the mere task of survival to be an exciting adventure. Even relatively young children were left to their own ingenuity to find something to eat. The invasion had meant a complete breakdown of the German food supply system, but the Allied forces, especially the Americans, also established, intentionally as well as unintentionally, new and different sources of supply. Often children went to the kitchens of army facilities to beg, scrounge, or steal food that the soldiers were discarding. To them the extensive waste of food by the occupier seemed incredible.

Sometimes soldiers with guns guarded the garbage to prevent children from picking it over, letting truckloads of oranges rot. Often, homeless boys attached themselves to American army units, following them from place to place. Teenage girls were proud to be seen with Allied soldiers; a package of cigarettes was a small price to pay for sexual favors.

The soldiers had a great deal to offer. Children and teenagers found them easy to trade with—and easy to steal from, too. There were many adults who were only too glad to exploit the children. Habitual criminals and men who in desperation had taken to crime—deserters from all the armies—competed in the huge racket that supplied the black markets of Europe. Among these men, children found employers who knew how to make use of their guileless regard, which averted suspicion, and of their nimble fingers and sharp wits. It was a tempting career choice for me!

Instead, I stayed in school, trying to make up for years of interrupted education. There were up to seventy youngsters in our class—of whom eight

A boy pushing a cart of looted groceries.

eventually graduated with a *Not Abitur* (emergency high school certificate). Lessons were given without maps or blackboards or chalk; the books we eventually received had been censored and partially deleted—history was once more rewritten with the imprimatur of the Allied occupation forces. The teachers—most of them elderly men and women and crippled war veterans—were exhausted. They could not give us much help.

Victor Gollancz, a British journalist who in that year explored "darkest Germany" and was appalled by what he saw, came to the conclusion in his book that the worst thing of all—worse than the malnutrition, the overcrowding, the gaping footwear in the schools—was the spiritual condition of the youth.[4] He may have been right from his vantage point. But what I remember from the year 1945 is that I was introduced to one of my favorite books, Antoine de St. Exupéry's *Little Prince*.[5] Some of my classmates and I would read it to each other, over and over again, by candlelight. Dedicated to his

*Children in a
Quaker-run school.*

friend "who is hungry and cold, and needs cheering up," St. Ex, the French pilot and poet, had two messages that stuck with me through a lifetime: "It is only with the heart that one can see rightly; what is essential is invisible to the eye"; and, "You become responsible, forever, for what you have tamed." Somehow those words made it possible for me to look at the devastation around me and not to lose hope.

Month after month, from the broken windows of our house, I could see masses of refugees and displaced persons wandering on the shattered streets along the Rhine. For the first time in my life I saw survivors from concentration camps in their striped pajamas. Like my friend, Peter Palmié, who is now a pediatrician in Bavaria and saw the same ghostlike figures on the

A child longing for candy.

road from Dachau to Garmisch, I wondered who they were and what hell they had left behind. It would take a lifetime to try to comprehend and to amend what had been done to them in the name of my people.

Events taking place in the aftermath of World War II resulted in the greatest dislocation of population ever recorded in human history. According to various estimates, between 30 and 40 million people were moved from their homelands to other areas of Europe and Asia. Among them were more than 8 million displaced persons in Western Europe, most of them in Germany. After a long nightmare of despair, millions of people—liberated at war's end from prisoner of war stockades, slave-labor enclosures, and concentration camps—became the responsibility of the Allied armies. The Allies began at once the immense task of feeding, clothing, and housing the survivors, of establishing identities and nationalities, and of reuniting the remnants of scattered families.[6]

ALTHOUGH SOME 7 MILLION displaced persons were eventually repatriated to their homelands, more than 1 million men, women, and children refused to return to their countries of origin. They remained in camps in the western zones of occupation, mostly in Germany, Austria, and Italy. These refugees were primarily natives of the Baltic states—Estonia, Latvia, and Lithuania—and of the eastern part of Poland—regions that had been forcibly incorporated into the Soviet Union. One out of four were children.

One of these children was Sara Glickstein, who had spent the first six years of her life on the road. Forcibly removed from Poland by the Soviets in 1939, when Sara was just a baby, her family had spent years in Siberia and then eventually made their way south through Kazakistan and back to Warsaw by the end of the war. They found a devastated city and their home in ruins. Sara remembered an abandoned doll in the rubble that she coveted. Her mother kept telling her that it didn't rightfully belong to her and that the child who owned the doll might come along and claim it someday!

The family eventually ended up in a Displaced Persons (DP) camp in Bavaria, and Sara went to school for the first time in her life. "It was very organized," she remembered. "I had a private tutor in math. The location of the camp was beautiful—my love of nature flowered there. We had a lot of excursions. They took us to see the arts and crafts of Bavaria—I remember being fascinated by the glassblowing. They really did a lot for us. I remember being a happy child there."

Sara's little family was lucky. They lived in a house with one room for the three of them and would eventually be joined by a younger sister who was born shortly after they arrived. They stayed in the same camp until they emigrated to the United States—her father learned a trade there. Other DP children, like Agate Nesaule from Latvia, happened to be in a group that the British moved from camp to camp, as private quarters were gradually returned to civilians. During five years she and her family moved a dozen times or so. Sometimes a few rooms in the army barracks or in Quonset huts were pleasant; other quarters were bleak because bomb-shattered windows were boarded up and didn't admit much light. Rooms were subdivided by blankets, sheets, plywood, or cardboard, anything that could be used to create the illusion of privacy.

In her memoirs, *A Woman in Amber*, Agate tells of the importance of learning that was stressed in each of the DP camps. "The riches of the heart do not rust," her teachers told her.[7] School became a reliable anchor for her. In every camp where she was placed, national groups organized their own schools, so that the children could catch up with what they had missed dur-

*Homeless children en
route to an unknown
destination.*

ing the war. Even first graders went to school six days a week, from early morning to noon, and plenty of homework was assigned to keep the children occupied in the afternoons. Standards were uniformly high, and discipline was strict. "Here at last was something positive," she remembered. "I knew that if I tried hard enough, I could master almost anything, and this gave me real satisfaction and a sense of control."

Most of the school-age children in the DP camps learned to master a great number of languages, which came in handy when they and their parents were resettled in other countries, especially in the United States. Marija Stankus-Saulaitis of Lithuania, who was eight years old when she left a Displaced Persons camp to emigrate with her ten-year-old brother to Waterbury, Connecticut, picked up a smattering of nine languages from her mother, who was an interpreter for the Americans. Her memories of school were not as happy as those of Sara and Agate: "We finally had school in the DP camp, but to get there, my brother and I had to pass the barracks in which the Americans lived. Their children would wait for us and run after us, jeering and throwing stones, as my brother, holding my hand tightly, pulled me through the streets."[8] Still, all three children never lost the love of books they had first acquired in the camps.

There were other children on the Allied side for whom the end of World War II did not bring the joy shared by their compatriots. Some, like the Japanese American children who had left their relocation camps, were like displaced persons in their own country, jeered by people who hated the "Japs." Isao Fujimoto remembered:

> For some people it was too dangerous to go back to their home towns; others really didn't have a place to go back to, because their homes and stores had been vandalized. . . . My dad first worked as an unskilled laborer, fixing railroad tracks, then we went back share cropping, farming strawberries. When we finally settled in Pleasanton, where there were naval bases, it was a very hostile environment. People would come up to us kids and yell, "What are you doing her, Jap? Get out of here!" They were yelling at me, who was 12 at the time, and at my little brother, age six—both of us native-born! But I knew judo, so people soon learned to leave me alone. . . . But what really saved me was baseball! We had played that in camp all the time. The principal put me on the school team, and when I scored all the runs, even the janitor who had called me names all the time, changed his attitude toward me. . . . I also had teachers who were very positive; some were veterans, but very broadminded and supportive. And, oh, the Catholic priest, who knew I was Buddhist, was very friendly to me and helped me get a job selling seeds. And when I went door to door selling seeds, I guess I realized that the people I was talking to were not all white people who hated me. They were Irish, German, Portuguese. . . . Then I realized how diverse this country is. I think that's what got me interested in the kind of work I do now—building multi-racial communities.[9]

Keith Barton was the son of a member of the Plymouth Brothers, who, like the Quakers, were conscientious objectors. His dad worked on agricultural projects in the south of England during World War II. When Keith entered grade school after the war had ended, he discovered that he was an outcast among the elementary school children.

There was a war my dad was supposed to have been in, but he wasn't. There was talk like, "What did *your* dad do during the war?" And I would say, "He was working down in the South." I was teased many times by the kids, who thought he was a coward, so I probably was a coward, too. I was in a lot of fights because of that. When I was eight, I remember getting into incredible trouble once when I took one of the slates that had come off our roof and threw it at one of my tormenters, and it cut his head.

For a while, in the summer and fall of 1945, there was an unlikely "war criminal" housed in detention in a Strasbourg jail. As a young teenager, my cousin Eddy, son of a German mother and a French army officer, had been drafted as a translator by the German occupation forces; he was bilingual, like everyone else in our family. When the war ended, the sixteen-year-old boy was branded a "collaborator." He was finally amnestied when his father, who had served with distinction as a captain with the Free French Forces, returned home and vouched for the fealty of his son. Eddy was released from jail before the year had ended.

On December 24, 1945, ten-year-old Regina Schwenke and her family celebrated their first Christmas Eve in peace. In Berlin, a Christmas tree was a rarity at that time, even rarer than a house that had not been damaged by bombs or artillery shells. Her two brothers decided to make a tree of their own. They bored holes in a broomstick and stuck fir branches in them. Just as they had accomplished this extraordinary feat, the broomstick broke into two pieces. The boys were not easily discouraged. They found another broomstick, tied the branches together like a pyramid, and put the stick in a bucket of sand. The "tree" was too wobbly to tolerate candles, but the children covered it with the tinfoil they had accumulated during the bombings.

Regina and her brothers and sisters marveled at the beauty of their Christmas tree, though a stranger might have thought it looked more like a scarecrow than an evergreen. The branches on the tree were stolen—the children had cut them from fir trees in the nearby park that had been sprayed with some protective fluid. The children covered the smell by sprinkling their "tree" with leftover perfume, homemade potato schnapps, and incense. It didn't help much, so they opened their windows and endured the freezing cold until they had sung their Christmas songs and received their homemade gifts.

That Christmas Eve was the most beautiful that Regina would remember throughout her life—even though the fumes from the fir branches became finally so unbearable that the boys had to move the tree to the balcony. Just as they were about to sit down for their meal, a stranger knocked at the door. He asked for his father, who had lived in their apartment building, and

An old man, invited to a Christmas party by GIs, shares his hot chocolate with a young girl.

he was told that the man had perished in the bombings. The stranger turned to leave, but the children insisted that he stay and share their meager rations. So his sadness turned to happiness.

The next morning, Regina and her family went to Christmas services. The sermon was about suffering and survival, about trust in God and hope in the future. And then the children sang, with great enthusiasm and joy, "Welt ging verloren, Christ is geboren. Freue Dich, Freue Dich, O Christenheit!" (The world was lost, but Christ is born today. Rejoice, rejoice, O Christendom!).[10]

On New Year's Eve 1945, a thirteen-year-old girl from Hamburg who had lost her sister and grandmother in the firestorm concluded her essay on the subsequent odyssey of her family with the following passage:

> When we arrived in Kiel with the remainder of our belongings, Vati said: "For seven years I have not had a family, now we will finally be together. . . . And so we are. I am now in the fifteenth school [after all my wandering] and I don't want to leave any more. My brother is now eight years old and we had—in spite of the hunger—a fine summer. Even Mutti is able to laugh once more, like other mothers did a long time ago, and dad is now at home in the evenings. This is absolutely wonderful! Although it was freezing in our rooms (5 degree Celsius) and we didn't have a cake, we had a wonderful Christmas. Mommy said "Children, remember the awful nights when the bombings didn't end, and we said we are willing to endure anything, if the ferocious attacks will finally end, remember?" We didn't miss the New Year's Eve cake either, but we hope that we will be able to bake one for Easter if we can finally get an oven. . . . In the meantime we begin to breathe more easily after all the horrible years and the deadly fears we had in the past. In spite of hunger and cold, we will stay put, and we will never make war again! And I would like to stay in my fifteenth school until I have passed the exams for my Abitur [high school graduation], but that will take some time. Meanwhile the four of us who survived rejoice that we are together again.[11]

At that same time, halfway around the world in southern Japan, Kiyoko Yamasaki went to a Buddhist shrine and said a prayer for the New Year. Kiyoko had come to Japan from San Francisco at the age of eight with her mother and two younger sisters before World War II broke out. Her mother had died in 1944, and her home had been destroyed by American bombs in 1945. She and her sisters had survived the war with their clothes on their back and a few belongings they had hidden in a suitcase in a hole dug under their house. They did not know what had happened to their father, who had stayed behind in California. No news had traveled back and forth between him and his family in Japan since the war broke out. Kiyoko said a prayer for her dead mother and her absent father.

When she returned to her uncle's home that day, she found a postcard. It was from her dad, who had been released from the internment camp at Tule Lake, California. He was sending a food package for his hungry daughters and money for the passage back to the United States. The long odyssey of the Yamasaki sisters, whose roots grew on both shores of the Pacific Ocean, among the victors and the vanquished, would soon be over!

II

The Kindness of Strangers

HERE IS AN ENGLISH PHRASE that has no equivalent in any other language in the world: It is "to be kind." To be kind means "to treat like kin." A simple cardboard box, a battered canteen, and a tin cup became for me symbols of the kindness of strangers when I was hungry and cold.

The cardboard box from an unknown donor came to me as a result of a unique venture by a consortium of twenty-two American charities that agreed to support a private, nonprofit organization to funnel food packages from individuals and families in the United States to friends and relatives in Europe: CARE (Cooperative for American Remittances to Europe) was born during the week Americans celebrated their first Thanksgiving after World War II.

After months of bureaucratic wrangling, CARE took possession of some 3 million surplus army ration packs that had been stored in a warehouse in Philadelphia in the event of a U.S. invasion of Japan—an invasion that was made unnecessary by the dawn of the nuclear age. Each "10-in-one package" contained enough food to feed ten men for a day, or one man for ten days: canned meat, dried milk, raisins, chocolate, and cigarettes.

By the time the first CARE Packages went on sale in the spring of 1946, an unlikely mix of people of goodwill would serve as the organization's first mission chiefs in Europe: Among them were former journalists, soldiers, foreign service officers, and members of religious groups. Barely six months after the agency's incorporation, one of its founders, Dr. Lincoln Clark, oversaw the delivery of the first CARE Packages to grateful civilians in Le Havre, a battered port in Normandy. The second American "invasion" of Europe had begun.

In 1946, CARE delivered nearly 1 million packages, most after the price had been lowered from $15 to $10. In the beginning, the donors had designated a specific recipient, for example, a niece or sister and her family in a particular country. But one order changed CARE's mission dramatically. Instead of a specific address, a donor wrote simply: "For a hungry person in Europe."

French children lining up in a classroom to be fed.

Austrian refugees receive CARE Packages.

In 1947, CARE sent 2.6 million packages. Americans placed their orders at railway stations, at department stores such as Macy's, and through many civic and religious organizations in their hometowns. Their anonymous generosity knew no bounds. After CARE had exhausted its army surplus stocks, it designed its own packages, which included not only food but tools, clothing, medicine, and, later, books. Eventually, more than 100 million CARE Packages would be delivered to people in need, many of them to citizens of countries with which the United States had been at war. Germany received more CARE Packages than any other nation in Europe: Some 40 million families, two-thirds of the German population, were recipients of these acts of kindness from a former enemy.[1]

Children unpacking a CARE Package in Germany.

Many children could not believe at first that an American they had never met would send them sustenance. Klaus P., a German youth, feared that the package his family received from an unknown donor was booby-trapped. For days, he and his friends were afraid to open it, until one of the boys concluded: "I think I have the answer: These Americans are just different. They want to help those in need."[2] Klaus and I, who have known saturation bombing, starvation rations, and the loss of fathers and brothers in World War II, have memories of CARE that are linked by a common thread: After all the misery and dying, compassion was alive: It came in a sturdy brown box!

When the war ended, sixteen-year-old Edith W. had walked 600 kilometers from her boarding school in Luxembourg to her childhood home near

Heidelberg, fleeing in front of the retreating German troops. "We slept in the daytime in barns, and we walked at night," she remembered. "Sometimes we got a ride in a tank or an ammunition train. . . . The country was absolutely torn up, and my mother had no idea where I was."

When she finally arrived home, her mother had sold all her jewelry to buy potatoes and milk from the local farmers. When school reopened, boiled potatoes were the standard fare for lunch. A family in Ohio sent her the first of many CARE Packages in 1946.

> I remember sitting around the table. . . . The extended family was always there: my grandfather who lost his eyesight in an air raid; my aunt and her son who had been a prisoner-of-war in Russia and came back ill; my mother, my brother, my younger sister and I; my father had been killed in the war. We were sitting around the kitchen table, waiting for the package to be opened. . . . We were anticipating all the goodies, and as children will do, we would sometimes get up in the middle of the night and snitch some peanut butter. . . . So CARE played a big part in my young life. It added the one bit of color and happiness to an otherwise horribly frightening time. Times when you felt dehumanized . . . when you hated your brother because my mother would sometimes give my brother an egg [from the three chickens she raised] and then she didn't have anything left for the rest of us.

In the bitter cold winter of 1946, Trudy M., age eleven, was a refugee in Bavaria. When her home was bombed out at the end of the war, her mother took her five children to friends in the hamlet of Pietzing, where they huddled together in two small, poorly heated rooms. Their father was in a detention camp. Trudy and her four siblings foraged for roots, berries, and mushrooms, and gleaned in the fields for leftover grain and potatoes.

A few days before Christmas, her mother was preparing a special treat—a cake made out of grain, carrots, and frozen potatoes—when the mailman brought a message that a CARE Package was waiting for them in the post office in the next town, some four miles away. Trudy remembered:

> The next morning my sister and I set out with our sled—a board with a rope tied to it. It was cold and the snow was deep. The journey took us most of the day. I remember how cold and hungry and tired we were, but how excitement sustained us until we returned home in the early winter darkness, bearing the heavy, stamped, betagged, taped and scuffed gift from an unknown stranger in America.

Finally the wrappings and the carton had been opened, and our room became bright and warm with the incredible treasures spilled all over our table: sugar, (peanut) butter, flour, canned meats and fruit cocktail, coffee and chocolate—REAL COFFEE AND REAL CHOCOLATE!!!

No one who hasn't been hungry . . . can possibly appreciate what that meant. My mother, who hadn't cried all those times when she couldn't feed us, cried now at the sight of all these wonderful things. And oh how we feasted that Christmas! No food will ever taste as good again as the food from that CARE Package.

For Ingeborg L., a teenager living in Vienna, the years 1946 and 1947 were "hell on earth." Babies were starving all around her because their mothers weren't nourished enough to have any milk. Her father developed scurvy from their diet of beans and oats, and she and her brother suffered from infectious hepatitis, spread by a plague of bedbugs that crawled through the ruins of the city. She remembered her mother saying, "If we survive . . . the one good thing that will come out of this [suffering] is that there will never be another war."

Ingeborg and her family began to receive monthly CARE Packages from an American cousin:

It had not only food, but blankets, it had sheets, it had medicine in it. . . . It was like magic: Dried milk, dried eggs, ham in cans, peanut butter. . . . We would ration it out, and we would literally exist on that food. The only thing we were totally mystified by was peanut butter. We had never seen or heard of peanut butter. . . . We were very suspicious about it until we tasted it, but we could still not understand why it was called butter, for in Austria, you know, butter comes from a cow. . . . And of course we loved it. I still do.

Ingrid S., a teenage girl in divided Berlin, whose father had survived a Russian prison camp, received her first CARE Package from an unknown donor in the United States: "We had been starving for a long time. We ate dandelions, oak leaves, anything green we could find. Our priest called me into his office one day and said, 'Bring your mother tomorrow and a knapsack.' I thought perhaps he would give us some firewood. He showed us a CARE Package and asked, 'Would you like one *with* or *without* coffee?' What a question!"

When money lost its value in postwar Germany, a tin of Nescafé from a CARE Package saved the life of a sick little girl in Hamburg. In the winter of 1946–1947, Susanna W. fell and developed a huge abscess on her leg that threatened to turn into gangrene. Her emaciated body succumbed to a seri-

Austrian children carrying a CARE Package.

ous infection and she developed a high fever. Friends in the United States had just sent her family a CARE Package. "It had . . . Spam, crackers, chewing gum, which we thought was candy," she remembered. "My sister and I, we swallowed it whole. Also some dried milk, some sugar and cocoa, and . . . what was really instrumental in saving my life . . . a little tin of Nescafé."

A doctor agreed to treat Susanna's leg when her mother promised him the coffee. "My mother kept the CARE Package under my bed, so he wasn't going to get it until he took care of me," she later wrote in a letter to her donors. "He came and performed surgery without anesthesia. But if he hadn't come, I probably would have died of this infection. He felt richly rewarded and I was cared for to live and gratefully tell about it. . . . So CARE

Packages were sent from heaven—they really were. They were better than Christmas."

Alfred W., who had earned his wings as a glider pilot at age fifteen, was 200 kilometers behind Soviet lines when the war ended. In two weeks he broke through Russian and American lines to return to his family. He arrived home to total destruction, "a life of misery in a ravished country, at the mercy of the conquerors, with everything we were taught to cherish torn down."

In the midst of starvation and despair the teenage boy received a CARE Package. A stranger in a faraway country rekindled his hope. Wrote he: "The lasting impact [of that package] was that someone I didn't know had spent their hard-earned money to send a package to a former enemy; that we were not forgotten and outcast, that there were human beings who cared for us as humans."[3]

Many of the children and young people whose lives were touched by CARE reciprocated the kindness of strangers when they grew into adulthood. Rainer E. was twelve years old and lived in a small coal-mining town in western Germany when CARE Packages allowed his parents to feed eight hungry children. They were all sent by a Chicago writer, named Gilfillan, who didn't know the boy's family until they wrote a thank-you note to him. After the first CARE Package that saved the lives of his twin baby brothers, others followed every month. Remembered Rainer:

> Eventually we didn't call them CARE Packages any more, we called them Gilfillan packages. We used to joke years afterwards that if somebody did something particularly good without knowing where that good act would wind up, we would call that a Gilfillan act. When I came to the States and got settled [in Baltimore], I decided that the one thing I could do to pay back was to send a monthly check to CARE to have somebody else somewhere in the world get the same help.

Today, former CARE recipients who are child survivors of World War II have forged their own chains of caring that extend from the needy in their community to the children of Asia, Africa, and Latin America, from the local food bank to the American Friends Service Committee, Caritas, the Lutheran World Relief, from UNICEF to a continuing steadfast support of CARE's efforts around the world. "When you survive the war, like I did, you want to pay back and do something for others," says one CARE Package recipient who fled, at age six, from war-torn Berlin after being bombed out. "I survived, so it's time to help other people to survive, too." CARE and

Austrian children unpacking a CARE Package.

CARE Packages are now registered marks of the Cooperative for Assistance and Relief Everywhere, Inc., and go to the needy in every part of the world.

CARE Packages also forged lifelong friendships between donors in the United States and recipients in Europe: A pair of mittens introduced eleven-year-old Eva B. from Pomerania to a couple in Minnesota and led to a friendship that has lasted more than fifty years.

At the end of World War II Eva, her sister, and her mother fled from Soviet-occupied Pomerania "with one blanket and whatever you had on your back." They slept out in the open for nearly a year until they reached a displaced persons camp in Lunden. The camp priest invited them to try out some clothing that had just arrived from the United States. Eva picked out a pair of mittens that a woman had knit in faraway Minnesota.

Eva's family wrote the woman a thank-you letter, describing their situation. "They had been gleaning food from the farmer's fields and scavenging in garbage piles," said their Minnesota donor. "To us the answer seemed to be to send them a CARE Package." Eva remembered:

> When we received a CARE Package, there was sometimes coffee in it. My mom would invite people in camp over for coffee. Everybody brought the one cup they owned, and the women would sit together and talk. They helped each other very much. There weren't many men in camp . . . mostly women with children and they suffered the most. They sent a Scottish plaid dress for my confirmation and also a green coat. . . . And on occasion even a beautiful piece of soap which smelled really good.

A red woolen coat with black trimmings sent in a CARE Package by an unknown donor kept me warm during the cold winters of 1946 and 1947, and a canteen filled with a midday meal from the Quakers kept me from the worst hunger pangs of a postwar diet of 900 calories. The Quakers fed millions of hungry school children in an unprecedented act of mercy that saved many from starvation. They considered their assistance simply as help extended from one caring human being to another, based on need, not on nationality, religion, or political persuasion.[4]

By the end of 1946, the food reserves in occupied Germany had shrunk to a bare minimum. President Truman sent former President Herbert Hoover to Europe to ascertain the needs of the civilian population. Upon his return in February 1947, Hoover made a passionate plea on behalf of millions of desperately hungry German children and assured the release of some 19 million dollars' worth of foodstuff, which made it possible to provide a 350-calorie meal each day for 3.5 million children in the American and British occupation zones. That meal, known as *Quäker Speisung* (Quaker feeding), represented more than a third of the calories in our daily diet.

As we lined up for our daily portions at the end of the school day, most of us thought that there must be millions of Quakers in the United States who cared enough to keep us alive. Little did I know that this represented the action of a small group of "silent helpers" who even today number only about 100,000 in the United States and 300,000 worldwide. Together with food, the American Friends Service Committee also sent thousands of tons of clothing, shoes, soap, and medical supplies to hungry children in Germany, and to Japan, where they were among the Licensed Agencies for Relief in Asia (LARA).

On Christmas Day 1946, young Hildegard Behr wrote a thank-you letter and decorated it with colorful drawings of flowers and candles: "Dear

'Kwäker.' I hope you like my letter. I wear the 'pulover' every Sunday and it keeps me very warm, and everyone likes it. We have no home of our own anymore and live in an old folks home. But the nice thing is that we live close to the woods. We play there during the summer and pick mushrooms. We also have a balcony. I greet you with a kiss."[5]

And in May 1947, another young German girl, Louise Appel, decorated her letter with drawings of chickens, eggs, and pussy willows, and wrote:

> On behalf of my mother I would like to thank you sincerely for the good soap which we received at Easter. Mama greatly rejoiced when we received the bar of soap. There are six of us children and she has lots of laundry to do. Soap is always scarce. All of the children are healthy, but Mama is greatly worried because our dear Papa has been missing in action for more than two years, and we have not heard from him. May God bless you!

One of the most elaborate "thank-you notes" in the archives of the American Friends Service Committee in Philadelphia was sent by a young German boy named Roland Straeke, who drew a picture of himself walking barefoot across the cobblestone square of his hometown. He wears an oversized coat and carries a pair of new shoes in his hand. His face has a radiant smile. He wrote: "Filled with gratitude and great joy, I come from the Red Cross. Now I don't have to walk barefoot anymore. I go to school in peace— I no longer shiver in the cold. Hurrah! Now I have a coat and pair of shoes. My dear parents and I are overjoyed!!"

Another thank-you letter to the Quakers came from Tokyo:

> *Dear all of Americans:*
> *We are Japanese night students. We have received much and dainty milk of L.A.R.A. goods from you and we thank you from the bottom of our heart for your kindness. Our country was suffered damages of war but now we are rebuilding a new and peaceful Japan by efforts of Marshal MacArthur and other very affectional and honorable gentlemen and we can live very happily and in safety.*

Perhaps the most enduring symbol of the kindness of strangers in post–World War II was a battered tin cup; I carried mine in my "survival kit." That cup contained the milk that was distributed by UNICEF to feed some 6 million European children in thirteen countries, from the fall of 1947 through the end of 1950. Poland was the largest aid recipient, followed closely by Yugoslavia, Italy, Germany, Austria, France, and Greece. Children of eastern European and "ex-enemy" countries predominated because their needs were the greatest.[6]

A German boy thanks the Quakers for a new coat and shoes.

One of the powerful figures who had spoken out for Europe's children was Herbert Hoover. "From the Russian frontier to the channel," he warned, "there are to-day millions of children not only badly undernourished, but steadily developing tuberculosis, rickets, anemia, and other diseases of subnormal feeding. If Europe is to have a future, something must be done about these children."[7] While Hoover, the politician, lobbied in Washington, D.C., on behalf of the children, Ludwik Racjchman, a Polish physician and one of the world's pioneers in public health, proposed to the General Assembly of the United Nations that an effort for children alone, consisting of food and medical assistance, should be undertaken by the UN.

On December 11, 1946, the assembly unanimously adopted a resolution creating the United Nations International Children's Emergency Fund

おいしかった
ミルク ミルク
ララ物資ありがとえ

A drawing of Japanese children dreaming of Quaker food.

(UNICEF). The resolution contained an eloquent statement of the need for an international effort on behalf of children:

> The children of Europe and China were not only deprived of food for several cruel years, but lived in a state of constant terror, witness to massacres of civilians, to horrors of warfare, and exposed to the progressive lowering of standards of social conduct. . . . With the hope of the world resting on coming generations, the problem of caring for children is international in scope and its solution must be found on an international basis.[8]

Between 1947 and 1950, UNICEF and its partner governments mounted the greatest relief operation for children ever conducted in human history, despite milk shortages, strikes, droughts, and civil wars that continued to ravage Europe. During these years, UNICEF shipped nearly 400 million pounds of milk powder, enough to make 6,400,000,000 cups of milk. UNICEF became known as the "cup of milk" organization, earning the nickname "milkman to the world's children." Some hungry children would ask for a glass of UNICEF, thinking that it was another word for milk. The

silhouette of a child holding a cup of milk to its lips became UNICEF's first symbol.

In the spring of 1947, armed with leather vaccination kits and good nerves, ninety-nine Danish nurses and doctors set out on behalf of UNICEF to vaccinate millions of children in Poland, Germany, and Yugoslavia against tuberculosis, which had reached near epidemic proportions. That same spring, Dr. Martha Eliot, the assistant chief of the U.S. Children's Bureau, visited Austria, Czechoslovakia, France, Greece, Italy, Poland, and Yugoslavia and learned that one out of every three infants and young children in these countries had rickets. Dr. Eliot knew how to stop the steady decline of these children. The cure was a daily dose of cod-liver oil: three to five milligrams for infants under the age of one, and five milligrams for one- to six-year-old children and pregnant women.

Norway, Canada, and New Zealand, the biggest producers of cod-liver oil in the late 1940s, came to the rescue and supplied huge metal drums of the oil as part of their governments' contributions to UNICEF. With their help, from December 1948 through 1950, UNICEF supplied the oil to millions of children in Eastern Europe, Greece, and Germany. German children wrote thank you letters: "Liebe UNICEF: . . . danke für den Lebertran. Euer Lebertran schmeckt sehr gut" (Dear UNICEF: Thank you for the Lebertran. It is very tasty).

In the bitter postwar winters from 1945 to 1948 many youngsters ran barefoot through rubble, rain, or snow because there was a chronic shortage of shoes. For want of shoes, children stayed home from school, missing not only their lessons but also the daily cup of milk from UNICEF. Some children who ran barefoot in subzero weather contracted respiratory infections; others developed pneumonia and died.

Two of the world's biggest leather producers, England and Australia, offered to ship quantities of precious cowhides as part of their contributions to UNICEF. Together they worked out a plan with individual governments to process that leather into shoes and boots and then to distribute them free to the poorest and neediest children.

More than 2 million pairs of shoes and boots were produced and distributed across the European continent to refugee children, particularly in Germany and Greece; to orphans in institutions; and to poor school children. When little Elefteria Tranopoulos, a four-year-old Greek girl, received her first leather shoes in 1948, she first hugged and kissed their sides, then the heels and soles, before she dared put them on.

A year earlier, in 1947, Jitka Samkova, a seven-year-old Czech girl, had composed a drawing on the theme: "Happiness in a country at peace." Her

A war orphan holding out an empty tin cup to receive milk.

UNICEF's first greeting card: "Happiness in a country at peace."

painting, done on glass, because paper was scarce, showed five little girls dancing around a maypole. It expressed so much joy that her teacher sent it to UNICEF's office in Prague. There it was reproduced on a poster that hung in UNICEF's feeding centers all over the country. It took two years for the news "of a wonderful drawing by a child" to reach UNICEF's offices in New York. When officials saw the poster in 1949, they decided to publish it as their first year-end greeting card.

As the bloodiest decade of the twentieth century drew to a close, a twelve-year-old girl from New Ipswich, New Hampshire, who had grown up oceans apart from the children of war-torn Europe and Asia, wrote a letter to UNICEF. Its message is still timely today:[9]

> *Dear UNICEF:*
>   *Please tell me why? Why do so many thousands and millions of parents, children and older people have to suffer? Can't something be done? I think you are doing a tremendous job of caring about these people. . . . I wish you great*

*luck in your work and think you are doing a great job! Maybe just maybe
NOBODY will have to suffer any more.*

Sincerely,
Carolyn M.

*P.S. Please if you do take time to write back, please promise me you will never
as long as there is tragedy in the world give up—*

THANK YOU

There is one special act of kindness that was commemorated in 1998 in the
Allied Museum in Berlin and on a special stamp issued by the U.S. Post Office. Fifty years earlier, American and British pilots had risked their lives to
save the beleaguered citizens of the western sector of Berlin, who had been
cut off from vital supplies by a Soviet blockade. From June 1948 until
September 1949, the Berlin Airlift, known as Operation Vittles, transported 2.3 million tons of basic necessities—from food to coal to medical
aid—to the capital of the former enemy. Some 200,000 CARE Packages
were delivered during the airlift. For 462 days and nights, rain or shine, in
good weather or bad, the pilots flew their missions of mercy to the 2.2 million Berliners who had been cut off from the world. For their courage and
caring, seventy-eight pilots and helpers on the ground paid with their lives.

An eight-year-old boy from Saint Louis, Missouri, was so concerned
about keeping the children of Berlin warm and well fed during the winter
of 1948–1949 that he wrote a letter to a fellow Missourian who happened
to occupy the White House at that time: "Dear President Truman. I think
we should have more *farms* in Berlin, Germany. So the people could raise
there own food. That way we can use all our planes to fly fuel and coal."[10]

The best-known pilot to the children of Berlin was an American from
Utah, Gail S. Halvorsen—a.k.a., "Uncle Wiggly Wings," "Mr. Candy
Bomber," or simply the "Chocolate Pilot."

A young lieutenant then, a retired air force colonel today, he remembered
his first meeting with a group of children who waved at him at the Tempelhof Airport as he was bringing in his supplies. In broken English, they
thanked him for the flour he had brought for their families, so they could
bake bread, but they did not beg him for candy as children in other cities of
war-torn Europe had done. The children of Berlin did not know what
candy tasted like!

Right then and there, Lt. Halvorsen devised a plan. He told the children
with gestures that on his next flights he would drop candy for them outside

A nine-year-old girl licking cabbage soup from a pot in Berlin.

the fence as he approached the airport. The children asked, "How can we tell your plane apart from all the others?" Halvorsen replied, "I'll wiggle my wings." With help from friends, and despite severe rationing, Halvorsen managed to scrape together two handfuls of chewing gum, lollipops, and chocolate. These he attached to small parachutes made of knotted handkerchiefs, so they would survive the fall. On the next flight to Berlin, he saw the children standing at the fence. He wiggled the wings of his airplane and dropped the little parachutes through the hatch before he landed. "As I flew back," he remembered, "I saw the children waving handkerchiefs, their little mouths making chewing movements—it had worked."

Soon there were neither enough handkerchiefs nor cut-up pilot shirts to make new parachutes. But once the news about the "Candy Bomber" got

Children in West Berlin watching an American plane during the airlift.

out, he received a flood of donations in the form of handkerchiefs and some twenty-three tons of candy from the United States. "It was hard to believe," Halvorsen recalled. "We received all kinds of hankies; plain ones, lace-bordered ones, some smelling of rose water. Young girls sent us hankies from their trousseaus." Before long, two secretaries were hired to answer all the thank-you letters from the children of Berlin to "Uncle Wiggly Wings."

One of the letters is on display in the Allied Museum in Berlin. It was written by a bedridden boy:

> *Herr Leutnant Halvorsen, Lieber Schokoladenflieger!*
> *[Dear Lieutenant Halvorsen, Dear "Chocolate pilot!]:*
>   *I have read in the newspaper that you have brought great joy to the chil-*
> *dren of Berlin with your gift of chocolates. . . . I would have liked to have*
> *eaten some chocolate myself, but none of your parachutes have landed in the*

garden of the hospital where I was staying. I was there for six weeks and watched your planes every day. I can now distinguish every type of plane, but unfortunately I can't come to the [Tempelhof] airport because of my illness.

And an enterprising seven-year-old girl wrote:[11]

We live near the airfield at Tempelhof and our chickens think your airplanes are chicken hawks and they become frightened when you fly over to land. They run in the shelter and some molt, with no more eggs from them. When you see the white chickens please drop it there, all will be O.K.

Your little friend,
Mercedes

Once the blockade was over, Gail Halvorsen went home to the United States. But the Berliners wanted him back, so he was appointed commander of the Tempelhof airport from 1970 to 1974. He returned to Berlin in the cockpit of a restored *Rosinenbomber* (Raisin Bomber) in 1998 for the 50th anniversary of the *Luftbrücke* (air-bridge). That summer I watched a group of gray-haired visitors at the Allied Museum as they encountered the exhibit of the old newsreels from the airlift. The men and women sat silently and wept—they had been the children who had gotten their first sweets from the "Chocolate Pilot." They never forgot his kindness—he never forgot their smiles.

12

Whatever Happened to the Children?

THERE ARE ONLY A HANDFUL OF STUDIES that follow children of World War II into adulthood and examine the impact of that war on their later lives. Included in these studies are some 2,000 individuals from Great Britain, the United States, Germany, Austria, Poland, and Japan, as well as Finnish child evacuees who were sent to Sweden when the Soviets invaded that small country in November 1939. These studies and my interviews with a dozen child survivors from these countries tell a similar story: Across the boundaries of time and place, the children of World War II have grown into adults with an extraordinary affirmation of life. But there are also some residual scars, even in the most resilient individuals.

The men and women whom I interviewed are in their late fifties and sixties now; a few have reached the biblical age of threescore and ten. They live in Berkeley and the Bavarian Alps, in London and Los Angeles, in California's Central Valley and in the midwestern Heartland. They come from all walks of life. They are Buddhists, Catholics, Protestants, Quakers, and Unitarians. Most have children and grandchildren—all love learning and books and like to grow things and nurture them along. Their stories give us a glimpse of the healing process that makes it possible, over a lifetime, to conquer the ghosts of war. Some shadows remain.[1]

This we have learned: The trauma of war appears to affect children differently, depending on the level of violence they have been exposed to and their capacity to cope with it. The effects tend to vary also with their age, gender, and temperament; their family and social support, and the political ideology and/or religious faith that provides the context of their lives.[2] Some war experiences in childhood tend to have a lasting impact: exposure to heavy bombing and combat; prolonged separation from the family; internment in refugee or detention camps; the loss of loved ones through acts of violence; and lack of proper schooling.

Half of the people I interviewed—the men and women who grew up in Great Britain, Germany, and Japan—had been exposed to heavy bombing in the metropoli-

Maimed children at play.

tan areas where they had lived as children. The memories of these experiences were still vivid in their minds after more than half a century, especially the frightening sounds of air raid sirens and the ak-ak-ak of machine gun fire from low-flying planes. All had been in the company of close family members—mothers, grandparents, and older siblings—when the air raids occurred. Their reports confirmed the clinical observations made by Anna Freud and Dorothy Burlingham during the London Blitz, which showed that the level of emotional upset or support displayed by the adult in a child's life, not the bombing itself, was most important in predicting the child's response and its impact on later life.[3]

Five years after the end of World War II, some 1,200 British school children who had been exposed to air raids were examined. Some 18 percent still showed disturbances caused or aggravated by the war experiences. They had war-related fears and nightmares, sleep disturbances, and exaggerated psychophysiological reactivity to sirens, loud noises, and explosions. That percentage is similar to the prevalence of post-traumatic stress disorder (PTSD) diagnosed in combat veterans of World War II and the Vietnam War.

We know little about how PTSD symptoms and other sequelae of war are affected by a person's age at the time of exposure, and what effects they have on coping over time.[4] Only about half of the Vietnam veterans with diagnosed PTSD, some 8 percent, still met the criteria for the diagnosis at a follow-up a decade and a half later. Among the persons I interviewed, only one reported such symptoms, which included recurrent episodes with hysterical blindness. She was also the person who, at a very young age, had experienced a cumulative number of war-related, stressful life events—from the bombing of Warsaw, to forced evacuation by the Soviets to Siberia, to a flight in bitter winter back to Poland, to the loss of her home and many family members, to life in a displaced persons camp in Germany—all before the age of six.

Shortly after Sara and her family had immigrated to the United States, when she was around the age of twelve, she became temporarily blind. She remembered: "When I was actually going blind, they first took me to a doctor who said, 'No, there is nothing wrong with her visually,' so they took me to a psychiatrist. He told my mother, 'She feels lonely here.' I sometimes feel that way even to-day. My fear and prayer is 'Please, God, don't let me go through this again, don't let me have this terrible reaction again."

For the others who were exposed to bombing—no matter at what age, whether as a preschooler or in grade school or high school—the sound of sirens still brought back the memory of war. Some reported physical effects, such as goose bumps or shivers, whereas others expressed a general dislike for the siren's high-pitched whine. Dinah Towns, whose home was halfway between London and Coventry, and who witnessed the bombing of both cities by the Germans, said, with a laugh, "When I hear a siren today, I listen to see if it's the 'all clear' sound. In England it was an even pitch, whereas the warning of approaching planes was up and down." I do the same today!

One of the other hazards children had to deal with, especially in Germany in the latter part of the war, were attacks by strafing planes. These were low-flying planes equipped with machine guns that shot at anything that moved, especially trains. Quite frequently, strafing planes announced an armada of approaching bombers. One of my recurrent nightmares occurs at German railroad stations, like Wiesbaden and Frankfurt, where I endured such attacks while traveling to and from school during World War II.

*Two German girls on their way to school pass a
totally leveled block of houses in Frankfurt.*

We know very little about the long-term effects of the atomic bomb on the
mental health of the children in Hiroshima and Nagasaki. In Japan, the survivors of the nuclear blast, the Hibakusha, and their offspring, the Hibakusha Nisei, have received payments for medical problems attributable to
atomic radiation, but the government has provided no economic or social
support for them.[5] Because of the physical weakness that can be a lasting effect of radiation from the A-bomb, the Hibakusha frequently cannot keep a
steady job. Most have below average incomes and cannot afford the expenses for their children's schooling, in a society that puts a premium on education.

Fears of genetic and chromosomal effects of atomic radiation have also
created a stigma for the Hibakusha. Arranged marriages and preservation of

the family name through children are still highly valued in Japan. The social stigma stemming from fears of continued radiation effects among subsequent generations has engendered unique psychological consequences for the Hibakusha and their families. Sensitive to potential rejection, many maintain secrecy and silence about their physical and mental suffering, especially the women.

The German children who survived the firebombing of Hamburg, Berlin, and Dresden have other psychological scars. In their late fifties and sixties now, they still have vivid memories of being "deathly afraid" at the time of the area bombing. In a 1994 follow-up of children of World War II in Germany, many respondents reported having nightmares well into midlife. On the positive side, the experience of having lived through the terror of bombing has generated in many child survivors of World War II a deep sense of compassion for children of contemporary wars, especially for youngsters who are in danger of becoming part of the "collateral damage" caused by long-range missile attacks.

A third of the individuals I interviewed had been child evacuees or refugees during World War II. They came from England, Germany, and Poland. What effect, if any, did the evacuation experience have on their later life? Though they came from countries that had been on opposing sides of the war, separation from loved ones was a shared experience for them. But, apart from that, there were other variables that affected both how each had responded to the situation when they were children and the long-term outcomes for each person.

Sir Michael Rutter was evacuated as a seven-year-old, together with a younger sister, and spent four years with a Quaker family in the United States. For him the seavacuation was a great adventure, though he missed his sister, who was placed in another family after their arrival in the United States. Upon his return to England, his family had to get used to a more "uppity" child. His grandmother wondered for a while if they might have sent the wrong boy back! He missed his foster family, who made a deliberate attempt not to interfere with the re-establishment of his bonds to his parents.

Annegret Ogden was a preschooler growing up in the heavily bombed Ruhr area of Germany when she was evacuated with her mother to Austria and, later, to southern Germany, where her village was occupied by French troops toward the end of the war. For her, the evacuation meant taking on a new identity to fit in with the other children in her new surroundings:

> They were all speaking a dialect I didn't understand, and they all treated me very badly, and they teased me a lot for two things: My

skirts were too short and I was a Protestant [in a Catholic region]. So the first thing was to hide from them that I was a Protestant—I went to Mass—and I had my mother lengthen my skirts. It took me only about four weeks to pick up the dialect and they said, "O well, she speaks already like the natives." My idea in each place was to blend in as fast as possible, which has served me very well [as an immigrant].

When Peter Palmié's home in Munich was bombed out, he was evacuated with his class to a KLV camp near Garmisch-Partenkirchen. He was thirteen by then, and he hated the regimentation of camp life: "We had morning flag and all these things, and we had to exercise like in the military. Some thirty-five boys lived together in one house, and we had school there, and we couldn't go home to Munich, so I couldn't see my parents." But he considers himself lucky that he had biology and chemistry lessons in camp, which made it possible for him to qualify for admission to the Gymnasium and, eventually, to medical school after the war was over.

There have been several follow-up studies of evacuee children in Great Britain, Australia, and Finland that confirm some of the impressions gained from my interviews. In general, children who were able to handle the evacuation experience best were those who had enjoyed positive relationships with their parents before the prolonged separation. Children in earlier conflict with their family fared more poorly in their new settings and after the reunion at the end of the war. But long-range effects in terms of persistent psychological disturbances in adults were not the *typical* outcome for either the British or the German child evacuees.

A follow-up study by Glen Palmer of some 100 child evacuees and refugees who came to Australia at the beginning of World War II from Britain, Germany, and Austria found that individuals who went from secure family environments to caring foster families felt generally positive about the overall experience in late adulthood.[6] It bears remembering that many of these children had numerous personal resources to fall back on. Their success in social relationships when they were child evacuees was closely linked with their ability to develop effective adult relationships and to create a network of social support in later life.

In the case of separation in the midst of a great sense of danger, fears for the child's and parents' safety, and lack of adequate preparation, the evacuation experience was viewed as less satisfactory. But even in this context, only a minority of the former child evacuees were pathologically disturbed in adulthood. Most found positive turning points in their lives through a supportive spouse and a career and have lived fulfilling and productive lives.

Ruth Inglis, on the basis of interviews with British child evacuees in late middle age, suggests, however, that long-term effects of the early disruption in the lives of child evacuees might be reflected in their attitudes toward separation from their *own* children. Many former evacuees who battened down the hatches of their grief and separation anxiety as children, she finds, relive the experience when they are parted from their own sons and daughters, making the parting doubly painful.[7]

Eila Räsänen's follow-up studies of Finnish child evacuees to Sweden complement the findings from Australia and Great Britain and the anecdotal evidence from my interviews. Some forty years after the end of World War II, the physical and mental health of 568 former child evacuees was compared with that of a control group of persons who had remained in their war-torn home country.[8] At midlife, the former child evacuees had fewer chronic somatic illnesses, especially of the cardiovascular system, than individuals in the comparison group who had grown up with poorer nutrition and who had experienced the horrors of war firsthand. The incidence of psychiatric illness was similar in both groups. But one of the major problems that confronted the evacuee children, both upon entry into Sweden and upon return to Finland, was a difficulty with language. Good language skills in both languages facilitated schooling in both countries—a lesson that Annegret Ogden had learned in Austria, Germany, and, finally, in the United States.

Sara, the Polish refugee, had to learn these lessons as well. By the time she immigrated to Chicago she spoke Polish, Russian, and German and now had to make sense of school lessons that were taught in American English. The richness of her language experiences stood in stark contrast to the poverty of her personal relationships. She had lost most members of her extended family during the war, and she still mourns that loss in late middle age. She is not alone: Glen Palmer's findings tell us that for most of the Polish and German refugee children who had come to Australia and who lost family members in World War II, the grieving and sorrowing goes on. Rather than healing with the passage of time, the pain of childhood loss can become more intense in later life.[9]

Despite the enormous number of casualties during World War II, there are few systematic studies of the effects of parental loss and bereavement on children and adolescents during wartime. The age of the child at the time at which the loss occurs and the circumstances under which the larger community shares the grief and respect for the lost one with the family may result in different consequences for bereaved children.

Younger children—under the age of six—tend to grieve with less intensity than do older children. This is a consistent finding that cuts across na-

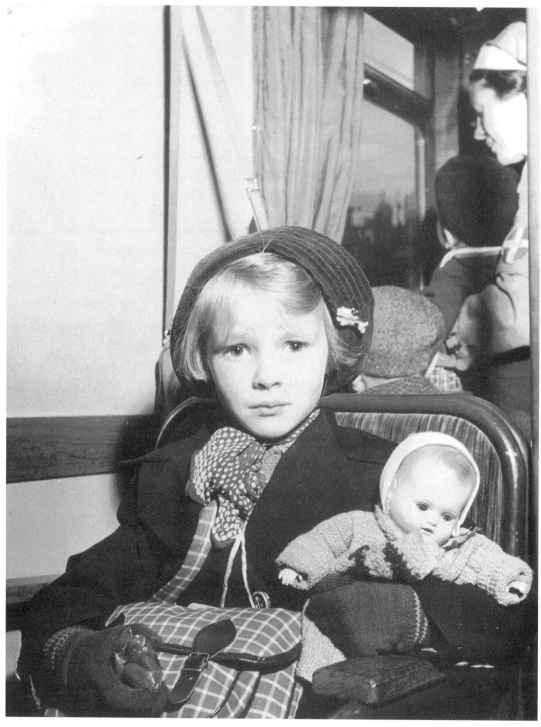

A Finnish child evacuee returning home.

tional borders and may be in part related to the level of a child's cognitive understanding of the concept of death. Older children have a greater awareness of the finality of death and can comprehend death as a universal and irreversible phenomenon—a concept that is understood by most children at age nine. That was the age at which Keiko Sasaki finally realized that her mother would never come back from Hiroshima. The ages of ten through fourteen seem to be the most vulnerable for daughters who have lost their mothers, and for boys who lost their fathers, in the war. The context and the meaning of the loss may have unique significance for the grieving child and may differ for the offspring of the victors in a "righteous cause"—the good war—and the children of the vanquished who are history's villains.

American families who lost a loved one in World War II generally hid their suffering. Many young war widows raised their families alone, despite social and economic hardships. The constant admonition to the widow tended to be, "If you can take it, your children can!" It was difficult for widows and fatherless orphans to fit in with the family-oriented U.S. postwar society. The same was true for German war widows. For them and their Russian counterparts, chances for remarriage were considerably smaller than for the war widows in the United States because of the enormous losses incurred among men of fighting age.

On all sides of the conflict, silence tended to characterize the war orphans' experience and intensify their loss. Dealing with the war-related loss of parents and siblings has turned out to be a lifelong job for those affected. The deaths of fathers and older brothers further disrupted childhoods already torn apart by the war. Often youngsters had to take on adult responsibilities at an early age—as providers of sustenance, as caretakers of younger brothers and sisters, and as emotional support. As a result of the loss, children often drew closer to their mother and resented the intrusion of any males that might become rivals for her attention.

In time, memories of fathers would be replaced by photos that hung on the wall or sat on a mantelpiece. Even as adults, those who lost their fathers and brothers in the war report a continued sadness of not knowing the final resting place of their loved ones. More than fifty years after the end of World War II—now that the Iron Curtain has lifted and the Wall no longer separates East from West—war orphans in Germany are making renewed efforts to find the graves of fallen family members.

In December 1991, "No Greater Love," a national organization in the United States that remembers the victims of war and terrorist attacks, held a memorial service at Arlington National Cemetery for families of World War II casualties. For most families, it was the first ceremony and the only "funeral" they had ever attended for their relatives who died in action in World War II, and the first time they had met others like themselves. Their stories are told in *Lost in the Victory: Reflections of American War Orphans of World War II*. The voices in this book are the voices of sons and daughters who for half a century have seldom spoken of their loss. Their reflections are filled with sadness, longing, and love.[10]

There were also teenage soldiers in combat in World War II who still mourn the loss of fallen comrades, and children like Tomiko Higa, who witnessed the awful casualties of the final ferocious battle of the war that killed her brother. My classmates in Germany were drafted into the air artillery batteries of the FLAK by age fourteen and fifteen or served in the Volkssturm at age sixteen and saw their comrades die. And there were American boys of fourteen and fifteen who participated in the Allied invasions in Sicily and on Normandy Beach—sailors like Eddie McCann and Gene Sizemore—who saw death all around them.

Aside from individual diaries and letters and a few oral histories, we know very little about the long-term impact of the combat experience on these youngsters. Barbara Elden Larney interviewed a sample of fifty-five German men and women, born between 1934 and 1939, when they were in their mid- and late fifties.[11] They vividly remembered being caught in combat as the Allied forces advanced into Germany and the sobering realization that their defense rested in the hands of "child soldiers" only a few years older than they were. "We watched them go down," recalled one of her respondents, "I remember hearing one of them crying out [when he was shot]."

Glen Elder, in *Children of the Great Depression*, found persistent symptoms of post-traumatic stress in late midlife among California veterans (from Berkeley and Oakland) who had seen heavy combat in their teens. During their sixth decade of life, one of five of those who had participated in heavy combat during World War II still had sleep disturbances and flashbacks involving combat scenes: "the hollering and screaming in the middle of the night." But front line service also taught them a positive lesson at an early age—the ability to survive adversity.[12]

Many of the children of World War II, especially in Europe, encountered not a single stressful life event but a combination of *trauma* (a threat to their own or loved ones lives), *loss* (of home, friends, or family members), and *deprivation* (of food, water, and housing). But there were also protective buffers in their lives that enabled them to survive and endure.

First and foremost among these protective factors were caring family members—mothers, grandmothers, older siblings—who stood by when the going got tough—during air attacks, on the run, and during periods of acute food shortage. They provided emotional support and a measure of physical sustenance. Teachers also lent a semblance of normalcy to the life of school-age children, whether they taught in air raid shelters in England or Germany, in resettlement centers for Japanese Americans in the Arizona desert, or in displaced persons camps in Austria. The lack of physical comfort and the absence of instructional material in a partially bombed-out school, or the cold and dust that penetrated the makeshift tents in an internment or refugee camp that served as classrooms, did not prevent children from experiencing the miracle of learning. Schooling gave some structure and focus to their lives. Books, no matter how tattered or torn, became a source of comfort and inspiration—for a little Russian girl in Leningrad, for a German boy in an air raid shelter in Frankfurt, and for Latvian, Estonian, and Polish children in DP camps in Bavaria.

A continuing sense of purpose in life, a sense of coherence and faith, appeared to make a difference in the way children of war managed the absurdities of what they saw, both during the war and in the postwar periods of deprivation. That faith was not bound to a narrow denominational interpretation of the Bible, and it did not depend exclusively on Christian tenets. The children of Hiroshima relied on their Buddhist faith; the children of Nagasaki prayed to a Christian God; the children of Dresden called upon Mary, the Mother of God; the children of nominally "atheist" Russia prayed for deliverance.

My friend and colleague Isao Fujimoto mused about how he and his four brothers and sisters and his twenty-five-year-old mother managed to survive without anger and bitterness in the internment camps:

> I think there are many factors here. I think there is something both in the Japanese culture and certainly in the Buddhist tradition, and that's something about the importance of family. And then there is the notion that you can't fight fate. You got dealt a hand and you make the most of it. The other one, coming from Buddhism, is the whole notion that the reality of life is suffering, but you don't have to take it, there is a way out of it. And so it's a way to face reality, and to move on. I think that's very important. And then a third one: how the family makes sense of all this. . . . Now when I look back at my mom, she was only 25 years old. She had five kids, her husband was taken away by the F.B.I., and we were trying to figure out what to do. . . . We kept on, we kept on working, we kept on going.

Over time, most child survivors of World War II took on responsibilities that were essential to the well-being of their family to a degree that may astound the contemporary reader.

Both during the fighting and in the postwar reconstruction period they looked out for younger siblings, found sustenance for their families, and took on jobs, both within the family and on the outside, that had once been held by adult males who were now absent, missing, or had been killed in action. That was true for girls as well as boys—especially in war-torn Europe.

In the long run it was access to continued schooling, the reaffirmation and strengthening of family ties, and the opportunity to do useful work that has enabled many child survivors of World War II to fashion an adult life that has had a sense of purpose. The individuals I interviewed have done so without hate and bitterness, but with a great deal of compassion. A sense of humor—generic in our family—proved helpful along the way. The resilient ones, like Scaramouche, were "born with the gift of laughter and the sense that the world was quite mad."

But there were important differences between the vanquished and the victors in the collective experience of men and women who were children or teenagers during World War II. Differences in educational opportunities after the war and available jobs on the labor market had a significant impact on their life course. An important component of the long-run cost of the war was the loss of human capital suffered by school-age children who received less education because of the war. Children in Germany and Austria (part of the former "Gross-Deutschland") who, like myself, were ten years old when the conflict began were significantly less likely to proceed into higher education than children of the same age who lived in neutral countries, like Sweden or Switzerland.

German children, especially girls, who had to complete their education and vocational training and start their careers in the immediate postwar period were the most disadvantaged in the long run. Youngsters who had to make the transition from elementary school to apprenticeships at age fourteen or fifteen, toward the end of or immediately after the war (between 1944 and 1946), found their educational opportunities sharply curtailed. The proportion of students obtaining a high school diploma (the Abitur) or a university degree was especially low for children who had to make the transition from elementary school to Gymnasium in that same period. Children—especially girls—who managed that feat made their way against all odds.[13]

World War II had an especially negative effect on the employment and occupational attainment of German girls who were between fourteen and sixteen years old when the war ended. Data on their work histories at midlife show that, compared to men of the same age, these women entered the labor market earlier and remained more frequently in unskilled jobs. The conditions of the immediate postwar period forced them to seek paid employment rather than vocational training or higher education. Their families often relied on their wages. Practical skills that allowed them to participate in the rebuilding process were preferred over occupations requiring higher learning. As a result, these women lacked the qualifications that would have enabled them to enter higher-status jobs later in life.

These women also had fewer children than their American counterparts. Unlike Great Britain and the United States, Germany did not experience a postwar baby boom. Instead it recorded a delayed effect of father absence during and after World War II. German men of my generation who were in their mid-teens during the war and living with only a mother had significantly fewer children than the average for their generation.

In the United States, in contrast, the GI Bill opened up undreamed-of educational and vocational opportunities to teenage veterans, like my husband, who had returned from war in the Pacific theater. For men of his generation, the GI Bill is remembered for its educational benefits. Created in 1944, it was prompted by fear of the social and political danger of widespread unemployment among returning veterans. The GI Bill of Rights gave my husband and his brother Richard a chance to obtain a college education. The brothers, who had both served in the navy, were the first in their family to leave their Minnesota farm and to enter professional careers.

For them, a college education represented an escape from the disadvantages of the past. This was true for other "children of the Great Depression" who had served in World War II. Glenn Elder examined the work histories of Berkeley veterans who are part of a longitudinal study at the University of California. He found that merely attending college, regardless of whether a degree was achieved, set these men on a course that produced substantial work-life achievement. They became significant contributors to one of the longest, steadiest periods of economic growth and prosperity that the United States enjoyed after World War II, a period that lasted about twenty-five years.

In contrast to a substantial postwar drop in the birth rate in vanquished Germany, the postwar prosperity in the United States created a "baby boom." From 1946 through 1964, a total of 75.9 million babies were born in the United States—a record high in the country's history. The family and the home had become a refuge—a refuge from the saber rattling of the Cold War and from the policy to contain the potential threats of Soviet communism and worldwide thermonuclear annihilation. Ironically, these threats appeared to be more menacing the farther away one lived from the divided city of Berlin, where the child survivors of World War II had learned to develop an especially refined form of gallows humor.

In the United States, the dreams of the men and women who had been children in World War II now centered on early marriage, large families, and a belief in upward social mobility. The values on which the "home-front" children had been brought up during the war were the ones they tended to profess as they came of age and entered adulthood: a strong belief in the essential goodness of the United States and its mission in the world; and respect for the leadership of government, education, religion, business, and labor. Subsequent events, like the civil rights movement and the Vietnam War and the assassinations of President Kennedy and Martin Luther King, Jr., would force these men and women to reevaluate the meaning of their patriotism—just as German children and teenagers had to do at the end of World War II.

Children from nations that suffered defeat in World War II differed from the victorious in how they dealt with events after the war. Their elders often used a strategy of silence about atrocities committed by their countrymen during or before the war, like the Holocaust in Germany or the rape of Nanking in Japan—a silence that was difficult to penetrate. German and Japanese children had come to terms not only with the destruction of their homeland, but also with the total defeat of the myths, ideologies, and values predominant in their societies. Children in the victorious United States were spared that experience—though events in a later war, Vietnam, would cause them some doubt about the righteousness of the American "cause." The Japanese American children, however, had reasons to doubt the professed American ideals of "justice for all" early on in World War II. They did not forget that lesson.

Tatsuko Anne Tachibana had a unique vantage point: She was nine years old when her family was removed from their home in Oceanside, California, and sent to the Poston, Arizona, internment camp, where they stayed for most of the war while her father was imprisoned by the FBI in a detention center in New Mexico as a "dangerous enemy alien." "As I look back over the years," says Anne, in William Tuttle's book *Daddy's Gone to War*, "I certainly harbor no bitterness or hatred toward this country, just a bit of sadness and many unanswered questions. . . . I hope our country has learned a lesson."[14]

It took a long time for the lesson to be learned by the representatives of the American people. On August 10, 1988, thirty-three years after the end of World War II, President Ronald Reagan finally signed the Civil Rights Act, with a formal apology from the U.S. Congress to the Japanese American community. Each camp survivor was granted a sum of $20,000. No one would be able to repay them for their loss of liberty and for the humiliation of being treated like traitors in their own country.

The psychological effects of the internment of the Japanese Americans has varied by generation.[15] The first-generation Issei lost all they had worked so hard to establish. Inside the camps, the roles of children and parents had often been reversed: The second-generation Nisei had been allowed positions of authority, for example as teachers and youth and recreation workers. But like the victims of rape, many Nisei felt somehow responsible for their fate. They often internalized their anger and chose a cooperative, obedient, quiet stance in coping with the demands of their post–World War II lives. Even the identity and self-concept of the members of the third generation (Sansei), who were either very young or born in camp, were affected. Some Sansei feel even today a sense of shame associated with their birthplace.

Yet another effect of the internment was its impact on the physical health of the internees, especially that of Nisei males. More than twice as many Sansei whose fathers were in camp have died before the age of sixty, compared to Sansei whose fathers were not interned. The internment experience created unusual stressors for Nisei fathers. On the whole, they have been much more reluctant to discuss the camp experience with their children than have Nisei mothers.

Although members of the third generation view their parents' internment generally as unjust and traumatic, they admire their postwar resilience and respect them as role models. The passage of the redress legislation in 1988 seems to have finally lifted some of the psychological burden of distrust that has been carried by Japanese Americans for decades, and has significantly strengthened intergenerational ties and ethnic pride.

One of the most remarkable aspect of my interviews with the child survivors of World War II was the absence of hatred and bitterness toward former "enemies" or toward people in their own country who had wronged them. Isao Fujimoto, who like Anne Tachibana had a father imprisoned by the FBI as an "enemy alien" and who spent his childhood years in two internment camps in Wyoming and California, remembers even today the small gift he received from the Quakers on Christmas Day 1942 when he was in the Heart Mountain Relocation Center. He has repaid this act of kindness a thousandfold by volunteering for the work of the American Friends Service Committee during the past forty years of his life.

The children of World War II did not lose their sensitivity to other people's suffering and could recognize the humanity of the enemy. Keith Barton, who was cruelly teased by his classmates in England because he was the son of a conscientious objector, learned an important lesson from his encounters with the German prisoners of war:

> I really believe having that early contact with those guys made me feel they were friendly, ordinary people. Now they tell me that they were prisoners of war, enemies, but they did all these nice things, like carving wooden toys for me. They did a lot more, like helping my mom—they did all these things like father surrogates, because they had kids of their own. I remember seeing their photographs. I *know* they had kids. This enemy business is ridiculous, because even if you are at war with a particular country, there are many people in that country that you could be close friends with, if you met them as people. So it is war, by definition, which is bad, it's the *war* that's doing the [hateful] things, *not* the *people*.

Larry Lauerhass Jr. grew up in southern California. During World War II his Japanese American neighbors were sent to internment camps:

> You become aware of the pain that war is causing human beings everywhere in the world. This experience was something that made me look more closely at the Far East and Europe. For me, it had the rather helpful end result that when I met people from these areas, I was much more open and willing to interact with them. I had a very good Japanese friend when I was in college. I think the war was quite the opposite of creating resentment. It was an opening for me.

The most striking quality shared by the child survivors of World War II that I interviewed was an active compassion for others in need. Sara Glickstein, the Polish refugee, had lost most of her family and her home in Warsaw, had been detained with her family in a labor camp in the Russian tundra, and had then spent five years of her childhood in a displaced persons camp. Kiyoko Yamasaki, born in San Francisco to Japanese parents, had been separated from her father, who was placed in a U.S. detention camp, and saw her house in Japan destroyed by American planes. Both Sara and Kiyoko would have had ample reasons to be bitter about what the war had done to their childhood. But it had not killed their spirit.

Said Sara:

> I think it helped, seeing all that suffering. I feel it has made me more of a compassionate person. I have actively tried throughout my life to be against war and for the people on the street, the ones who

are homeless. I understand what it is not to have a home. . . . I am also trying to help animals who are cruelly treated. . . . I feel that they are in the same position that a lot of humans are in who suffer [in wars], and they are even more helpless.

Kiyoko remembered fondly her Japanese relatives who didn't hate her for being American during World War II, and her American friends who didn't hate her for being Japanese when she returned home to California after the war. "I think I am fortunate that I have met all those nice people," she said. "So, as long as I live, I like to be nice to people. I'm coming to an age where I don't know how long I am going to live, so I try to be extra nice. I just appreciate that I was fortunate enough to meet so many nice people in my life."

During the lifetime of the children of World War II there would be no lasting peace on earth. In the second half of the twentieth century more than 100 armed conflicts have been fought in Africa, Asia, Europe, and the Middle East. Nine out of ten casualties in contemporary wars are now noncombatants.[16] Millions of children today will bear the physical and psychological scars of war for the rest of their lives. For some, the impact will be disabling; others will learn to live with their painful memories, as did most of the children of World War II.

UNICEF—founded by individuals who had seen the effects of war on the children of Europe and Asia, and renamed the United Nations Children's Fund—has been a ceaseless advocate for the rights of the youngest victims of armed conflict. In September 1990, government leaders met at the United Nations headquarters in New York to participate in the first-ever World Summit for Children. There they signed the Convention on the Rights of the Child—a declaration aimed at the protection of the most vulnerable members of the human race.

The Convention commits the world's leaders to demobilizing child soldiers, reuniting child refugees with their families, healing the mental and physical wounds of the youngest victims of war, and restarting schools for them. The task is daunting, for in the last decade of the twentieth century civil wars have killed and maimed millions of children. Millions are refugees, have been orphaned, or are unable to locate their parents. Millions more have seen their homes destroyed and mourn the death of loved ones.

Yet we need not despair. For the stories of the child survivors of World War II teach us that war- and violence-induced physical and psychological trauma are not irreversible. We *can* feed and clothe the children of war, find shelter for those in need of refuge, bind the wounds of the hurt and

A quartet of survivors: orphans of the war.

maimed. People of goodwill did that for the children of World War II. *We can do it again.*

We *can* give hope to the children of war, provide them with the love of caring adults—a member of the family, a teacher, someone who will listen and hold their hand. We *can* use schools as places to restore structure and routine in young lives, where the children can learn the skills to rebuild their world in peace. We did it before, when the whole world lay in ruins. *We can do it again!*

But if we want a lasting peace on earth in the years to come, we need to listen to the children of war, who—in each generation—are wise beyond their years. They can tell us better than any politician, diplomat, or military strategist what war does to the human spirit. They have seen it close up. They have seen, wide-eyed and defenseless, the slaughter of the innocent.

Some fifty years after the end of World War II, three children from the former Yugoslavia whose country had been ravaged by civil wars that seemed to have no end, wrote an eloquent plea to people all over the world. Their poems were published by UNICEF in a heart-wrenching book with the title *I Dream of Peace.*[17] "Stop the war and the fighting," wrote eleven-year-old Ivana. "Stop the planes and the shells for a smile on a child's face. . . . Stop everything that kills and destroys for a smile of happiness on a child's face."

Ten-year-old Roberto knew just how that dream of peace could come true: "If I were President," he wrote, "the tanks would be playhouses for the kids. Boxes of candy would fall from the sky. The mortars would fire balloons, and the guns would blossom with flowers. All the world's children would sleep in a peace unbroken by alerts or by shooting. The refugees would return to their villages, and we would start anew."

Who knows? The children of Berlin once saw candy fall from the sky, dropped by an American pilot with a generous heart. Perhaps the dream of peace can still come true—perhaps we can start anew. Millions of boys and girls in war-torn countries all over the world would smile again—just as my cousins and I did so long ago. Will anybody listen? Will we ever learn that *no* war is good for children? "I send you this message," writes Sandra, age ten, in the midst of the fighting: "Don't ever hurt the children. They are not guilty of anything."

Select Chronology of World War II

The events listed below provide context for the eyewitness accounts related in this book.

1939

September 1	Germany invades Poland.
September 3	France and Great Britain declare war on Germany.
September 17	The USSR invades Poland.
September 27	Warsaw falls.
November 30	Finnish-Soviet war starts.

1940

March 12	Finnish-Soviet war ends.
April 9	Germany invades Norway and Denmark.
May 10	Germany launches an offensive in the west. Churchill becomes prime minister.
May 15	British air offensive against Germany starts. Dutch army surrenders.
May 20	Dunkirk evacuation starts.
May 28	Belgian army surrenders.
June 4	Dunkirk evacuation is complete.
June 14	German troops enter Paris.
June 22	France signs armistice treaty with Germany.
July 10	Battle of Britain begins.
September 7	Blitz on London begins.
November 14	Air raid on Coventry.

1941

June 22	Germany invades the USSR.
October 2	Germans start their offensive to capture Moscow.
October 19	State of siege is announced in Moscow.
November 28	Fourth Panzer Group is 12.5 miles from Moscow.
December 5	Red Army counteroffensive in front of Moscow starts.
December 7	Japanese attack Pearl Harbor.

| December 8 | United States declares war on Japan. |
| December 11 | Germany declares war on the United States. |

1942

January 1	United Nations declaration is signed by China, Great Britain, the United States, and the USSR.
January 26	U.S. troops arrive in Northern Ireland.
February 13	Roosevelt signs an executive order that results in evacuation of 110,000 Japanese Americans from the West Coast.
March 17	General MacArthur is appointed to command southwest Pacific.
May 30	First RAF thousand-bomber raid on Germany.
June 4	Battle of Midway starts.
November 8	Allied landings in Algeria and Morocco start North African campaign.

1943

January 27	Eighth USAAF mounts its first raid on Germany.
February 2	German forces capitulate at Stalingrad.
May 13	Axis forces capitulate in North Africa.
May 24	U-boats are withdrawn from the North Atlantic.
July 24	RAF raids on Hamburg.
September 3	Allies land on the Italian mainland.
September 8	Italy surrenders.
November 9	UNRRA is established.
December 24	Eisenhower is named as supreme commander for Normandy landings.

1944

January 27	Leningrad siege ends after 900 days.
January 31	U.S. forces land on the Marshall Islands.
February 20	"Big Week," Anglo-U.S. air offensive against Germany starts.
April 22	MacArthur's forces land at Hollandia, New Guinea.
June 6	Allies land in Normandy.
June 13	Start of V-1 bombardment against England.
June 15	Strategic air offensive against Japan begins.
July 20	Attempt to assassinate Hitler fails.
August 25	Germans surrender in Paris.
September 8	First V-2 rocket lands on England.
October 20	U.S. troops land in the Philippines.
October 21	First German city is captured, when Aachen falls to U.S. troops.
December 16	Germans launch Ardennes campaign. Battle of the Bulge begins.

1945

January 14	Red Army attacks into eastern Prussia.
February 13	Air raid on Dresden.
February 19	U.S. forces land on Iwo Jima.
February 26	U.S. Ninth Army reaches the Rhine south of Düsseldorf.
March 7	U.S. Third Army crosses the Rhine at Remagen.
April 1	U.S. forces land on Okinawa.
April 12	Roosevelt dies; Truman becomes president.
April 25	San Francisco UN conference starts.
April 30	Hitler commits suicide.
May 2	Red Army takes Berlin.
May 7	At 2:41 Jodl signs unconditional surrender of Germany at Reims to take effect at 0001 on May 9.
August 6	Atomic bomb dropped on Hiroshima.
August 9	Atomic bomb dropped on Nagasaki.
August 14	Emperor Hirohito announces Japan's unconditional surrender.
September 2	Japanese surrender signed aboard the USS *Missouri* in Tokyo Bay.

Notes

Prologue

1. Martin K. Sorge, *The Other Price of Hitler's War: German Military and Civilian Losses Resulting from World War II* (New York: Greenwood Press, 1986).

2. See, for example, Laurel Holliday, ed., *Children of the Holocaust and World War II: Their Secret Diaries* (New York: Pocket Books, 1995); Sarah Moskovitz, *Love Despite Hate: Child Survivors of the Holocaust and their Adult Years* (New York: Schocken Books, 1983).

Chapter 1

1. Hannes Heer, ed., *Als Ich Neun Jahre Alt War, Kam Der Krieg: Schulaufsätze 1946: Ein Lesebuch Gegen Den Krieg* (Köln: Prometh Verlag, 1980), chap. 7. The reader should be aware that in an attempt not to overburden this book with annotations, I have not included a note for every quotation. As a general rule, I note a source only the first time I draw from it in each chapter; subsequent quotations drawn from the same source are not marked with a note, unless a note was prudent in order to avoid confusion. Also, all translations from German sources are my own.

2. William L. Shirer, *The Rise and Fall of the Third Reich: A History of Nazi Germany* (New York: Simon and Schuster, 1959).

3. Janine Philipps, *My Secret Diary* (London: Shepheard-Walwyn, 1982).

4. Kurt Homburg, *Aus Kindertagen vor 50 Jahren* (Herford: Maximilian Verlag, 1992).

5. Interview with Dinah Towns, October 10, 1997.

6. Jean-Louis Besson, *October 45: Childhood Memories of the War* (Mankato, Minn.: Creative Editions, 1995).

7. Eleanor Allen, *Wartime Children: 1939–1945* (London: A & C Black, 1975).

8. Bessie Shea, "War at Scapa Flow," in *Children of the Blitz: Memories of Wartime Childhood*, ed. Robert Westall (New York: Viking, 1985), 60–71.

9. Lucien Hut, "The Netherlands," in *No Longer Silent: World-Wide Memories of the Children of World War II*, ed. C. LeRoy Anderson, Joanne R. Anderson, and Yunosuke Ohkura (Missoula, Mont.: Pictorial Histories Publishing Co., 1995), 118–133.

10. Jules, "Belgium," in Kati David, *A Child's War: World War II Through the Eyes of Children* (New York: Avon Books, 1989), 83–90.

11. Regina Schwenke, *Und Es Wird Immer Wieder Tag: Kindheitserinnerungen an Berlin's Dunkelsten Tage* (Berlin: Arani, 1983).

12. Jill, "Letter to Dear Mummy and Daddy, September 1, 1940," in *Children of the Blitz: Memories of Wartime Childhood,* ed. Robert Westall (New York: Viking, 1985), 92.

13. Alice Brady, *Children Under Fire* (Los Angeles: Columbia Publishing Co., 1942).

14. Ibid.

15. Jennifer J. Borchert, "Dear Diary." URL: http://www.msu.edu/user/borcher3.

Chapter 2

1. Michael Foreman, *War Boy: A Country Childhood* (New York: Arcade Publishing Co., 1991), 7–8.

2. Robin, "England," in Kati David, *A Child's War: World War II Through the Eyes of Children* (New York: Avon Books, 1989), 39.

3. Interview with Keith Barton, November 1997.

4. Interview with Dinah Towns, October 10, 1997.

5. Christian Søe, "A Relatively Civilized War," in *Children in War: Reminiscences of the Second World War,* ed. David Childs and Janet Wharton (Nottingham, U.K.: University of Nottingham, 1989), 161–170.

6. Jytte Christensen Johansen, "Denmark," in *No Longer Silent: World-Wide Memories of the Children of World War II,* ed. C. LeRoy Anderson, Joanne R. Anderson, and Yunosuke Ohkura (Missoula, Mont.: Pictorial Histories Publishing Co., 1995), 100–102.

7. Lucien Hut, "The Netherlands," in *No Longer Silent: World-Wide Memories of the Children of World War II,* ed. C. LeRoy Andersen, Joanne R. Anderson, and Yunosuke Ohkura (Missoula, Montana: Pictorial Histories Publishing Co., 1995), 118–133.

8. "SS 5: Pages from Jan's Diary," in *Children of the Resistance,* ed. Lore Cowan (New York: Meredith Press, 1969), 106–127.

9. Willemien van de Zand, "Witness to an Invasion," in *Children in War: Reminiscences of the Second World War,* ed. David Childs and Janet Wharton (Nottingham, England: University of Nottingham, 1989), 135–145.

10. Ola Austbo, "Norway," in *No Longer Silent: World-Wide Memories of the Children of World War II,* ed. C. LeRoy Anderson, Joanne R. Anderson, and Yunosuke Ohkura (Missoula, Mont.: Pictorial Histories Publishing Co., 1995), 112–116.

11. Yuri Kirshin, "Russia," in *No Longer Silent: World-Wide Memories of the Children of World War II,* ed. C. LeRoy Anderson, Joanne R. Anderson, and Yunosuke Ohkura (Missoula, Mont.: Pictorial Histories Publishing Co., 1995), 276–280.

12. N. P. Dovbenko, "Russia," in *No Longer Silent: World-Wide Memories of The Children of World War II,* ed. C. LeRoy Anderson, Joanne R. Anderson, and Yunosuke Ohkura (Missoula, Mont.: Pictorial Histories Publishing Co., 1995), 44–48.

13. Lyudmila Anopova, "Siege of Leningrad Survivor Relives Her Childhood Terror." URL: http://www.sptimes.ru/archives/sppress/siege.html.

14. Ina Konstantinova, "Diary," in *Children of the Holocaust and World War II. Their Secret Diaries*, ed. Laurel Holiday (New York: Pocket Books, 1995), 249–254.

15. Elsbeth Emmerich, *My Childhood in Nazi Germany* (New York: Bookwright Press, 1991).

16. Jean-Louis Besson, *October 45: Childhood Memories of the War* (Mankato, Minn.: Creative Editions, 1995).

Chapter 3

1. In *Children of the Blitz: Memories of Wartime Childhood*, ed. Robert Westall (London: Viking, 1985), chap. 3.

2. Bertha Leverton and Shmuel Loewenson, *I Came Alone: The Story of the Kinder Transports* (Lewes, Sussex: The Book Guild, 1998).

3. Interview with Dinah Towns, October 10, 1997.

4. Westall, *Children of the Blitz*, 41–56.

5. Susan Isaacs, ed., *The Cambridge Evacuation Survey: A Wartime Study in Social Welfare and Education* (London: Methuen, 1941).

6. Michael Fethney, *The Absurd and the Brave: CORB–The True Account of the British Government's World War II Evacuation of Children Overseas* (Lewes, Sussex: The Book Guild, 1990).

7. Geoffrey Bilson, *The Guest Children: The Story of the British Child Evacuees Sent to Canada During World War II* (Saskatoon, Saskatchewan: Fifth House, 1988).

8. Carlton Jackson, *Who Will Take Our Children?* (London: Methuen, 1985), 99.

9. Margaret Beal, "Diary," in *The Day They Took the Children*, ed. Ben Wicks (London: Bloomsbury, 1989), 144–155.

10. Jack Keely, "Interview," in *The Children's War: Evacuation, 1939–1945*, ed. Ruth Inglis (London: Collins, 1989), 120–122.

11. Caroline Bell and Eddie Bell, *Thank You Twice or How We Like America* (New York: Harcourt, Brace and Company, 1941), 109–112.

12. Ruth Inglis, "Effects of Evacuation," in *The Children's War: Evacuation, 1939–1945* (London: Collins, 1989), 147–166.

13. B. S. Johnson, ed., *The Evacuees* (London: Victor Gollantz Ltd., 1968).

14. Inglis, "Effects of Evacuation."

15. "Bomben und Kinderlandverschickung," in *Heil Hitler, Herr Lehrer: Volksschule 1933–1945*, ed. Arbeitsgruppe Pädagogisches Museum (Reinbeck by Hamburg: Rowohlt Verlag, 1983).

16. Hannes Heer, ed., *Als Ich Neun Jahre Alt War, Kam Der Krieg: Schulaufsätze 1946: Ein Lesebuch Gegen Den Krieg* (Köln: Prometh Verlag, 1980), chap. 12.

17. Ibid.

18. Ibid.

19. Ibid.

20. Claus Larass, *Der Zug Der Kinder: KLV—Die Evakuierung 5 Millionen Deutscher Kinder im 2. Weltkrieg* (Frankfurt: Ullstein, 1992), 62–63.

21. Ibid.

22. Annemarie Landenberger, *Als Hamburger Lehererin in Der Kinderlandver-schickung: Tagebuch 1943* (Hamburg: Verein für Hamburger Geschichte, 1992).

23. Larass, *Der Zug Der Kinder.*

24. Georg Klitta, "Das Finale des Zweiten Weltkriegs in Schwandorf" in *Die erweiterte Kinder-Land-Verschickung: KLV-Lager 1940–1945,* edited by Gerhard Dabel (Freiburg: Schillinger, 1981), 293.

25. "Inge L." in Claus Larass, *Der Zug Der Kinder: KLV—Die Evakuierung 5 Millionen Deutscher Kinder im 2. Weltkrieg* (Frankfurt: Ullstein, 1992), 141-157.

26. "Erfahrungen, Auswirkungen and Lehren aus der Sicht von Teilnehmern," in *Die erweiterte Kinder-Land-Verschickung: KLV-Lager 1940–1945,* ed. Gerhard Dabel (Freiburg: Schillinger, 1981), 309–312.

Chapter 4

1. Richard Tamabayashi, "December 7" in *Boy Scouts: My Diary: December 7–15, 1941,* File 50 (Honolulu: Hawaii War Records Depository, University of Hawaii at Manoa).

2. Dorinda Makanaōnalani Nicholson, *Pearl Harbor Child* (Honolulu, Hawaii: Arizona Memorial Museum Association, 1993), 15–20.

3. George Fujimoto, "My First War Experience," in *University of Hawaii Themes, Pearl Harbor Attack*, File 24.01 (Honolulu: Hawaii War Records Depository, University of Hawaii at Manoa).

4. Marjorie Bond, "Wartime Hawaii," in *Punahou School Essays, April 23–24, 1944,* File 24.02 (Honolulu: Hawaii War Records Depository, University of Hawaii at Manoa).

5. Helen Jean Stubblefield, quoted in *Victory Gardens and Barrage Balloons,* ed. Frank Wetzel (Bremerton, Wash.: Perry Publishers, 1996).

6. Boy Scouts, *My Diary: December 7–15, 1941,* File 50 (Honolulu: Hawaii War Records Depository, University of Hawaii at Manoa).

7. Sacred Hearts Academy, *Diary: December 1941–January 1942,* File 24.02 (Honolulu: Hawaii War Records Depository, University of Hawaii at Manoa).

8. *San Francisco Chronicle,* December 9, 1941, cited in Ella Leffland, *Rumors of Peace* (New York: Harper and Row, 1979), 18–19.

9. Barbara Crozier, "My Schooling After the War Began," in *Punahou School Essays, April 23–24, 1944,* File 24.02 (Honolulu: Hawaii War Records Depository, University of Hawaii at Manoa).

10. This quotation and the following one are from William M. Tuttle Jr., *Daddy's Gone to War: The Second World War in the Lives of American Children* (New York: Oxford University Press, 1993), chap. 1.

11. Cited in Tuttle, *Daddy's Gone to War.*

12. Ibid.

13. Robert W. Kirk, *Earning Their Stripes: The Mobilization of American Children in the Second World War* (New York: Peter Lang, 1995).

14. Herbert A. Werner, *Iron Coffins: A Personal Account of the German U-Boat Battles of World War II* (New York: Da Capo Press, 1998).

15. Bruce Smith, *The History of Little Orphan Annie* (New York: Ballantine, 1982).

16. Clive Oldroyd, "Letter to General MacArthur, July 22, 1942," Douglas MacArthur Memorial Archives and Library, Norfolk, Va.

17. Patricia A. Coyle, "Letter to General MacArthur, August 9, 1942," Douglas MacArthur Memorial Archives and Library, Norfolk, Va.

18. Joan Dooley, "Letter to General MacArthur, November 10, 1942," Douglas MacArthur Memorial Archives and Library, Norfolk, Va.

19. Robert W. Kirk, "Getting in the Scrap: The Mobilization of American Children in World War II," *Journal of Popular Culture* 29 (1995): pp. 223–233.

20. This "Dear Poppy" letter and the other Berman family letters that I quote in the pages that follow are collected in Ruth Berman, *Dear Poppa: The World War II Berman Family Letters* (Saint Paul: Minnesota Historical Society Press, 1997).

21. Robert Puchmond, "Why We Should Live Up to Our War Bond Pledge." Douglas MacArthur Memorial Archives and Library, Norfolk, Va.

22. Joshua Akana, "A Student Letter from Honolulu," *Weekly News Review*, March 29, 1943.

23. Kirk, *Earning Their Stripes.*

24. Interview with Nancy Rogers, November 1997.

25. Interview with Larry Lauerhass Jr., June 1997.

26. Lloyd Hornbostel, *War Kids, 1941–1945: World War II Through the Eyes of Children* (Lakeville, Minn.: Galde Press, 1996), 108.

Chapter 5

1. Sacred Hearts Academy, *Diary: December 1941–January 1942,* File 24.02 (Honolulu: Hawaii War Records Depository, University of Hawaii at Manoa).

2. Maisie Conrat and Richard Conrat, *Executive Order 9066: The Internment of 110,000 Japanese Americans* (Cambridge, Mass.: MIT Press, 1972).

3. Interview with Isao Fujimoto, January 1998.

4. Quoted in Michael O. Tunnell, *The Children of Topaz: The Story of a Japanese American Internment Camp Based on a Classroom Diary* (New York: Holiday House, 1996).

5. Quoted in Grace Nakamura, "Testimony," in *Personal Justice Denied*, Report of the Commission on Wartime Relocation and Internment of Civilians (Washington, D.C.: Government Printing Office, 1982).

6. Quoted in Tunnell, *The Children of Topaz*, 9–11.

7. Quoted in John Tateishi, ed., *And Justice for All: An Oral History of the Japanese American Detention Camps* (New York: Random House, 1984).

8. Michi Weglyn, *Years of Infamy: The Untold Story of American Concentration Camps* (Seattle, Wash.: University of Washington Press, 1996).

9. Reprinted in *Through Innocent Eyes: Writings and Art from the Japanese American Internment by Poston I Schoolchildren*, edited by Vincent Tajiri (Los Angeles: Keiro Services, 1990).

10. Father High T. Lavery, "Letter to President Truman," *Pacific Citizen*, September 24, 1949.

11. Renee Tawa, "Childhood Lost: The Orphans of Manzanar," *Los Angeles Times*, March 11, 1997.

12. Francis Honda, "Testimony," in *Personal Justice Denied,* Report of the Commission on Wartime Relocation and Internment of Civilians (Washington, D.C.: Government Printing Office, 1982).

13. Jeanne Wakatsuki Houston and James D. Houston, *Farewell to Manzanar* (Boston: Houghton Mifflin, 1973), 82.

14. Cited in Tawa, "Childhood Lost."

15. Helen Elizabeth Whitney, "Care of Homeless Children of Japanese Ancestry During Evacuation and Relocation" (Ph.D. diss., University of California, Berkeley, 1948).

16. Kinya Noguchi, "Testimony," in *Personal Justice Denied.*

17. Houston and Houston, *Farewell to Manzanar.*

18. Report of the War Relocation Administration, cited in Whitney, "Care of Homeless Children of Japanese Ancestry During Evacuation and Relocation."

19. Tateishi, *And Justice for All.*

20. Elizabeth C. Evanson, "Scrapbook" (Seattle, Wash: University of Washington Libraries, Manuscript and Archives Division, 1942).

21. Elizabeth Willis Bayley, "Letters of Japanese American Students" (Seattle, Wash.: University of Washington Libraries, Manuscript and Archives Division, 1942–1943).

22. High Third Grade, Mountain View School, Topaz, Utah, *Our Daily Diary: March 8–August 12, 1943* (Salt Lake City, Utah: Utah State Historical Society).

23. Donald Nakahata, quoted in John Tateishi, ed., *And Justice for All: An Oral History of Japanese American Detention Camps* (New York: Random House, 1984), 53–55.

24. Yoshiko Uchida, *The Invisible Thread* (Englewood Cliffs, N.J.: Julian Mesner, 1991).

25. Emiko Kamiya, "My First Christmas in Poston," in Tajiri, *Through Innocent Eyes.*

26. Kazue Tsuchiyama, "Winter Life in Poston," in Tajiri, *Through Innocent Eyes.*

27. Bebe Reschke, "Testimony," Public Hearings of the Commission on Wartime Relocation and Internment of Civilians, 1981. Washington National Archives, National Archives and Records Service, General Service Administration, 1983.

28. Ben Takeshita, quoted in John Tateishi, ed., *And Justice for All: An Oral History of the Japanese American Detention Camps* (New York: Random House, 1984), 243–247.

29. "Our Flag," in *Manzanar Whirlwind*, February 1945.

30. Erica Harth, "Children of Manzanar: Experiences in an Internment Camp During World War II," *Massachusetts Review* 34 (3): p. 390.

Chapter 6

1. Mary Louise Koehnen, "Letters to General Eisenhower: April 8, 1942–June 22, 1943" (Abilene, Kans.: Dwight D. Eisenhower Library).

2. Dwight D. Eisenhower, "Letters to Mary Louise Koehnen: April 15, 1942–August 2, 1943" (Abilene, Kans.: Dwight D. Eisenhower Library).

Chapter 7

1. Anthony D. Duke, "Oral History" (New Orleans: Eisenhower Center Archives, University of New Orleans).

2. Joseph McCann, Jr., "Oral History" (New Orleans: Eisenhower Center Archives, University of New Orleans).

3. Kurt Homburg, *Aus Kindertagen vor 50 Jahren* (Herford: Maximilian Verlag, 1992).

4. Herbert Meier, "Oral History" (New Orleans: Stephen and Hughes Ambrose German Veterans Collection, Eisenhower Center Archives, University of New Orleans).

5. Walter Henschke, "So kämpft deutsche Jugend!" *Völkischer Beobachter,* 7 März 1945.

6. Ewald Becker, interview by Hughes Ambrose (New Orleans: Stephen and Hughes Ambrose German Veterans Collection, Eisenhower Center Archives, University of New Orleans).

7. Willy Dittgen, *Der Kinderkäfig von Attichy: Ein Erlebensbericht* (Rheinberg: Michael Schiffer, 1957), 8.

8. *Westfälische Neueste Nachrichten,* 8 März 1945.

9. Stephen E. Ambrose, *Citizen Soldiers* (New York: Simon and Schuster, 1997), 439.

10. Al Ptak, *Firestorm* (Rosedale, B.C.: Arashida Publications, 1996), 42–43.

11. Hans Dietrich Nicolaisen, *Die Flakhelfer: Luftwaffenhelfer und Marinehelfer im Zweiten Weltkrieg* (Berlin: Ullstein, 1981), 132–133.

12. Hannes Heer, ed., *Als Ich Neun Jahre Alt War, Kam Der Krieg: Schulaufsätze 1946: Ein Lesebuch Gegen Den Krieg* (Köln: Prometh Verlag, 1980), chap. 17.

13. Erich Womelsdorf, interview by Hughes Ambrose (New Orleans: Stephen and Hughes Ambrose German Veterans Collection, Eisenhower Center Archives, University of New Orleans).

14. Dieter Borkowski, *Wer Weiss Ob Wir Uns Wiedersehen* (Berlin: Das Neue Berlin, 1990).

15. Klaus Granzow, *Tagebuch Eines Hitlerjungen: Kriegsjugend in Pommern: 1943–1945* (Bremen: Claus Schüneman Verlag, 1986).

16. Tomiko Higa, *The Girl With the White Flag* (Tokyo: Kodansha International, 1991).

Chapter 8

1. Alice Brady, *Children Under Fire* (Los Angeles: Columbia Publishing Co., 1942).

2. Quoted in Ingrid Horst, *Born Under Hitler: A German Childhood Connected with History* (Boston: Perspective Publishers International, 1988), 250.

3. William L. Shirer, *The Rise and Fall of the Third Reich: A History of Nazi Germany* (New York: Simon and Schuster, 1959).

4. Leopold Banny, *Dröhnender Himmel, Brennendes Land* (Wien: Österreichischer Bundesverlag, 1988); Hans Dietrich Nicolaisen, *Die Flakhelfer: Luftwaffenhelfer und Marinehelfer im Zweiten Weltkrieg* (Berlin: Ullstein, 1981); Ludwig Schatz, *Schüler-Soldaten: Die Geschichte der Luftwaffenhelfer im Zweiten Weltkrieg* (Frankfurt am Main: Thesen Verlag, 1972).

5. Rita Bake, ed., *Aber Wir Müssen Zusammen Bleiben: Mütter und Kinder im Bombenkrieg: 1943–1945: Gespräche* (Hamburg: Landeszentrale für Politische Bildung, 1993).

6. Regina Schwenke, *Und Es Wird Immer Wieder Tag: Kindheitserinnerungen an Berlin's Dunkelsten Tage* (Berlin: Arani, 1983).

7. Dieter Borkowski, *Wer Weiss Ob Wir Uns Wiedersehen* (Berlin: Das Neue Berlin, 1990).

8. Kurt Vonnegut Jr., *Slaughterhouse 5 or The Children's Crusade* (New York: Dell, 1966).

9. Kurt Vonnegut Jr., "Memoirs," *Faces of Indiana and Midwestern History* 3, no. 4 (special issue, fall 1991).

10. Johanna Mittmann, quoted in Ingrid Horst, *Born Under Hitler*, 248.

11. Uta Wutherich, in Christine Lipp, ed., *Kindheit und Krieg: Erinnerungen* (Frankfurt am Main: Fischer, 1992), 158.

12. Willy A. Schauss, *My Side of the War: How Meatballs Saved My Life* (Kalispell, Mont.: Scott Publications, 1994).

13. Klaus Granzow, *Tagebuch Eines Hitlerjungen: Kriegsjugend in Pommern, 1943–1945* (Bremen: Claus Schüneman Verlag, 1986).

14. Katherine Kaoru Morooka Reyes, "Japan," in *No Longer Silent: World-Wide Memories of the Children of World War II*, ed. C. LeRoy Anderson, Joanne R. Anderson, and Yunosuke Ohkura (Missoula, Mont.: Pictorial Histories Publishing Co., 1995), 206–219.

15. Shinsuke Tani, *Seasons Unforgotten* (Tokyo: Toju-sha, 1976).

16. Arata Osada, ed., *Children of the A-Bomb: The Testament of the Boys and Girls of Hiroshima* (New York: G. P. Putnam's Sons, 1980).

17. Takashi Nagai, ed., *Living Beneath the Atomic Cloud: Testimonies of the Children of Nagasaki* (Tokyo: SAN-YU-SHA, 1979).

18. Fuiji Tsumimoto, "I squat down on the spot . . . ," in Takashi Nagai, *Living Beneath the Atomic Cloud,* 2–6.

Chapter 9

1. N. P. Dovbenko, "Russia," in *No Longer Silent: World-Wide Memories of the Children of World War II,* ed. C. LeRoy Anderson, Joanne R. Anderson, and Yunosuke Ohkura (Missoula, Mont.: Pictorial Histories Publishing Co., 1995), 46–47.

2. Elsbeth Emmerich, *My Childhood in Nazi Germany* (New York: Bookwright Press, 1991).

3. Elizabeth Shelfer Morgan, *Uncertain Seasons* (Tuscaloosa: University of Alabama Press, 1994).

4. Lorraine Fader, "Letter to General MacArthur, January 12, 1943" (Norfolk, Va.: Douglas MacArthur Memorial Archives and Library).

5. Charmaine Leavitt, "Letter to Dear Justin, December 29, 1943," in *World War II Letters from American Women on the Home Front*, ed. Judy Barrett Litoff and David C. Smith (New York: Oxford University Press, 1991), 236.

6. John Nichols Jr., quoted in *Lost in the Victory: Reflections of American War Orphans of World War II*, ed. Calvin L. Christman, 133–134 (Denton: University of North Texas Press, 1998).

7. Robert G. Raymond, *Scouting, Cavorting, and Other World War II Memories* (Billings, Mont.: R. G. Raymond, 1994).

8. Ulla Ellersdorfer, quoted in *Kindheit und Krieg: Erinnerungen*, ed. Christine Lipp, 37–38 (Frankfurt am Main: Fischer, 1992).

9. Annie Bennett, quoted in Calvin L. Christman, *Lost in the Victory*, 89–92.

10. Nancy Rougvie, quoted in Calvin L. Christman, *Lost in the Victory*, 129–132.

11. Hannes Heer, ed., *Als Ich Neun Jahre Alt War, Kam Der Krieg: Schulaufsätze 1946: Ein Lesebuch Gegen Den Krieg* (Köln: Prometh Verlag, 1980), chap. 8.

12. Irene Grudzinska-Gross, ed., *War Through Children's Eyes: The Soviet Occupation of Poland and the Deportations: 1939–1941* (Stanford, Calif.: Hoover Institute Press, 1981).

13. Alice Brady, *Children Under Fire* (Los Angeles: Columbia Publishing Co., 1942).

14. Laurencia Abatayo Baltazar, quoted in C. LeRoy Anderson et al., *No Longer Silent*, 202–206.

15. Hans Sester, *Als Junge im Sogenannten Dritten Reich* (Frankfurt am Main: H. A. Herchen, 1987).

16. Quoted in Heer, *Als Ich Neun Jahre Alt War*, chap. 11. The two following quotations are from the same source.

17. Keiko Sasaki, quoted in *Children of the A-Bomb: The Testament of the Boys and Girls of Hiroshima*, ed. Arata Osada (New York: G. P. Putnam's Sons, 1980).

Chapter 10

1. Judith M. Spiegelman and UNICEF, "Survivors of World War II: The Rescue of a New Generation," chap. 1 in *We Are the Children: A Celebration of UNICEF's First Forty Years* (Boston: Atlantic Monthly Press, 1986).

2. Hannes Heer, ed., *Als Ich Neun Jahre Alt War, Kam Der Krieg: Schulaufsätze 1946: Ein Lesebuch Gegen Den Krieg* (Köln: Prometh Verlag, 1980), chap. 2.

3. Sibylle Meyer and Eva Schulze, *Von Liebe Sprach Damals Keiner: Familienalltag in der Nachkriegszeit* (München: C. H. Beck, 1985), 100–101.

4. Victor Gollancz, *In Darkest Germany* (London: Victor Gollancz Ltd., 1947).

5. Antoine de Saint-Exupéry, *The Little Prince* (New York: Harcourt Brace and Co., 1943).

6. U.S. House, *Displaced Persons in Europe and Their Resettlement in the United States,* 81st Cong., 2nd sess., 1950, H. Rept. 1507.

7. Agata Nesaule, *Woman in Amber: Healing the Trauma of War and Exile* (New York: Penguin, 1995).

8. Maria Stankus-Saulaitis, "Forgotten Faces of the War," *America,* July 1995, 6–8.

9. Interview with Isao Fujimoto, January 1998.

10. Regina Schwenke, *Und Es Wird Immer Wieder Tag: Kindheitserinnerungen an Berlin's Dunkelsten Tage* (Berlin: Arani, 1983).

11. Erna Stahl, *Jugend im Schatten von Gestern: Aufsätze Jugendlicher zur Zeit* (Hamburg: Hans Köhler Verlag, 1948), 72–73.

Chapter 11

1. David Morris, ed., *A Gift from America: The First Fifty Years of CARE* (Atlanta, Ga.: Longstreet Press, 1996).

2. The quotes from CARE Package recipients come from interviews conducted on the occasion of the fiftieth anniversary of CARE's founding. The transcripts are in the archives of CARE's headquarters in Atlanta, Georgia.

3. Alfred P. Wehner, *From Hitler Youth to U.S. Citizen* (New York: Carlton Press, 1972).

4. Deutsches Historisches Museum, "Stille Helfer: 350 Jahre Quäker," *Deutsches Historisches Museum* 6, no. 15 (1995–1996).

5. The "thank-you letters" and drawings from German and Japanese children are located in the archives of the American Friends Service Committee in Philadelphia, Pennsylvania.

6. Judith M. Spiegelman and UNICEF. *We Are the Children: A Celebration of UNICEF's First Forty Years* (Boston: Atlantic Monthly Press, 1986).

7. Quoted in UNICEF, *The State of the World's Children,* 50th anniversary issue (New York: Oxford University Press, 1996).

8. Ibid.

9. Carolyn Marsh, "Letter to UNICEF" (n.d.). New York: UNICEF Headquarters.

10. Richard Wallace, "Letter of President Truman" (Independence, Mo.: Harry S. Truman Library, n.d.).

11. Gail S. Halvorsen, *The Berlin Candy Bomber* (Bountiful, Utah: Horizon Publishers, 1997).

Chapter 12

1. The quotations in the following pages are excerpts from interviews I conducted between June 1997 and October 1998.

2. Peter S. Jansen and Jon Shaw, "Children as Victims of War: Current Knowledge and Future Research Needs," *Journal of the American Academy of Child and Adolescent Psychiatry 32,* no. 4 (July 1993): pp. 697–708.

3. Anna Freud and Dorothy T. Burlingham, *War and Children* (New York: Medical War Books, 1943).

4. Philip A. Saigh, John A. Fairbank, and Anastasia E. Yasik, "War Related Post-Traumatic Stress Disorder Among Children and Adolescents," in *Children in the Urban Environment: Linking Social Policy and Clinical Practice*, edited by Norman Philipps and Shulamith L. A. Strausner (Springfield, Ill.: Charles Thomas Publisher, 1997), 119–140.

5. Mikihashiro Tatara, "The Second Generation of Hibakusha Atomic Bomb Survivors," in *International Handbook of Multigenerational Legacies of Trauma*, ed. Yael Daniel (New York: Plenum Press, 1998), 141–146.

6. Glenn Palmer, "The Impact of Ethnic and Political Violence on Children Who Found Refuge in Australia During World War Two," in *Landscapes of Development*, ed. Laura E. Berk (Belmont, Calif.: Wadsworth Publishing Co., 1999), 431–441.

7. Ruth Inglis, *The Children's War: Evacuation, 1939–1945* (London: Collins, 1989), 182.

8. Eila Räsänen, "Excessive Life Changes During Childhood and Their Effects on Mental and Physical Health in Adulthood," *Acta Paedopsychiatrica* 55 (1992): pp. 19–24.

9. Jean L. Athey and Frederick L. Ahear, "The Mental Health of Refugee Children: An Overview," in *Refugee Children: Theory, Research, and Services*, ed. Frederick L. Ahear and Jean L. Athey (Baltimore, Md.: Johns Hopkins University Press, 1991), chap. 1.

10. Calvin L. Christman, ed., *Lost in the Victory: Reflections of American War Orphans of World War II* (Denton: University of North Texas Press, 1998).

11. Barbara Elden Larney, "Children of World War II in Germany: A Life Course Analysis" (Ph.D. diss., Arizona State University, 1994).

12. Glenn H. Elder Jr., *Children of the Great Depression: Social Change in Life Experience*, 25th anniversary edition (Boulder, Colo.: Westview Press, 1999), 320–330.

13. Karl Ulrich Meyer, "German Survivors of World War II: The Impact on the Life Course of the Collective Experience of Birth Cohorts," in *Social Structure and Human Lives*, ed. M. W. Riley (Newbury Park, Calif.: Sage Publications, 1988), 229–246.

14. William M. Tuttle Jr., *Daddy's Gone to War: The Second World War in the Lives of American Children* (New York: Oxford University Press, 1993), 254–261.

15. Donna Nagata, "Intergenerational Effects of the Japanese-American Internment," in *International Handbook of Multigenerational Legacies of Trauma*, ed. Yael Daniel (New York: Plenum Press, 1998), 125–139.

16. UNICEF, *The State of the World's Children*, 50th anniversary issue (New York: Oxford University Press, 1996).

17. UNICEF, *I Dream of Peace—Images of War by Children of Former Yugoslavia* (New York: Harper Collins, 1994).

Bibliography

Akana, Joshua. 1943. "A Student Letter from Honolulu." *Weekly News Review,* March 29.

Allen, Eleanor. 1975. *Wartime Children: 1939–1945.* London: A & C Black.

Ambrose, Stephen. 1997. *Citizen Soldiers.* New York: Simon and Schuster.

Anderson, C. LeRoy, Joanne R. Anderson, and Yunosuke Ohkura, eds. 1995. *No Longer Silent: World-Wide Memories of the Children of World War II.* Missoula, Mont.: Pictorial Histories Publishing Co.

Arbeitsgruppe Pädagogisches Museum, ed. 1983. *Heil Hitler, Herr Lehrer: Volksschule 1933–1945.* Reinbeck by Hamburg: Rowohlt Verlag.

Athey, Jean L., and Frederick L. Ahear. 1991. "The Mental Health of Refugee Children: An Overview." In *Refugee Children: Theory, Research, and Services,* edited by Frederick L. Ahear and Jean L. Athey, chap. 1. Baltimore, Md.: Johns Hopkins University Press.

Austbo, Ola. 1995. "Norway." In *No Longer Silent: World-Wide Memories of the Children of World War II,* edited by C. LeRoy Anderson, Joanne R. Anderson, and Yunosuke Ohkura, 112–116. Missoula, Mont.: Pictorial Histories Publishing Co.

Bake, Rita, ed. 1993. *Aber Wir Müssen Zusammen Bleiben: Mütter und Kinder im Bombenkrieg: 1943–1945: Gespräche.* Hamburg: Landeszentrale für Politische Bildung.

Banny, Leopold. 1988. *Dröhnender Himmel, Brennendes Land.* Wien: Österreichischer Bundesverlag.

Bayley, Willis Elisabeth. 1942–1943. "Letters of Japanese American Students." Seattle: University of Washington Libraries, Manuscript and Archives Division.

Beal, Margaret. 1989. "Diary." In *The Day They Took the Children,* edited by Ben Wicks, 144–155. London: Bloomsbury.

Bell, Caroline, and Eddie Bell. 1941. *Thank You Twice or How We Like America.* New York: Harcourt, Brace & Co.

Berman, Ruth. 1997. *Dear Poppa: The World War II Berman Family Letters.* Saint Paul: Minnesota Historical Society Press.

Besson, Jean-Louis. 1995. *October 45: Childhood Memories of the War.* Mankato, Minn.: Creative Editions.

Bilson, Geoffrey. 1988. *The Guest Children: The Story of the British Child Evacuees Sent to Canada During World War II.* Saskatoon, Saskatchewan: Fifth House.

Birdsall, James. 1988. *The Boys and the Butterflies: A Wartime Rural Childhood.* London: Pavillion.

———. 1990. *Moths in the Memory: A Postwar Spring.* London: Pavillion.

Boge, Volker. 1992. *Bunkerleben und Kinderlandverschickung.* Hamburg: Dolling und Galitz.

Bond, Marjorie. 1944. "Wartime Hawaii." In *Punahou School Essays, April 23–24, 1944*. File 24.02. Honolulu: Hawaii War Records Depository, University of Hawaii at Manoa.

Bonney, Thérèse. 1943. *Europe's Children: 1939–1943*. New York: Plantin Press.

Borkowski, Dieter. 1990. *Wer Weiss Ob Wir Uns Wiedersehen*. Berlin: Das Neue Berlin.

Boy Scouts. 1941. *My Diary: December 7–15, 1941*. File 50. Honolulu: Hawaii War Records Depository, University of Hawaii at Manoa.

Brady, Alice. 1942. *Children Under Fire*. Los Angeles: Columbia Publishing Co.

Childs, David, and Janet Wharton, eds. 1989. *Children in War: Reminiscences of the Second World War*. Nottingham, U.K.: University of Nottingham.

Christman, Calvin L., ed. 1998. *Lost in the Victory: Reflections of American War Orphans of World War II*. Denton: University of North Texas Press.

Commission on Wartime Relocation and Internment of Civilians. 1981. Public Hearings. Washington National Archives, National Archives and Records Service, General Service Administration, 1983.

———. 1982. *Personal Justice Denied*. Washington, D.C.: Government Printing Office.

Conrat, Maisie, and Richard Conrat. 1972. *Executive Order 9066: The Internment of 110,000 Japanese Americans*. Cambridge, Mass: MIT Press.

Cowan, Lore. 1969. *Children of the Resistance*. New York: Meredith Press.

Coyle, Patricia. 1942. "Letter to General MacArthur, August 9." Norfolk, Va.: Douglas MacArthur Memorial Archives and Library.

Crozier, Barbara. 1944. "My Schooling After the War Began." In *Punahou School Essays, April 23–24, 1944*. File 24.02. Honolulu: Hawaii War Records Depository, University of Hawaii at Manoa.

Dabel, Gerhard, ed. 1981. *Die erweiterte Kinder-Land-Verschickung: KLV-Lager 1940–1945*. Freiburg: Schillinger.

David, Kati. 1989. *A Child's War: World War II Through the Eyes of Children*. New York: Avon Books.

Deutsches Historisches Museum. 1995–1996. "Stille Helfer: 350 Jahre Quäker." *Deutsches Historisches Museum* 6 (15).

Dittgen, Willy. 1957. *Der Kinderkäfig von Attichy: Ein Erlebensbericht*. Rheinberg: Michael Schiffer.

Dooley, Joan. 1942. "Letter to General MacArthur, November 10." Norfolk, Va.: Douglas MacArthur Memorial Archives and Library.

Dovbenko, N. P. 1995. "Russia." In *No Longer Silent: World-Wide Memories of the Children of World War II*, edited by C. LeRoy Anderson, Joanne R. Anderson, and Yunosuke Ohkura, 44–48. Missoula, Mont.: Pictorial Histories Publishing Co.

Duke, Anthony Drexel. 1992. "Oral History." New Orleans: Eisenhower Center Archives, University of New Orleans.

Eisenhower, Dwight D. 1942–1943. "Letters to Mary Louise Koehnen: April 15, 1942–August 2, 1943." Abilene, Kans.: Dwight D. Eisenhower Library.

Elder, Glenn H., Jr. 1999. *Children of the Great Depression: Social Change in Life Experience.* 25th anniversary edition. Boulder, Colo.: Westview Press.

Emmerich, Elsbeth. 1991. *My Childhood in Nazi Germany.* New York: Bookwright Press.

Evanson, Elizabeth C. 1942. "Scrapbook." Seattle: University of Washington Libraries, Manuscript and Archives Division.

Fader, Lorraine. 1943. "Letter to General MacArthur, January 12, 1943." Norfolk, Va.: Douglas MacArthur Memorial Archives and Library.

Fethney, Michael. 1990. *The Absurd and the Brave: CORB–The True Account of the British Government's World War II Evacuation of Children Overseas.* Lewes, Sussex: The Book Guild.

Foreman, Michael. 1991. *War Boy: A Country Childhood.* New York: Arcade Publishing Co.

Freud, Anna, and Dorothy T. Burlingham. 1943. *War and Children.* New York: Medical War Books.

Fujimoto, George. 1947. "My First War Experience." In *University of Hawaii Themes, Pearl Harbor Attack.* File 24.01. Honolulu: Hawaii War Records Depository, University of Hawaii at Manoa.

Gesenway, Deborah, and Mindy Roseman. 1987. *Beyond Words: Images from America's Concentration Camps.* Ithaca: Cornell University Press.

Gollancz, Victor. 1947. *In Darkest Germany.* London: Victor Gollancz Ltd.

Granzow, Klaus. 1986. *Tagebuch Eines Hitlerjungen: Kriegsjugend in Pommern, 1943–1945.* Bremen: Claus Schüneman Verlag.

Greenfield, Meg. 1955. "Childhood Tempered by Anxiety." *Washington Post,* July 26.

Grudzinska-Gross, Irene, ed. 1981. *War Through Children's Eyes: The Soviet Occupation of Poland and the Deportations: 1939–1941.* Stanford, Calif.: Hoover Institute Press.

Halvorsen, Gail S. 1997. *The Berlin Candy Bomber.* Bountiful, Utah: Horizon Publishers.

Harth, Erica. 1993. "Children of Manzanar: Experiences in an Internment Camp During World War II." *Massachusetts Review* 34 (3): pp. 367–391.

Heer, Hannes, ed. 1980. *Als Ich Neun Jahre Alt War, Kam Der Krieg: Schulaufsätze 1946: Ein Lesebuch Gegen Den Krieg.* Köln: Prometh Verlag.

Hershey, John. 1964. *Here to Stay.* New York: Bantam Books.

Higa, Tomiko. 1991. *The Girl with the White Flag.* Tokyo: Kodansha International.

High Third Grade, Mountain View School, Topaz, Utah. 1943. "Our Daily Diary: March 8–August 12." Salt Lake City, Utah: Utah State Historical Society.

Hochhuth, Maili. 1985. *Schulzeit Auf Dem Lande, 1933–1945.* Kassel: Gesamthochschulbibliothek.

Holliday, Laurel, ed. 1995. *Children of the Holocaust and World War II: Their Secret Diaries.* New York: Pocket Books.

Hollingsworth, Hilda. 1991. *They Tied a Label on My Coat.* Camden Town, London: Virago Press.

Homburg, Kurt. 1992. *Aus Kindertagen vor 50 Jahren.* Herford: Maximilian Verlag.

Honda, Francis. 1982. "Testimony." In *Personal Justice Denied.* Report of the Commission on Wartime Relocation and Internment of Civilians. Washington, D.C.: Government Printing Office.

Hornbostel, Lloyd. 1996. *War Kids, 1941–1945: World War II Through the Eyes of Children.* Lakeville, Minn.: Galde Press.

Horst, Ingrid. 1988. *Born Under Hitler: A German Childhood Connected with History.* Boston: Perspective Publishers International.

Houston, Jeanne Wakatsuki, and James D. Houston. 1973. *Farewell to Manzanar.* Boston: Houghton Mifflin.

Hughes, Marian. 1994. *No Cake, No Jam.* London: Heineman.

Hut, Lucien. 1995. "The Netherlands." In *No Longer Silent: World-Wide Memories of the Children of World War II,* edited by C. LeRoy Anderson, Joanne R. Anderson, and Yunosuke Ohkura, 118–133. Missoula, Mont.: Pictorial Histories Publishing Co.

Inglis, Ruth. 1989. *The Children's War: Evacuation, 1939–1945.* London: Collins.

Ippish, Hanneke. 1996. *Sky: A True Story of Resistance During World War II.* New York: Simon and Schuster.

Ipsen, Anne. 1998. *A Child's Tapestry of War.* Edina, Minn.: Beaver's Pond Press.

Isaacs, Susan, ed. 1941. *The Cambridge Evacuation Survey: A Wartime Study in Social Welfare and Education.* London: Methuen.

Jackson, Carlton. 1985. *Who Will Take Our Children?* London: Methuen.

Jansen, Peter S., and Jon Shaw. 1993. "Children as Victims of War: Current Knowledge and Future Research Needs." *Journal of the American Academy of Child and Adolescent Psychiatry 32,* no. 4 (July): pp. 697–708.

Johansen, Jytte Christensen. 1995. "Denmark." In *No Longer Silent: World-Wide Memories of the Children of World War II,* edited by C. LeRoy Anderson, Joanne R. Anderson, and Yunosuke Ohkura, 100–102. Missoula, Mont.: Pictorial Histories Publishing Co.

Johnson, B. S., ed. 1968. *The Evacuees.* London: Victor Gollantz Ltd.

Kamiya, Emiko. 1990. "My First Christmas in Poston." In *Through Innocent Eyes: Writings and Art from the Japanese American Internment by Poston I Schoolchildren,* edited by Vincent Tajiri. Los Angeles: Keiro Services.

Keely, Jack. 1989. "Interview." In *The Children's War: Evacuation, 1939–1945,* edited by Ruth Inglis, 120–122. London: Collins.

Kirk, Robert W. 1995. *Earning Their Stripes: The Mobilization of American Children in the Second World War.* New York: Peter Lang.

——. 1995. "Getting in the Scrap: The Mobilization of American Children in World War II." *Journal of Popular Culture* 29: pp. 223–233.

Kirshin, Yuri. 1995. "Russia." In *No Longer Silent: World-Wide Memories of the Children of World War II,* edited by C. LeRoy Anderson, Joanne R. Anderson, and Yunosuke Ohkura, 276–280. Missoula, Mont.: Pictorial Histories Publishing Co.

Klitta, Georg. 1981. "Das Finale des Zweiten Weltkriegs in Schwandorf." In *Die erweiterte Kinder-Land-Verschickung: KLV Lager 1940–1945,* edited by Gerhard Dabel. Freiburg: Schillinger.

Klug, Lilo. 1989. *Surviving the Fire: Mother Courage and World War II.* Seattle: Open Hand Publishing Co.

Koehnen, Mary Louise. 1942–1943. "Letters to General Eisenhower, April 8, 1942–June 22, 1943." Abilene, Kans.: Dwight D. Eisenhower Library.

Koerber, Hilda. 1948. *Kindheit und Jugend: 1941–1947: Briefe und Aufzeichnungen Junger Menschen.* Berlin: F. A. Herbig Verlagsbuchhandlung.

Konstantinova, Ina. 1995. "Diary." In *Children of the Holocaust and World War II: Their Secret Diaries,* edited by Laurel Holliday, 249–254. New York: Pocket Books.

Koster-Hetzendorf, Maren, ed. 1995. *Ich Habe Dich So Gesucht-Der Krieg und Seine Verlorenen Kinder.* Augsburg: Pattloch.

Kuppers, Waltraud. 1964. *Mädchentagebücher der Nachkriegszeit.* Stuttgart: Ernst Klett Verlag.

Kurt, Alfred. 1994. *Offenbacher Luftwaffenhelfer im Kriegseinsatz.* Offenbach am Main: Offenbacher Geschichtsverein.

Lambert, Derek. 1965. *The Sheltered Days: Growing Up in the War.* London: Andre Deutsch.

Landenberger, Annemarie. 1992. *Als Hamburger Lehrerin in der Kinderlandverschickung: Tagebuch 1943.* Hamburg: Verein für Hamburger Geschichte.

Larass, Claus. 1992. *Der Zug Der Kinder: KLV—Die Evakuierung 5 Millionen Deutscher Kinder im 2. Weltkrieg.* Frankfurt: Ullstein.

Larney, Barbara Elden. 1994. "Children of World War II in Germany: A Life Course Analysis." Ph.D. diss., Arizona State University.

Lavery, Father High T. 1949. "Letter to President Truman." *Pacific Citizen,* September 24.

Leavitt, Charmaine. 1991. "Letter to Dear Justin, December 29, 1943." In *World War II Letters from American Women on the Home Front,* edited by Judy Barrett Litoff and David C. Smith, 236. New York: Oxford University Press.

Leffland, Ella. 1979. *Rumors of Peace.* New York: Harper and Row.

Leverton, Bertha, and Shmuel Loewenson. 1998. *I Came Alone: The Story of the Kinder-Transports.* Lewes, Sussex: The Book Guild.

Lipp, Christine, ed. 1992. *Kindheit und Krieg: Erinnerungen.* Frankfurt am Main: Fischer.

Litoff, Judy Barrett, and David C. Smith, eds. 1991. *World War II Letters from American Women on the Home Front.* New York: Oxford University Press.

Macardle, Dorothy. 1951. *Children of Europe.* Boston: The Beacon Press.

Marsh, Carolyn n.d. "Letter to UNICEF." New York: UNICEF Headquarters.

Marx, Trish. 1994. *Echoes of World War II.* Minneapolis: Lerner Publications.

Massey, Victoria. 1978. *One Child's War.* London: British Broadcasting Corporation.

McCann, Joseph Jr. 1992. "Oral History." New Orleans: Eisenhower Center Archives, University of New Orleans.

Meier, Herbert. 1995. "Oral History." New Orleans: Eisenhower Center Archives, Stephen and Hugh Ambrose German Veterans Collection.

Merson, Elizabeth. 1983. *Children in the Second World War.* Harlow: Longman.

Meyer, Karl Ulrich. 1988. "German Survivors of World War II: The Impact on the Life Course of the Collective Experience of Birth Cohorts." In *Social Structure and Human Lives*, edited by M. W. Riley, 229–246. Newbury Park, Calif.: Sage Publications.

Meyer, Sibylle, and Eva Schulze. 1985. *Von Liebe Sprach Damals Keiner: Familienalltag in der Nachkriegszeit*. München: C. H. Beck.

Mills, Pamela Kirk. 1990. *Orphan of the Storm: The Experience of a Little Girl in Wartime England*. Torrens, A.C.T.: A. Mills.

Mittag, Detlef. 1995. *Kindheit und Jugend um 1945: Kriegskinder: Zehn Überlebungsgeschichten*. Berlin: Internationale Liga für Menschenrechte.

Monham, Kathleen. 1979. *Growing Up in World War II*. Hove: Wayland.

Morgan, Elizabeth Shelfer. 1994. *Uncertain Seasons*. Tuscaloosa: University of Alabama Press.

Morris, David, ed. 1996. *A Gift from America: The First Fifty Years of CARE*. Atlanta: Longstreet Press.

Moskovitz, Sarah. 1983. *Love Despite Hate: Child Survivors of the Holocaust and Their Adult Years*. New York: Schocken Books.

Moss, Miriam. 1988. *A School Child in World War II*. Hove: Wayland.

Nagai, Takashi, ed. 1979. *Living Beneath the Atomic Cloud: Testimonies of the Children of Nagasaki*. Tokyo: SAN-YU-SHA.

Nagata, Donna. 1998. "Intergenerational Effects of the Japanese American Internment." In *International Handbook of Multigenerational Legacies of Trauma*, edited by Yael Daniel, 125–139. New York: Plenum Press.

Nakamura, Grace. 1982. "Testimony." In *Personal Justice Denied*. Report of the Commission on Wartime Relocation and Internment of Civilians. Washington, D.C.: Government Printing Office.

Nesaule, Agate. 1995. *Woman in Amber: Healing the Trauma of War and Exile*. New York: Penguin.

Nicholson, Dorinda M. 1993. *Pearl Harbor Child*. Honolulu, Hawaii: Arizona Memorial Museum Association.

Nicolaisen, Hans Dietrich. 1981. *Die Flakhelfer: Luftwaffenhelfer und Marinehelfer im Zweiten Weltkrieg*. Berlin: Ullstein.

Noguchi, Kinya. 1982. "Testimony." In *Personal Justice Denied*. Report of the Commission on Wartime Relocation and Internment of Civilians. Washington, D.C.: Government Printing Office.

Oldroyd, Clive. 1942. "Letter to General MacArthur, July 22." Norfolk, Va.: Douglas MacArthur Memorial Archives and Library.

Osada, Arata, ed. 1980. *Children of the A-Bomb: The Testament of the Boys and Girls of Hiroshima*. New York: G. P. Putnam's Sons.

Palmer, Glenn. 1999. "The Impact of Ethnic and Political Violence on Children Who Found Refuge in Australia During World War Two." In *Landscapes of Development*, edited by Laura E. Berk, 431–441. Belmont, Calif.: Wadsworth Publishing Co.

Perkins, Charles, ed. 1998. *Children of the Storm: World War II in the Words of the Children Who Lived Through It*. Osceola, Wis.: Motorbooks International.

Pettit, Jayne. 1996. *A Time to Fight Back: True Stories of Wartime Resistance*. Boston: Houghton Mifflin Co.

Philipps, Janine. 1982. *My Secret Diary*. London: Shepheard-Walwyn.

Priamus, Heinz-Jürgen. 1985. *Die Ruinenkinder*. Düsseldorf: Droste Verlag.

Ptak, Al. 1996. *Firestorm*. Rosedale, B.C.: Arashida Publications.

Public Hearings of the Commission on Wartime Relocation and Internment of Civilians. 1983. Washington, D.C. National Archives and Records Service, General Service Administration.

Puchmond, Robert. 1943. "Why We Should Live Up to Our War Bond Pledge." Norfolk, Va.: Douglas MacArthur Memorial Acrhives and Library.

Räsänen, Eila. 1992. "Excessive Life Changes During Childhood and Their Effects on Mental and Physical Health in Adulthood." *Acta Paedopsychiatrica* 55: pp. 19–24.

Rautenberg, Ilse. 1990. *Hämmert Man Hart Dich zu Stahl*. Aachen: Fischer.

Raymond, Robert G. 1994. *Scouting, Cavorting, and Other World War II Memories*. Billings, Mont.: R. G. Raymond.

Sacred Hearts Academy. 1941–1942. *Diary: December 1941–January 1942*. File 24.02. Honolulu: Hawaii War Records Depository, University of Hawaii at Manoa.

Saigh, Philip A., John A. Fairbank, and Anastasia E. Yasik. 1997. "War Related Post-Traumatic Stress Disorder Among Children and Adolescents." In *Children in the Urban Environment: Linking Social Policy and Clinical Practice*, edited by Norman Philipps and Shulamith L. A. Strausner, 119–140. Springfield, Ill.: Charles Thomas Publisher.

Saint-Exupéry, Antoine de. 1943. *The Little Prince*. New York: Harcourt Brace and Co.

Schatz, Ludwig. 1972. *Schüler-Soldaten: Die Geschichte der Luftwaffenhelfer im Zweiten Weltkrieg*. Frankfurt am Main: Thesen Verlag.

Schauss, Willy A. 1994. *My Side of the War: How Meatballs Saved My Life*. Kalispell, Mont.: Scott Publications.

Schmidt, Hellmut. 1992. *Kindheit und Jugend unter Hitler*. Berlin: Siedler.

Schnorback, Herman. 1983. *Lehrer und Schüler unterm Hakenkreuz: 1933–1945*. Königstein, Taunus: Atheneum.

Schwenke, Regina. 1983. *Und Es Wird Immer Wieder Tag: Kindheitserinnerungen an Berlin's Dunkelsten Tage*. Berlin: Arani.

Sester, Hans. 1987. *Als Junge im Sogenannten Dritten Reich*. Frankfurt am Main: H. A. Herchen.

Shea, Bessie. 1985. "War at Scapa Flow." In *Children of the Blitz: Memories of Wartime Childhood*, edited by Robert Westall, 60–71. New York: Viking.

Shirer, William L. 1959. *The Rise and Fall of the Third Reich: A History of Nazi Germany*. New York: Simon and Schuster.

Søe, Christian. 1989. "A Relatively Civilized War." In *Children in War: Reminiscences of the Second World War*, edited by David Childs and Janet Wharton, 161–170. Nottingham, U.K.: University of Nottingham.

Sorge, Martin K. 1986. *The Other Price of Hitler's War: German Military and Civilian Losses Resulting from World War II.* New York: Greenwood Press.

Smith, Bruce. 1982. *The History of Little Orphan Annie.* New York: Ballantine.

Smith, Lucinda. 1942. "A Honolulu School in Wartime." *Radcliffe Quarterly,* May, pp. 22–26.

Spiegelman, Judith M., and UNICEF. 1986. *We Are the Children: A Celebration of UNICEF's First Forty Years.* Boston: Atlantic Monthly Press.

Stahl, Erna. 1948. *Jugend im Schatten von Gestern: Aufsätze Jugendlicher zur Zeit.* Hamburg: Hans Köhler Verlag.

Stankus-Saulaitis, Maria. 1995. "Forgotten Faces of War." *America,* July, pp. 6–8.

Stanley, Jerry. 1994. *I Am an American.* New York: Crown.

Tajiri, Vincent, ed. 1990. *Through Innocent Eyes: Writings and Art from the Japanese American Internment by Poston I Schoolchildren.* Los Angeles: Keiro Services.

Tamabayashi, Richard. 1941. "December 7." In *Boy Scouts: My Diary: December 7–15, 1941.* File 50. Honolulu: Hawaii War Records Depository, University of Hawaii at Manoa.

Tani, Shinsuke. 1976. *Seasons Unforgotten.* Tokyo: Toju-sha.

Tatara, Mikihashiro. 1998. "The Second Generation of Hibakusha Atomic Bomb Survivors." In *International Handbook of Multigenerational Legacies of Trauma,* edited by Yael Daniel, 141–146. New York: Plenum Press, 1998.

Tateishi, John, ed. 1984. *And Justice for All: An Oral History of the Japanese American Detention Camps.* New York: Random House.

Tawa, Renee. 1997. "Childhood Lost: The Orphans of Manzanar." *Los Angeles Times,* March 11.

Tedder, Valerie. 1994. *The Pantry Under the Stairs: Childhood Memories of World War II.* Leicester, England: City Council, Living History Unit.

Townsend, Peter. 1980. *The Smallest Pawns in the Game.* Boston: Little Brown.

Tsuchiyama, Kazue. 1990. "Winter Life in Poston." In *Through Innocent Eyes: Writings and Art from the Japanese American Internment by Poston I Schoolchildren,* edited by Vincent Tajiri. Los Angeles: Keiro Services.

Tunnell, Michael O. 1996. *The Children of Topaz: The Story of a Japanese American Internment Camp Based on a Classroom Diary.* New York: Holiday House.

Tuttle, William M., Jr. 1993. *Daddy's Gone to War: The Second World War in the Lives of American Children.* New York: Oxford University Press.

Uchida, Yoshiko. 1991. *The Invisible Thread.* Englewood Cliffs, N.J.: Julian Mesner.

UNICEF. 1994. *I Dream of Peace—Images of War by Children of Former Yugoslavia.* New York: Harper Collins.

———. 1996. *The State of the World's Children.* 50th anniversary issue. New York: Oxford University Press.

U.S. House. 1950. *Displaced Persons in Europe and Their Resettlement in the United States.* 81st Cong., 2nd sess. H. Rept. 1507.

van de Zand, Willemien. 1989. "Witness to an Invasion." In *Children in War: Reminiscences of the Second World War,* edited by David Childs and Janet Wharton, 135–145. Nottingham, England: University of Nottingham.

Vonnegut, Kurt Jr. 1966. *Slaughterhouse Five or The Children's Crusade*. New York: Dell.

———. 1991. "Memoirs." *Faces of Indiana and Midwestern History* 3, no. 4 (special issue, fall).

Wallace, Richard. n.d. "Letter to President Truman." Independence, Mo.: Harry S. Truman Library.

Wasilewska, Irena. 1946. *Suffer the Little Children*. London: Maxlowe.

Weglyn, Michi. 1996. *Years of Infamy: The Untold Story of American Concentration Camps*. Seattle: University of Washington Press.

Wehner, Alfred P. 1972. *From Hitler Youth to U.S. Citizen*. New York: Carlton Press.

Werner, Herbert A. 1998. *Iron Coffins: A Personal Account of the German U-Boat Battles of World War II*. New York: Da Capo Press.

Westall, Robert, ed. 1985. *Children of the Blitz: Memories of Wartime Childhood*. London: Viking.

Wetzel, Frank, ed. 1996. *Victory Gardens and Barrage Balloons*. Bremerton, Wash.: Perry Publishers.

Wharton, William. 1982. *A Midnight Clear*. New York: Alfred A. Knopf.

Whitney, Helen Elizabeth. 1948. "Care of Homeless Children of Japanese Ancestry During Evacuation and Relocation." Ph.D. diss., University of California, Berkeley.

Wicks, Ben, ed. 1989. *The Day They Took the Children*. London: Bloomsbury.

Index